John Knight and Carolyn Jenkins
ECONOMIC POLICIES AND OUTCOMES IN ZIMBABWE
Lessons for South Africa

Jo Ann Paulson (*editor*)
AFRICAN ECONOMIES IN TRANSITION
Volume 1: The Changing Role of the State

Jo Ann Paulson (*editor*)
AFRICAN ECONOMIES IN TRANSITION
Volume 2: The Reform Experience

Crisis, Adjustment and Growth in Uganda

A Study of Adaptation in an African Economy

Arne Bigsten
Professor of Development Economics
Gothenburg University
Sweden

and

Steve Kayizzi-Mugerwa
Associate Professor (Development Economics)
Gothenburg University
Sweden

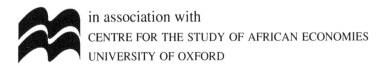

in association with
CENTRE FOR THE STUDY OF AFRICAN ECONOMIES
UNIVERSITY OF OXFORD

First published in Great Britain 1999 by
MACMILLAN PRESS LTD
Houndmills, Basingstoke, Hampshire RG21 6XS and London
Companies and representatives throughout the world

A catalogue record for this book is available from the British Library.

ISBN 0–333–76384–X

First published in the United States of America 1999 by
ST. MARTIN'S PRESS, INC.,
Scholarly and Reference Division,
175 Fifth Avenue, New York, N.Y. 10010

ISBN 0–312–22134–7

Library of Congress Cataloging-in-Publication Data
Bigsten, Arne.
Crisis, adjustment and growth in Uganda : a study of adaptation in
an African economy / Arne Bigsten and Steve Kayizzi-Mugerwa.
p. cm. — (Studies on the African economies)
"In association with the Centre for the Study of African
Economies, University of Oxford."
Includes bibliographical references and index.
ISBN 0–312–22134–7 (cloth)
1. Uganda—Economic conditions. 2. Income—Uganda. I. Kayizzi
-Mugerwa, Steve. II. Title. III. Series.
HC870.B535 1999
338.96761—dc21
98–47235
CIP

This book is printed on paper suitable for recycling and made from fully managed and
sustained forest sources.

10   9   8   7   6   5   4   3   2   1
08   07   06   05   04   03   02   01   00   99

Printed and bound in Great Britain by
Antony Rowe Ltd, Chippenham, Wiltshire

Contents

Contents

List of Figures

List of Tables

Acknowledgements

This work was initiated in 1988, in the first year of the economic reform programme begun by the National Resistance Movement the previous year, and we have since undertaken a number of extended research trips to Uganda. We gratefully acknowledge assistance from officials at the Bank of Uganda and at the Ministry of Finance and Economic Planning, especially the Department of Statistics. Discussions with officials from other ministries, too many to list, were very useful. Assistance from the World Bank Resident Mission in Kampala, notably that of Chukwuma Obidegwu, is also acknowledged. The survey on which Appendices A and B are based was undertaken in collaboration with the Department of Economics of Makerere University. We would like to thank Dr Germina Ssemogerere, the Head of Department at the time, Mohammed Kalyango, Anthony Balayo and their students for assistance rendered. For research assistance we thank Kupukile Mlambo and Negatu Makonnen, former graduate students at Göteborg University, and now PhDs in economics. We also thank Eva-Lena Neth for assistance at the many stages of this work.

This book was mainly financed by a research grant from the Swedish Agency for Research Cooperation with Developing Countries (SAREC) and additional financial assistance was also received from the Swedish International Development Cooperation Agency (Sida), the Scandinavian Institute of African Studies, Stiftelsen Futura and Göteborg University.

Several chapters of the study were presented in earlier versions at conferences in Stockholm and Elsinore (Denmark), while earlier drafts of the entire manuscript were presented at seminars at the Department of Economics, Göteborg University, Sweden. We also especially thank our colleagues Per-Åke Andersson and Lennart Flood for their comments and Haji Semboja for his collaboration. Aili Mari Tripp, of the University of Wisconsin at Madison, made useful comments on parts of the manuscript, in discussions at Makerere University, while colleagues at the African Development Bank suggested useful improvements. The final version of this book benefited from extensive comments by Paul Collier, Simon Appleton, Jan Willem Gunning, an anonymous referee, and copy editing by Rick Wicks.

Some of the material included in the book has appeared in *World Development, Journal of International Development, Canadian Journal of Development Studies* and two conference volumes published by Routledge. We have also drawn freely on our reports on Uganda published by Sida in its Macroeconomic Studies series.

In no way are the people and institutions named above implicated in the shortcomings of the study, which remain ours alone. The authors are listed alphabetically.

Arne Bigsten and Steve Kayizzi-Mugerwa
Göteborg, May 1997

List of Acronyms

ADB	African Development Bank
ADF	African Development Fund
AIDS	Acquired Immune-deficiency Syndrome
BOU	Bank of Uganda
CMB	Coffee Marketing Board
CPI	Consumer price index
DAAPCB	Departed Asians' Abandoned Properties Custodian Board
DANIDA	Danish International Development Agency
EPADU	Export Policy Analysis Unit
EPRC	Education Policy Review Commission
ERP	Economic Recovery Programme
ESAF	Enhanced Structural Adjustment Facility
GDP	Gross domestic product
IDA	International Development Agency
ILO	International Labour Organisation
IMF	International Monetary Fund
M0	Currency in circulation
M1	Narrow measure of money supply
M2	Broad measure of money supply
NEC	National Enterprise Corporation
NGO	Non-governmental organisation
NRA	National Resistance Army
NRM	National Resistance Movement
NURP	Northern Uganda Reconstruction Programme
OGL	Open general licensing
PAC	Public Accounts Committee
PAPSCA	Programme for the Alleviation of Poverty and the Social Costs of Adjustment
PSIP	Public Sector Investment Programme
PTA	Preferential trade area
PTAs	Parents and Teachers Associations
RC	Resistance Council
SAF	Structural Adjustment Facility

SAREC	Swedish Agency for Research Cooperation with Developing Countries
SIP	Special Import Programme
UCB	Uganda Commercial Bank
UDC	Uganda Development Corporation
UIA	Uganda Investment Authority
UN	United Nations
UNICEF	United Nations Children and Education Fund
UPDF	Uganda People's Defence Forces
URA	Uganda Revenue Authority
USAID	United States Agency for International Development
VAT	Value added tax

The Republic of Uganda

In addition to the districts shown above, six new districts were created in 1997: Sembabule, Busia, Katakwi, Nakasongola, Koboko and Bukholi.

Chapter 1: Introduction

Uganda in the 1980s and before that in the 1970s was one of Africa's sadder economic stories, but at Independence in 1962 it had been optimistic with a relatively buoyant economy and effective socioeconomic infrastructure.[1] Emerging from civil war, it had the added problem of embarking on reform in the early to mid-1980s from a position of severe political weakness. Policy-makers saw the need to build coalitions in support of adjustment, but potential benefits for powerful groups such as the army seemed remote. Uganda is thus a good example of the dilemmas facing a poor economy attempting to achieve internal and external balance.

Uganda's post-Independence optimism was based largely on a mutually beneficial relationship between government and smallholders:[2] peasants produced food and export crops, while the government ensured adequate producer prices and provided the crucial infrastructure services. The country was overwhelmingly agricultural: coffee was the mainstay, while other important cash crops included cotton, tobacco and tea. In the small but robust industrial sector, which was mainly import-substituting except for copper mining in the west, there was processing of sugar and cement and manufacturing of soap, beverages and textiles. The textile industry not only supplied domestic needs but also had a substantial surplus for export. A good climate and rich wildlife made the country a potential tourist destination, while economic cooperation with Kenya and Tanzania promised some economic advantages as well.

In the period 1960–70, real GDP grew at an annual average of close to 5 per cent, domestic investment at 7.5 per cent, and private consumption at 5.2 per cent. With the population growing at 3 per cent there was an improvement in welfare in the first years of independence, at least for some groups. Judging from the perspective of the 1960s, there was thus little to prepare one for the brutal realities of the 1970s and 1980s. In retrospect, however, there were many problems under the surface. As in most developing countries, there was an urban-rural gap and regional gaps as well, mainly here between the northern and southern parts of the country. Unresolved political conflicts from the 1950s, complicated by the new challenges of nationhood, were to prove too much for the brittle alliances that had assumed leadership at Independence (see for instance Uganda Protectorate, 1961). The first change was Milton Obote's seizure of the presidency in 1966, followed by Idi Amin in 1971.

After Independence the new regime pursued a mixed-economy strategy, with emphasis on state-ownership of the 'commanding heights', which led to the nationalisations of the late 1960s and early 1970s. The period was also marked by an increasing 'radicalisation' of the economic and political debate. Whether 'African Socialism' — as the new mood came to be known — would have kept the country on the path of economic growth and prosperity is doubtful (see for instance Oberschall, 1969). But in any case Idi Amin's rise to power put an end to the economic experimentation of the 1960s, and ushered in a decade of political and economic chaos.

Besides increasing lawlessness and expansion of the coercive institutions of government, notably the army, the main effect of the Idi Amin era was the collapse of traditional trade links. Peasants also turned their backs on official marketing channels, because of declining domestic terms of trade, poor payment systems, inadequate supply of inputs, and growing insecurity. The concurrent decline of the modern sector — the public sector and manufacturing — increased unemployment and underemployment, lowering wages across the board. In response to the increasingly confused state of affairs, parallel markets (*magendo*) grew up and, with time, the underground economy came to dominate in the cities, which was devastating for public services, as collection of taxes became extremely cumbersome. Public-sector wages fell drastically in real terms, and the morale of civil servants sank. Competition for diminished resources weakened public institutions, and by the end of the 1970s, corruption and other rent-seeking activities had become rampant. Neighbouring economies were performing better than Uganda, so skilled labour emigrated, leaving hospitals, schools and colleges, as well as government departments, seriously understaffed.

By the early 1980s it had become clear that to bring producers back into the market and improve the government's capacity to manage economic policy, serious measures had to be taken. Thus beginning with Obote's return to power in 1980, all regimes have attempted economic reform, based on the IMF/World Bank model. The policy packages, which have been extensively debated,[3] were similar to those adopted in the 1980s in many other Sub-Saharan countries. Studies of adjustment have shown that the bureaucratic and import-substituting sectors tend to lose while agriculture and labour-intensive manufacturing gain from resulting relative-price changes, which of course implies that pre-adjustment political and business elites have much at stake. Indeed much like in neighbouring Kenya (see Bigsten, 1993), some aspects of the adjustment programme in Uganda directly threatened the livelihoods of rent-seekers. Trying to improve efficiency, while paying attention to welfare or distributional criteria, left little room for political manoeuvre. Reforms had opportunity costs which went well beyond those measured in traditional cost-benefit analysis.

Uganda's adjustment debate has been intensive (see for example Mamdani, 1989; Tumusiime-Mutebile, 1990; Hansen and Twaddle, 1991; Henstridge, 1994a), ranging from the contention that economic reform was the only alternative to decline to the view that adjustment was creating difficult social conditions for the majority of people, but without the benefit of structural transformation. In the heat of debate, it was not always clear, at least to the uninitiated, exactly what it was that the government wished to achieve, which conditions were being imposed with IMF/World Bank loans, or whether in fact there were feasible alternative strategies for addressing the crisis.

Most African governments reached similar agreements with the IMF/World Bank, but many chose not to implement them, even when aid and loans had been received. Uganda's willingness to implement the programmes has had much to do with its success: In the last five years Uganda has been one of the best-performing economies in Africa. In the 1996 budget speech, the Finance Minister announced that the economy had almost doubled since 1986.

Foreign funding has been crucial in returning Uganda to stability and growth. However, some neighbouring countries, such as Tanzania, and Kenya before the aid embargo of 1992/93 (see Agrawal *et al.*, 1993), enjoyed relatively higher inflows, but with less impressive results. It is also true that recent rapid progress in Uganda came from a very low base, but this was due to a level of political chaos hardly known in, for instance, Tanzania or Kenya. Uganda embarked on economic adjustment even as it struggled to bring about political stability. Compared with most other countries in the region, therefore, the economic rehabilitation and structural adjustment required in Uganda were of another order of magnitude.

In assessing the impact of adjustment, it is often difficult to show with much certainty, because of lack of a counterfactual history in real life, what the alternative or 'no-adjustment' outcome would have been. Uganda's case is perhaps more clear-cut: 'no adjustment' would probably have meant continued economic decline, destruction of infrastructure, and even more widespread civil conflict. Possibly poverty and social dislocation were already so widespread in Uganda that people were willing to support a reform, economic liberalisation backed by more disciplined government, that promised a turnaround.

Uganda's experience shows that there are always conflicts between what is desirable in the short versus the long run. The elimination of shortages was an essential first step towards stabilisation and recovery, and in this regard Uganda's adjustment efforts were successful. By the mid-1990s, most consumer goods were available, with no price controls. The government managed to bring down inflation, while keeping growth reasonably high. However, a central aim of adjustment was also to create a stable environment for long-term growth. Investors abhor uncertainty, and thus it seemed rational to avoid short-term expansionary measures in order to achieve long-term growth, via higher investment. Thus, when the time perspective is sufficiently long, the best strategy is rapid growth: eventually most groups in society benefit when total production becomes much larger.

The problem is that, starting from a low base, the time it takes before all groups benefit may be quite long. Thus, in spite of the good record on growth of Museveni's government, poverty continues to afflict large sections of the population. Therefore, one can sometimes make a good case for short-term distributional measures even if they have a cost in terms of long-term growth. Measures to help the poor, such as the provision of affordable basic health care and primary education, may even have beneficial long-term growth impacts. Still, there are seldom any clear-cut answers as to how the balance should be struck. Short-term improvements in the welfare system, not backed by a functioning economy, might soon be reversed. Ultimately, policy moves in these critical areas are political, in a different way from, say, interest-rate policy where a simple conditionality could be applied. Thus, although the IMF and the World Bank have in the past decade urged the government to increase spending on health, education, and economic infrastructure, the truth is that ultimately the government has chosen the expenditure patterns that reflected its political constraints, as indeed do governments everywhere.

Adaptation is the key. The government has adjusted to donor policy, including aid conditionality; the Ugandan economy as a whole has responded to policy changes and to changes in the external environment; and above all, households have changed their behaviour in response to government policies. In the study, the effects of economic policy at the aggregate level are discussed in detail, but 'snapshot' empirical analyses of responses at the household level, both urban and rural are also presented. The latter is done with the help of a household-based survey.

By 1997, more than ten years after embarking on its first adjustment programme, Uganda had attained some economic stability, and the confidence of policy-makers had increased markedly. Many challenges remain, however, including fragility of the peace and still rampant poverty. Yet our conclusion is optimistic, that even the severest cases of socioeconomic decline can be overcome by a willingness to change direction, by setting free the productive capacities of the country, especially in the countryside, and by nurturing good-will among neighbours and the international community. Uganda was for many years considered to be Africa's 'worst case'. Its recent recovery thus provides hope for similar countries in the region.

Notes

1. Uganda achieved self-government in 1961, while full independence came a year later. Akena Ojok noted

   the late Benedicto Kiwanuka on his becoming Prime Minister of Uganda in 1961, inherited from the Colonial Government a working government system, an economy pregnant with life and an education system full of hope and promise (Uganda, 1979a).

2. See for instance *Uganda's Second Five-Year Development Plan 1966–71* (Uganda, 1966b).
3. See World Bank (1994a and 1994b) on adjustment in Africa. Nelson (1984) provides an early overview of issues in the political economy of adjustment.

Chapter 2: The Years of Optimism (1960–71)

1. Introduction

In Uganda, there has been a tendency in recent years to look back at the 1960s as something of a 'golden age', when the economy, especially the modern sector, saw unprecedented expansion. At the time, it was hoped that this would generate employment for the youthful and increasingly better-educated labour force and also — in a bid to redress the colonial legacy — help to create a viable basis for a more equitable distribution of national resources (Uganda, 1966a). In the countryside, peasants were becoming more involved in cash-crop production.[1] This was encouraged partly because it was believed that increased rural demand for modern-sector goods, made possible by rising rural cash incomes, was crucial for the well-being of the small but expanding import-substituting manufacturing sector. Industrialisation was itself thought to be a key element of development policy. Social, administrative and educational services were expanding rapidly along with the rest of the public sector (Uganda, 1965a). The policy of Ugandanisation led to rapid advancement for many individuals and groups in both the civil service and the parastatals. The administrative strata in government and industry enjoyed a high standard of living.

A number of factors jeopardised this seemingly robust start, however (Mudoola, 1988a, 1988b, 1993). On the political front, the post-1962 euphoria was brought to an abrupt end by restiveness in the military, collapse of the political alliance between the radical and conservative streams of Uganda's political elite, and rising disaffection, both within and outside the party, with the ruling and increasingly powerful and monolithic Uganda People's Congress, led by Milton Obote (see, for example, Kabwegyere, 1974; Bunker, 1991).

Beyond that, there was a major struggle for power and influence (the 'Uganda Crisis') between the central government and the Kabaka of Buganda. Increasing animosity between the Uganda government and the Kabaka's headquarters at Mengo, a Kampala suburb, culminated in a brief but serious military confrontation in 1966. Thus the political agenda of the 1960s was contested. This was not in itself the bane of Uganda — much the same was happening in other countries in the region — but the tendency to resort to violence presaged future problems.

The political and administrative institutions inherited at Independence were in many respects mere extensions of those used earlier as instruments of coercion by the colonial regime. Deemed repressive before Independence, they did not become more palatable with the change of regimes. The military continued to be used to contain the threat of insurrection in the various parts of the country, for instance. More than before, however, it became a crucial instrument for the preservation of political power. Increasing in numbers from 700 to 7000 men in the first seven years of independence, it became 'the critical nerve centre of power' (Mudoola, 1988b: 16). Military expenditure claimed a large share of the total budget, far exceeding social expenditures. This set an unfortunate pattern for the leaner economic years ahead (Brett, 1994). Despite these developments, the 1960s were on the whole, and in retrospect, a decade of optimism.

2. Economic Policy in the 1960s

Pressures to raise wages were beginning to mount even before Independence. The departure of expatriate administrators enabled some Ugandans to embark on 'comet' careers, thus markedly increasing their remuneration, while compassion for lower-level employees also led to a desire for minimum-wage legislation. The 'living-wage' debate, which would return with a vengeance decades later, was very much alive in the 1960s. Of most concern then was the economic plight of unskilled wage earners. The Kennedy commission, set up to suggest remedies, had advocated a radical upward revision of the minimum wages (Uganda Protectorate, 1962).[2] This recommendation was rejected by the protectorate government, and only minor adjustments were made; with Independence only a few months away, the wages headache was left to the newcomers. The incoming government soon discovered that a combined policy of employment expansion and a generous socially-conscious wage legislation could meet with only limited success. Nevertheless, the minimum wage was increased fourfold in real terms between 1957 and 1970.

Uganda adopted a mixed-economy strategy at Independence and private ownership was sanctioned by the new constitution. The Foreign Investment (Protection) Act of 1964 and a related Industrial Charter seemed to have all the necessary guarantees for free private enterprise. Nevertheless, the policy thrust of the 1960s, like that of many other newly-independent African countries, was *dirigiste*, favouring the government's lead in all major economic activities, with emphasis on creation of employment and the generation and allocation of investment. Yet, since the economy was based on peasant-dominated agriculture, spread all over the country, government control of the economy never quite reached the levels of, say, Zambia. This was to prove a blessing. In the 1970s and 1980s, with the economy beset by a multitude of setbacks, the bulk of the population could survive even as the modern sector retreated.

The first national development plan was launched soon after achieving self-government in 1961, months before full independence. One of the main goals of the plan, and of economic policy more generally, was improvement of the standard of living for all Ugandans, with a view to 'eliminating poverty' altogether (Uganda, 1965b). In a peasant economy, this presupposed some policy initiatives towards the agricultural sector. Among the earliest of these were increased subsidisation of agricultural equipment and fertiliser, expansion of agricultural research and extension services, and diversification of the crop portfolio.

Optimism increased in Uganda as the economic depression of the first years of the decade was replaced by a boom in 1963. However, the new government was increasingly concerned with the slow pace of employment creation. As elsewhere in Africa, economic diversification and import-substitution policies were followed, based on simple premises. The government would undertake the 'liberal granting of tariff protection, customs refunds on imported raw materials, and temporary employment permits for key expatriate personnel' (Uganda, 1965b). According to the model used to project economic development in the post-Independence decade, manufacturing was to undergo rapid growth (see Elliot, 1973: 9).

The import-substitution stage, it was hoped, would soon be replaced by increased ability to export to the rest of the East African Economic Community. Throughout the 1960s the share of exports in GDP was above 20 per cent, but exports still consisted mainly of traditional commodities. The economy was still able to exploit its comparative advantages and to pay for the bulk of its imports with its own resources, but already by the end of the decade Uganda had built up a fairly sizeable foreign debt (see Table 2.1).

Monetary policy, what there was of it, was controlled by an East African Currency Board shared with Kenya and Tanzania.[3] While limiting domestic leeway in the determination of economic policy, it helped keep inflation at bay. The government simply had no way of financing its deficits by printing money, which was controlled by the joint currency board. Inability to regulate credit was often a source of frustration to policy-makers, especially during harvest seasons, when there was invariably a shortage of credit. In 1966, the country established its own central bank, The Bank of Uganda, 'which would be used cautiously but effectively' (Uganda, 1966a: 6) to undertake a more active steering of money supply via interest rate and credit policies.[4] The Bank began issuing its own currency in 1967. But while the government pursued this inward-looking policy, it also tried to broaden cooperation with its East African neighbours, with a treaty for East African Cooperation signed on 6 June 1967. It formalised existing arrangements between the three countries, including a free-trade area, a common external tariff and the removal of quantitative restrictions on inter-territorial trade. Then in May 1970, exchange controls on transactions with Kenya and Tanzania were introduced, so that, in effect, the currencies ceased to be at par.

Besides the increasingly difficult political terrain, the government was now also grumbling about the low level of private-sector savings and the slow rate of investment. The business community, then mainly of Asian origin, was blamed for 'sitting on the fence', and for indulging in 'anti-Uganda' transfers of capital abroad. Asians, some with Ugandan citizenship but a substantial number without, had traditionally dominated business, especially daily commerce in the major urban centres. In announcing his 'new political culture', Obote himself had referred to the Asian British passport holders as those who 'have no roots, nor have they had any desire to have, in this country' (Uganda, 1970: 7).[5] There was now a determined strengthening of the control apparatus, with restrictions on currency and property transfers.

During the latter half of the 1960s, the government introduced broad legislation which ensured it a substantial measure of control in most spheres of the economy, a trend similar to that in Tanzania. However, the government's insistence on greater involvement in 'development efforts' was essentially euphemism for the anti-Asian (and anti-pluralist) strategy. The Produce Marketing Board was established in 1968 and charged with the responsibility of marketing over 30 commodities that were not traditional cash crops. In 1969, cooperative unions were given the monopoly of collecting and processing coffee, cotton, and tobacco. Both measures cut out the bulk of the Asian middlemen and traders.[6]

The definitive move towards total control of economic activity by the state was made when Obote presented his *Common Man's Charter* in 1969, the Ugandan expression of a leftist tendency that had swept through Africa in the 1960s. This was followed by the Nakivubo Pronouncements of May 1970, by which the government acquired a controlling stake in all the major enterprises in the country, including the mainly British-owned commercial banks. The Cooperative Statutes Act of 1970 gave discretionary powers to the Minister of Cooperatives in all matters pertaining to the cooperative movement, at the expense of farmer-owned institutions, such as Bugisu Cooperative Union (Bunker, 1991). The Trade Unions Act of 1970 and the Banking Act of 1969 also emphasised government control. In industry, government involvement was mainly through the Uganda Development Corporation (UDC), established already in 1952. As Kalule-Settala had put it in his budget speech, 'The control of the economy by our citizens is our cornerstone for stability and prosperity' (Uganda, 1969: 1).

It can be argued that this frenetic activity at the end of the decade was in part an attempt to address the complex of challenges (and contradictions) arising from the brief, but eventful, post-Independence experience: how to preserve state power; how to expand investment and thereby increase economic growth; how to prevent the 'leakage' of national resources abroad; how to incorporate peasants and the rural sector in the development process; how to redress the inequalities in incomes and opportunities; and finally, how to bridge the regional economic gaps. Unfortunately for Uganda, the 'heights' acquired in the nationalisation drive, which included manufacturing and transport companies as well as banks, were not sufficiently 'commanding' even in government hands. The key sector, agriculture, which was mainly in the hands of smallholders, was not much affected by these shifts in ownership. In any case, before any useful assessment of the changes could be undertaken, Obote's government was replaced in a *coup d'etat* in January 1971, by Idi Amin.

3. Economic Performance (1960–71)

Table 2.1 shows estimates of growth, inflation, investment, money supply, and other macroeconomic variables for the period 1960–71. At the beginning of the 1960s a recession beset Uganda, due mainly to adverse weather conditions and declining terms of trade. Domestic-producer prices for coffee fell in nominal terms from an average of 80 cents per pound in 1957 to 50 cents in 1961 and 43 cents in 1965 (Uganda, 1967a). Even given the relatively low inflation of those days, coffee prices fell sharply in real terms. The investment climate was also rather depressed due to worries about the economic policies that would be pursued after Independence. However, coffee production rose during this period, a reflection of the increasing incorporation of the countryside into the market economy. Real GDP fell in 1961, picked up somewhat in 1962, and then grew by the unprecedented rate of close to 12 per cent in 1963. GDP per capita fell even more in the first year of self-government, but recovered in 1963. In spite of this, formal-sector employment fell even in that year and grew only slowly in 1964. Real wages were 44 per cent higher in 1964 than in 1960, which was having a cost in terms of employment. In

1965, a total of 240,990 individuals were engaged in the formal sector, comprising only about 4 per cent of the labour force.

After embarking on the Second National Development Plan with the slogan 'Work for Progress' in 1965 (Uganda, 1966), formal employment increased at a rate of 5 per cent per year over the next six years — most of it in the public sector — raising its share in the labour force to about 5 per cent at the end of the period.[7] But real wages peaked in 1966 and 1967, then gradually declined as market forces began to assert themselves. This pattern is similar to that observed for Kenya (Collier and Lal, 1986).

Investment recovered after the early 1960s and then showed a small but steady rise for most of the decade. The share of investment in GDP is also somewhat misleading, since the subsistence sector (included in GDP) undertook little investment. Thus, as a share of modern-sector GDP, investment was much greater. Average annual GDP growth was above 5 per cent from 1962 to 1969.

With import substitution and weak international coffee prices, it was not possible to bring about much improvement in the rural-urban terms of trade, but there was no sharp fall either.[8] Money supply growth was under reasonable control, although there was a rather rapid growth of credit to the government at the end of the decade. Still, on the whole, the 1960s were a period of low inflation, an average of less than 3 per cent. In 1970 inflation started to accelerate, however, and reached 12 per cent by the end of the year.

Tables 2.2 and 2.3 show data on wage incomes to illustrate the disparities in earning opportunities in both sectoral and regional terms. Table 2.2 presents a summary of income surveys for unskilled workers in a number of Ugandan towns from 1958–65. At that time regular employment was the main source of wage income, in contrast to the 1980s, when informal employment was high. For Kampala and Jinja, the capital and the main industrial town, regular employment provided over 90 per cent of incomes. For the smaller towns, Mbale, Fort Portal and Gulu, the share was smaller but still substantial, and casual employment still only about 3 per cent of incomes. Sale of produce was a major source of income for unskilled workers in the smaller towns, but not in Kampala and Jinja. The possibility to grow crops while also holding a job, was often used as an excuse for the

Table 2.1: *Economic Performance Indicators 1960–71 (indices: 1960=100)*

	1960	1961	1962	1963	1964	1965	1966	1967	1968	1969	1970	1971
GDP growth (%)	3.2	-1.1	4.1	11.7	7.5	0.9	6.3	5.1	3.2	11.7	0.7	-0.2
GDP per capita index	100	96	97	103	106	102	104	105	104	112	109	106
Gross domestic investment/GDP (%)	11	10	11	13	12	11	12	13	13	14	13	15
Gross domestic savings/GDP (%)	16	13	14	17	19	12	12	14	14	15	16	11
Exports/GDP (%)	26	24	23	27	29	26	26	25	24	21	22	19
Terms of trade	100	91	91	84	93	85	97	90	94	94	102	103
Net foreign direct investment (US$ million)	–	–	–	–	–	–	–	1.5	0.9	3.3	4.2	-1.2
Total external debt (US$ million)	–	–	–	–	–	–	–	–	–	–	151.7	172.4
Formal sector wage employment (index)	100	96.6	94.3	90.8	91.8	98.6	100.6	105.1	115.4	120.8	127.8	132.8
Real modern sector wages index	100	110.1	120.0	133.3	144.2	147.1	153.3	153.7	141.2	139.1	136.9	135.5
Inflation (GDP deflator)	-1.1	6.0	-2.8	2.9	5.7	11.6	-0.8	-0.8	3.7	1.2	12.4	11.7
Growth of money supply (M1) (%)	–	–	–	–	–	–	–	8	21	10	14	2
Growth of domestic credit (%)	–	–	–	–	–	–	–	–	22	13	23	26
Growth of credit to government (%)	–	–	–	–	–	–	–	–	35	77	77	64
Bank deposit interest rate (%)	–	–	–	–	–	–	3.5	3.5	3.5	3.5	3.5	3.5
Population (millions)	6.6	6.8	7.1	7.4	7.7	8.0	8.4	8.7	9.1	9.4	9.8	10.1

Sources: Uganda (1965b), *Background to the Budget 1965–66*; Uganda (1966c), *Statistical Abstract, 1965*; Uganda (1967a), *Statistical Abstract 1966*; Uganda (various issues), *Quarterly Economic and Statistical Bulletin*; World Bank (1982); *World Data 1995*.

differentiated wage and benefits structure under the protectorate government (Uganda Protectorate, 1962). Except for Mbale, 'other cash incomes' were roughly even across towns.

Table 2.2: *A Comparison of Unskilled Workers' Income by Source in Ugandan Towns, 1958–65 (Ushs and per cent)*

	Kampala (1964)	Jinja (1965)	Mbale (1958)	F. Portal (1960)	Gulu (1961)
Regular employment (%)	91.0	94.2	61.7	72.6	67.2
Casual employment (%)	0.6	0.5	3.5	3.0	2.4
Sales of produce (%)	1.8	1.6	24.8	19.7	24.9
Other cash income (%)	6.6	3.7	–	4.7	5.5
Cash income (UShs/month)	139.0	161.0	93.6	59.7	85.6
Total expend. (UShs/month)	158.2	186.9	97.0	62.0	83.2
Cash income/total expend. (%)	87.9	86.0	96.5	96.4	102.9
Food/total expenditure (%)	50.1	47.2	49.9	59.5	43.6

Note: food expenditure does not include own produced food.
Source: Uganda (1967a), *Statistical Abstract 1966*.

It is noteworthy that cash income is exceeded by total expenditure in all cases but one, most notably for Kampala and Jinja. Thus for unskilled workers this meant that part of the food consumed was grown at home. So even in the early 1960s unskilled workers did not survive solely on their formal sector wages (Uganda Protectorate, 1962). For the upper echelons, corruption was already a form of income diversification (Greenstone, 1966).

In the 1960s, the average share of the private sector in formal employment was 60 per cent, though its share in the total wage-bill was much smaller; mean earnings in private employment were much lower than in the public sector. Presumably the government was not in a position to enforce its minimum wage legislation outside the public sector. Table 2.3 shows that in 1965, 27 per cent of private sector employees earned less than 100 Ushs/month, but only 15 per cent of public-sector employees. The median employee earned somewhat less than 150 Ushs/month in the private sector, and just over that in the public sector. No registered employees earned 2,000 Ushs/month or more in 1965. From 1965 to 1971 the distribution of employment by wage group shifted markedly, reflecting increased Ugandanisation in the upper brackets and, in the lower ones, a general shift upwards due to increased minimum wage levels. In 1971, 23 per cent of the employees earned above 400 Ushs/month, as opposed to 10 per cent in 1965 (quite an increase even given the average inflation rate of 2.5 per cent). In 1971 50 per cent earned less than 150 Ushs, compared with 57 per cent in 1965.

Table 2.3: *Per Cent Distribution of Wage Employment by Wage Group 1965/1971 (Ushs/month)*

Sector	<100	100–149	150–199	200–399	400–999	1000–1999	2000–2999	3000+
Private (1965)	27	38	12	15	7	1	–	–
Public (1965)	15	31	19	23	9	3	–	–
All (1965)	22	35	15	18	8	2	–	–
All (1971)	13	18	19	27	15	5	1	2

Note: prices were 30 per cent higher in 1971 than in 1965.
Sources: Uganda (1967a), *Statistical Abstract 1966*, and Uganda (1972c), *Enumeration of Employees, June 1971*

4. Conclusions

Independent Uganda had inherited an overwhelmingly agricultural economy. The spread of cash-crop production, generally steady commodity-terms-of-trade in the 1960s and the rapid growth of the small import-substituting manufacturing sector, had together lent the country an aura of relative prosperity. The economy was growing rapidly and the social infrastructure was expanding at an unprecedented pace. However, many of the problems that would turn up in subsequent decades were already well-rooted: the regional and urban-rural economic gaps, disparities in access to services such as education and health care and, tragically, the increasingly politicised role of the military.

The establishment of a national central bank to replace the East African Currency Board — in the belief that a national institution would be more amenable to government persuasion, especially in the area of deficit financing — marked the removal of an external 'agency of restraint' (see Collier, 1995). It was hoped that it would help alleviate the perceived shortage of credit in the economy as a whole, and reduce the fear that some of the national profits were somehow being siphoned off. In Kenya, the powers of the central bank were countervailed to some degree by the relatively more developed financial institutions and markets. However, in Uganda, as in Tanzania, the growth of the financial sector had been slow, with government institutions dominating. The emphasis on national, government-controlled institutions meant that no new private financial institutions would be forthcoming. Lack of competition led to a decline in efficiency and to a smaller range of services. The anti-Asian sentiments of the 1960s, as well as the government's eradication of independent cooperative unions and trade unions, revealed increasing intolerance of all potential competitors for the attention of 'workers and peasants'.

All these trends of the 1960s — anti-Asian, anti-cooperatives, anti-currency board — were examples of the concentration of power in the government. The developments of the 1970s were more the consequences of this concentration of power than the weakening of the institutions of the 1960s.

Notes

1. Cotton was introduced earlier in the century and spread rapidly throughout the country, but coffee eventually overtook it in economic importance, especially in southern and eastern Uganda. Tobacco was mostly grown in the north-western region, while tea, predominantly a plantation crop, was grown on estates in western and southern Uganda.
2. This was presented as follows (p. 6):

   > We believe that in order to encourage the development of a permanent wage earning class, the Government should take the lead in paying wages sufficient to meet these obligatory and socially desirable expenditures as well as enabling the worker to feed and clothe his family to a level consistent with the general level of wealth and development in the country as a whole.

3. The East African Currency Board was established in London in 1919 to issue and redeem East African currency in exchange for UK pounds sterling (see Bank of Uganda, 1970).
4. In August 1965, the Uganda Commercial Bank was launched.
5. Obote went on to add that

   > they have never shown any commitment to the cause of Uganda or even to Africa. Their interest is to make money, which they exported to various capitals of the world on the eve of our independence.

6. President Obote (Uganda, 1970: 6) stated:

   > Like in the case of the Cooperative Movement, with regard to the ginning of cotton and the processing of coffee, some of the parastatal bodies will in future have monopoly in the fields of their activities, to the exclusion of any countrywide private enterprise ... Courage and boldness must be the essence in the consolidation of our independence.

7. The plan also envisaged the doubling of per capita income from 520 to 1050 Ushs by 1970.

8. During the period the rural-urban terms of trade, measured as the agricultural price index divided by manufactures price index, was as follows.

1960=100	1964=103	1968=100
1961=96	1965=110	1969=98
1962=91	1966=110	1970=108
1963=90	1967=107	1971=130

Chapter 3: Crisis and Decline (1972-80)

1. Introduction

Uganda's capital base and infrastructure, which had expanded rapidly in the 1960s, began to deteriorate with Amin's assumption of power in 1971, along with the professionalism which had once characterised the civil service. Unfortunately, Amin's rule of 1971-79 coincided with several severe international economic disturbances: the oil shock of 1973/74, the international recession which followed, and fluctuations in the terms of trade for commodity exporters.[1]

As a notable Ugandan political scientist has argued (Mamdani, 1976), Amin was not some momentary aberration in Uganda's public affairs, but very much a product of the country's socio-political evolution. Whether nations deserve the leaders they produce is, of course, another matter altogether. But it is not surprising that Amin's coup was initially popular among certain key groups, especially in the south of the country, bureaucrats, businessmen, the royal worthies of Buganda, and even Western diplomats. These groups had experienced a decline in political influence, and some in their economic fortunes as well during Obote's seemingly well-orchestrated radical onslaught on 'the privileged and the feudal classes' at the end of the 1960s. Also, mistakenly, some expected Amin to end the human rights violations, which were common under Obote. Soon after taking power, Amin included a number of top academics in his government — the key word at the time was efficiency — and he had quickly moved to reverse Obote's 'socialism' by reducing to 49 per cent the 60 per cent state participation in major businesses, which had been declared in the Nakivubo Pronouncements of May, 1970. This assuaged the apprehension of the large, mostly Asian-owned companies and the multinationals, but the respite was short-lived.

Amin was in a populist mood, blaming Obote (Uganda, 1972a) for 'over-concentration on politics, at the expense of taking care of our economic life'. But the military regime was about to embark on

20

policies that would drastically transform the structure of the economy and reduce the well-being of the people for decades. With its anti-socialist rhetoric, the Amin regime frightened neighbouring Tanzania, with which Obote had enjoyed particularly good relations — Obote had patterned his *Common Man's Charter*, as well as the *Nakivubo Pronouncements*, on Nyerere's *Arusha Declaration* of 1967. Amin's relations with Kenya were not much improved, either, by his wild territorial claims on the western parts of that country. This alienation of Uganda from its neighbours weakened the East African Community, which remained dysfunctional until its final collapse in 1977. Domestically, Amin began to eliminate, often by extra judicial executions, real and potential enemies, including key members of his initially civilian-dominated government. He soon got rid of his stiffly academic ministers, replacing them with his own military men. Foreign diplomatic missions began to pack their bags (Kayizzi-Mugerwa and Bigsten, 1992).

2. Economic Policy in the 1970s

In the culmination of a decade of anti-Asian sentiment, Amin expelled Asians from Uganda at the beginning of his 'Economic War' in August 1972. The expulsion clearly marked an end to Uganda's post-independence decade of relative prosperity. Jamal (1976) saw the expulsion of the Asians, as a consequence of the long history of economic inequalities between them as a group and the rest of the population, but he also notes (1987: 127) that it was 'difficult to say that urban income distribution improved after the expulsion of the rich Asian class'.

Amin also further expanded the public sector. A large number of formerly Asian-owned companies fell into government hands. There were only 10 parastatals in 1972, but by the mid-1970s there were 23, responsible for about 250 different business enterprises (Katumba, 1988). The government also created a Departed Asians' Abandoned Properties Custodian Board (DAAPCB) to administer the smaller ventures and interests, not otherwise allocated. As predicted in an uncharacteristically candid policy analysis undertaken during the

Amin era (Uganda, 1977), this expansion of the public sector was to prove disastrous. The managers of the new parastatals lacked both managerial competence and entrepreneurial skill.

There were three main effects of the Asian expulsion. First, as Wakhweya indicated in the first budget speech of the Amin era (Uganda, 1971: 10), the task facing the government was 'to re-establish the credibility and national honour of Uganda' after the coup, but instead this admitted loss of reputation was aggravated by the expulsion of the Asian entrepreneurs; access to their formal and informal lines of credit was also lost. Second, the manner in which former Asian businesses were acquired created insecurity of tenure, leading to asset stripping, followed by slow decay of buildings and businesses, especially in Kampala. Third, skilled managers were replaced by largely unskilled and relatively uneducated people, often drawn from the military.

The companies were now run with a plethora of motives, which did not include the need to make profits or contribute to the government treasury. Previously they generated government revenue in the form of corporate taxes, rent, licences and fees (Uganda, 1977: 45), but now they became dependent on government subsidies to meet running costs.

In an effort to expand the tax base, the government introduced the Commercial Transactions Levy in 1972, initially as a surcharge on services, but later extended to cover sales of goods by traders and manufacturers. It was a form of VAT with a rate of 20 per cent on most goods, 50 per cent on some categories. More taxes were introduced in 1973, such as an export duty on arabica coffee, airport service charges, and a special once-and-for-all business levy on institutions and persons who had acquired properties of the departed Asians. Income-tax deposits were introduced in 1976 as a way of 'dealing with a poor tax culture and weak administrative capacity' (Uganda, 1995a). These deposits were a unique creation of the Uganda tax authorities: in the absence of audited records, most business owners paid a deposit to the tax authorities, to be adjusted when the final tax assessment was done. Since the latter almost never happened, deposits became the actual taxes due, which left considerable margin for arbitrariness and collusion. Meanwhile, the private individuals who acquired some of the smaller businesses soon stripped them of most assets. A shortage of foreign exchange and loss of foreign credit led to a general lack of spare parts. By the mid-1970s, with poor maintenance in the parastatals and elsewhere, only a small portion of installed capacity could be utilised.

To counteract the resulting decline of employment in the private sector, the government increased its own labour force. Between 1971 and 1975 public-sector employment increased at an annual rate of 11 per cent, from 134,030 to 209,300, while other formal employment fell from 190,500 to 161,900.

Economic imbalances emerged early in Amin's regime, but instead of attempting to correct them via normal stabilisation policies, the government chose to use administrative controls instead. In 1972 import restrictions were introduced on a range of products, and exchange control regulations were tightened. Licences were introduced for importers and exporters, as well as advance cash deposits for imported goods. Foreign travel allowances were reduced by 50 per cent. Money supply increased over the decade at a rate of 30 per cent annually, from 1.7 billion shillings at the end of 1970 to over 12 billion by the end of 1979 (Sentongo, 1979). At the same time a decrease in the supply of goods and services, was aggravated by the fact that many peasants shifted from the monetary economy into subsistence production, so overall decline in the demand for money was greater than the reduction in GDP. This combination of an expansionary monetary policy with a decline in money demand led to a generally rising rate of inflation over the 1970s (Table 3.1). Since fighting inflation was also a government priority, increasingly tighter price controls were introduced. Sugar was a politically sensitive commodity, but the expulsion of its Asian producers had reduced supply from over 120,000 tonnes in 1972 to barely 20,000 in 1976. Various sugar allocation mechanisms were then devised in a bid to halt the escalation of prices, but this only increased the sugar scarcity. Thus, though price controls were sometimes brutally enforced, they failed to improve supply or to correct the resulting imbalances.

In 1973, to provide Amin's close friends with highly visible positions and to get potential rivals out of the barracks, the administrative structure of the country was re-organised into provinces — led by powerful governors — parallel structures to the central administration, but with little local participation in decision-making. First and foremost, the governors saw themselves as enforcers of measures ranging from price control to anti-smuggling. The governor of Kampala was known to inspect the city's *matooke* markets to make sure that the prices charged were 'justified'; his counterparts in the border regions would sometimes arrest smugglers and cattle rustlers.

Attempts at socioeconomic legislation, such as the Land Reform Decree of June, 1975, though earning the regime some radical credentials, proved of little worth in practice. Amin's populist agenda began to fail him, because he had challenged too many forces, both internally and externally. His policies and actions failed to generate the economic resources necessary to finance the civil service and the army and to maintain political support. The steady decline of the economy began to hurt even his diehard supporters. The value of salaries and the quantity of imports fell, reducing the resources available to the elite.

The ambitious Action Programme of 1977 was the military government's final attempt to stabilise the economy. It was an all-embracing investment programme based on domestic savings, including those from increased competition in the parastatal sector and higher efficiency in government. There were also plans to improve incentives for saving in banks and pension schemes. The total cost of the programme — of which the foreign exchange component would be 80 per cent — was estimated at Ushs 11 billion, that is, almost three times recurrent expenditure, or nine times development expenditure. The Action Plan was totally unrealistic, particularly its reliance on foreign exchange availability. The exchange rate had remained fixed at about 8 shillings to the US dollar for over a decade, while the dollar traded at up to 100 shillings on the parallel market. This obviously had a strongly negative effect on official exports and the rationality of resource allocation. Ugandan export incomes were dwindling throughout the 1970s, except for the temporary reprieve during the coffee boom from 1975 to 1977 when terms of trade almost tripled (Table 3.1). By 1978, the share of (official) exports in GDP was a meagre four per cent — down from over 20 per cent in the 1960s — which could not possibly sustain the import-intensive investment programme.

With the imminent collapse of the East African Economic Community and the increased political tension in the region, Uganda expanded its military rapidly, though military expenditure did not rise as fast. Uganda's military expenditure as a ratio to GDP was 3.6 per cent in 1971, and had risen to 4.6 per cent in 1972, but then fell to 2 per cent by 1978. In Kenya the ratio had risen from 1.2 per cent in 1971 to 4.5 per cent in 1978, and in Tanzania from 2.4 to 7 per cent (see Mohammed, 1995). The much lower expenditure in Uganda was reflected in increasing pauperisation of the soldiers and deterioration of their equipment, perhaps explaining the relative ease with which they were defeated by a combined force of Tanzanian troops and Ugandan exiles in 1979.

3. Economic Performance (1972–80)

Table 3.1 and Figures 3.1 and 3.2 show the main indicators of economic performance for the period from 1972, when Amin declared persons of Asian origin *personae non gratae*, to 1980, when Milton Obote assumed power for the second time.[2] Real gross domestic product fell for most of these years, with a virtual collapse at the end of the 1970s: GDP fell by 5.5 per cent in 1978, then by 11 per cent in 1979, and a further 3.4 per cent in 1980, during the war with Tanzania and the subsequent period of political instability. With population growth of about 3 per cent per year, GDP per capita fell by more than 25 per cent in just these three years.

The decline of the 1970s was partly due to the falling investment rate: from about 11 per cent in 1972, gross domestic investment fell to only 6 per cent of GDP by 1976, and stayed at that level for the rest of the period. Since gross investments thus were far from enough to cover depreciation, the real capital stock was shrinking rapidly in the second half of the 1970s, clearly indicating a collapse of investor confidence. After the Asian expulsion, Amin was generally regarded as a predator: no private investor would invest long-term in a country where security of ownership had become so tenuous. The situation was further aggravated by the fact that insecurity and general lawlessness were particularly severe in the most productive areas of the country. Second, the Ugandan business class, which traditionally was Asian in origin, was expelled from the country in 1972. It was replaced by other groups, including soldiers, ministers, erstwhile chiefs etc., that were too preoccupied in other arenas and too distracted by the political confusion to have upheld a high rate of domestic investment. Third, economic policies pursued during this period were also detrimental to savings: with the interest rate paid on bank deposits fixed at 3.5 per cent, while inflation was much higher — over 50 per cent in some years — real interest rates were extremely negative.

The main donors — Great Britain, Canada, the United States — then withdrew, soon followed by many other Western countries, with a direct negative impact on investment, since a substantial portion of fixed capital creation depended on aid disbursements. In the period 1972–80 total net long-term capital inflows amounted to only US$190 million, in stark contrast to the amounts of aid received by Uganda in the 1960s, and to the increasing amounts received by other countries in the region, such as Kenya and Tanzania.

With deterioration of the macroeconomic environment, the volume of exports also began to fall, especially cotton and tobacco, which are annual crops. Low producer prices and political instability in the main growing areas in northern Uganda led to decreasing acreage under these crops during the 1970s, and their total output fell by more than 50 per cent. Coffee, on the other hand, is a perennial crop: trees were mostly not uprooted, but were neglected so that output fell and some output was diverted outside official marketing channels. Henstridge (1995) analysed the response of coffee producers in Uganda to high taxation in the context of an increasingly overvalued exchange rate. Besides affecting output negatively, this form of double taxation led to extensive coffee smuggling to neighbouring countries. Henstridge estimates (p. 217) that between 1974/75 and 1987/88 roughly US$115 million worth of coffee was smuggled out of Uganda each year as much as half of the output in some years. According to the 1979 budget speech, 27,000 tonnes of coffee were smuggled out of the country in the 1975/76 season, and

Table 3.1: *Indicators of Economic Performance 1972-1980* (indexes: 1960=100)

	1972	1973	1974	1975	1976	1977	1978	1979	1980
GDP growth (%)	1	-1	-2	-2	1	-1.6	-5.5	-11	-3.4
GDP per capita (index)	104	100	95	90	88	84	77	66	62
Gross domestic investment/GDP (%)	11	8	11	8	6	6	8	6	6
Gross domestic savings/GDP (%)	13	11	10	5	7	7	3	8	0
Export/GDP (%)	18	16	14	8	11	8	4	3	7
Terms of trade (1960=100)	94	88	76	78	108	186	119	117	113
Net foreign direct investment (million US$)	-11.9	5.2	1.7	2.1	1.2	0.8	1.0	1.6	–
Total external debt (US$ million)	177.6	177.4	204.4	211.5	246.5	338.1	449.7	590.2	702.5
Wage employment (index)	135.0	143.2	150.8	150.5	149.6	150.4	–	–	–
Inflation (GDP deflator)	4.2	15.5	23.5	45.3	16.3	57.5	24.5	68.6	51.0
Money supply (M1) (growth %)	36	38	43	8	37	30	21	52	31
Domestic credit (growth %)	35	37	34	18	27	25	24	23	64
Credit to government (growth %)	55	49	35	24	33	15	30	28	59
Interest, bank deposit rate	3.5	3.5	3.5	3.5	3.5	3.5	3.5	3.5	3.5
Population (million)	10.3	10.6	10.9	11.2	11.5	11.9	12.3	12.7	13.1

Sources: Uganda (various years), *Background to the Budget*; World Bank (1989b), *World Tables 1988-89*; Uganda (various years), *Budget Speech*; World Bank (1982); *World Data 1995*.

Figure 3.1: *Shares of Investment, Exports and Government Expenditures in GDP, 1972–80*

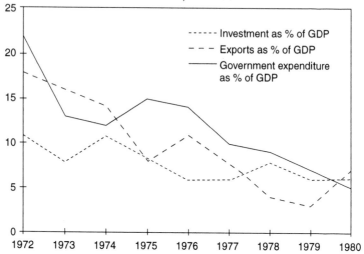

Source: Uganda (various years) *Background to the Budget.*

Figure 3.2: *Inflation and Money, 1972–80*

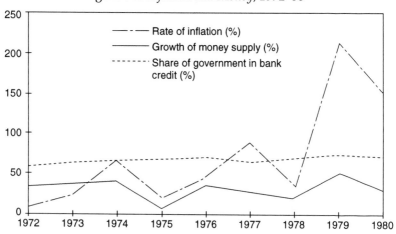

Source: Uganda (various years) *Background to the Budget.*

another 51,000 tonnes were smuggled in the following crop season. At the height of the coffee price boom, 1977/78, yet another 47,500 tonnes were said to have been taken out of the country illegally. Coffee smuggling did not end with the overthrow of the Amin regime, and the crop year 1978/79 saw the disappearance of another 50,000 tonnes of coffee. This is just one example, of several, of the population retreating from the official economy to subsistence or parallel markets.

Thus, in spite of the tremendous improvement in coffee prices between early 1975 and the peak in 1977 (prices quadrupled), and thereby also in the overall terms of trade, the country's official export volume fell, intermittently, to extremely low levels by the end of the decade. Peasants had abandoned the annual cash crops, such as cotton and tobacco, so the coffee that was produced constituted an increasing share of exports. Tea production also declined sharply, so that coffee was virtually the only export commodity by the end of the 1970s. The once promising tourist industry, formerly one of the highest earners of foreign exchange, crumbled as well under the twin pressures of security difficulties and poor maintenance of hotels and game parks.

The first sharp reversal in the current account followed the oil crisis of 1973-74 and the world-wide economic recession of 1975. However, in spite of the substantial smuggling of coffee out of the country, the boom years of 1976 and 1977, saw a marked improvement, with a surplus of US$43 million in the current account in 1976, and US$68 million in 1977. The years 1978-80 saw a deterioration again, as coffee prices weakened and oil prices rose strongly once again. Amin's government found it difficult to borrow, although some countries were still willing to provide credit.

The 1970s were particularly difficult for government revenue. The African businessmen who had taken over Asian companies managed to resist taxation, so the corporate sector contributed less and less to tax revenue, and income taxes had an even smaller share in revenue generation. Coffee became the main source of revenue, via controlled producer prices and export levies; the latter had contributed less than 10 per cent in the mid-1960s (Uganda, 1965b). Still, as is well known from standard trade theory, the incidence of import taxes is on the export sector, so the peasants were also the main financiers of government in the 1960s and 1970s. This role of the peasants was to continue in the 1980s.

With large military outlays, government expenditures invariably exceeded revenue, although, as a ratio to GDP, government expenditure was becoming smaller and smaller in the 1970s (Figure 3.1). This was mainly because the monetary part of the economy was contracting. The state found itself in a vicious circle. Its mismanagement of the economy led to economic decline and lower tax revenues, which forced it to devise new ways, such as increased export taxation, to collect revenue, which, however, further accelerated the decline and made it even more difficult to collect taxes. The government, therefore, had increasingly to rely on domestic loans to finance its expenditures, and this took the bulk of domestic credit (Figure 3.2); the banking system's claims on government were, on average, 65 per cent of total domestic credit during this period.

4. Conclusions

In the African context, Amin's rule was, in some respects, not exceptional. In less than a decade of independence, military dictatorships had taken over in a number of countries. The relatively weak civilian governments had brought little prosperity, and the only viable institution was the military. Military regimes thrived on extreme forms of nationalism, including the suppression of minorities. In Uganda, this led to the mass expulsion of an important group of producers, financiers and artisans of Asian descent. However, massacres of peasants in the countryside and killing of political opponents set Uganda apart. This and a general lack of focused economic policies set Uganda on a path of rapid decline (Kasfir, 1983). Though Mazrui (1975) saw some redeeming features in this otherwise gloomy era, including the spread of the Swahili language, with its favourable implications for East African unity, and resistance to super power interference, most judgements have so far been unwaveringly harsh.

For the length of its existence, Amin's regime had had bad relations with Tanzania, where Obote and the bulk of Uganda's political elite had taken refuge when Amin took power in 1971. Amin's claims on Tanzanian territory and the raid on the Kagera region provided the Tanzanian government, as well as Uganda's exiled groups, the opportunity to oust Amin. The invading force made a rapid advance towards Kampala, where Amin's troops were dislodged with little difficulty. Pain (1987) argued that Amin's domestic allies used his period in power to realise their corporate interests in business via the military. But with business brought to a virtual standstill by the economic chaos during Amin's last years in power, military power itself did not seem worth defending. The bulk of Amin's troops went into exile in Southern Sudan and parts of Zaire.

Notes

1. A number of multi-disciplinary studies of the Ugandan economy covering this period have begun to put the Amin years in perspective, including the resulting challenges facing subsequent regimes, see for example Hansen and Twaddle (1988), Wiebe and Dodge (1987), and Campbell (1979). A more traditional study is Sathyamurthy (1986); see also Brett (1989), Mamdani (1988), and Ofcansky (1996).
2. From the mid-1970s Ugandan statistics suffered from inadequate data collection and lost records. As part of later adjustment efforts, the government has put strong emphasis on rehabilitation of the data gathering units, especially the Statistics Department based at Entebbe.

Chapter 4: Reform Without Stability: Obote II to the NRM (1981–86)

1. Introduction

The leadership vacuum left by the rapid collapse of Amin's military government in early 1979 increased the level of insecurity, weakening attempts at economic reform by the regimes that followed. There were three governments in less than two years: the Lule government was in office for only about 70 days (April to June, 1979), followed by Binaisa who ruled for close to a year, and the Military Commission which ushered in the elections of 1980. The war and the failure to contain corruption resulted in political and economic chaos. Power continued to be seen as a means to private enrichment (Tindigarukayo, 1988). The period from April 1979 to December 1980 demonstrated the futility of undertaking economic reform in a political vacuum.

Despite Amin's absence since early 1979, coordinated economic reforms were not embarked upon until 1981, when a military-civilian coalition under Obote (Obote II) sought and received technical and financial support from the IMF and the World Bank. Except for brief periods when Uganda's leaders changed, the IMF and the World Bank have continued to be major actors in Uganda's adjustment efforts. The adjustment experience can be divided into two distinct phases. The first was the period 1981–86, which began with a degree of optimism as the economy responded, from a low base, to newly-introduced economic incentives, but which quickly gave way to policy regression as domestic political difficulties relegated economic concerns to the background; and beginning in 1987 the second, more successful phase under the NRM (National Resistance Movement), which will be discussed in the next chapter.

2. Initiating Economic Reform

In Uganda's adjustment debates, the Obote II period is often ignored for the more promising results of the NRM era, yet as the first real attempts at reform in Uganda, there are lessons to learn from the Obote II experience as well. At the start of his second period in power, Obote saw his government's priorities as raising efficiency in the goods producing sectors, prudent use of funds, and the creation of incentives for both domestic and foreign investors (Uganda, 1981a).[1] To achieve and maintain these goals, the economy needed market reforms. A Commonwealth team that visited Uganda in 1979 to survey its rehabilitation needs had made similar suggestions (Commonwealth Secretariat, 1979; Uganda, 1979b), as had IMF and World Bank missions of the early 1980s.

A key issue in the early 1980s was how to arrive at an exchange rate that would enable more efficient resource allocation. A vocal group argued for reigning in the black currency market (via controls) to put some order into the economy (Green, 1981; Banguire, 1989). However, to meet the terms of the initial IMF-supported 13-month stabilisation programme, starting in June 1981, the Obote II government undertook a number of measures, including floating the shilling, increasing producer-prices for export crops, removal of price controls, rationalisation of tax structures, and better control of government expenditure, accompanied by increased accountability in the public sector. The shilling immediately depreciated from 8 to 80 shillings to the US dollar (see Figure 4.1 and Appendix 4B). This was a 'dirty float', with a committee of the Bank of Uganda managing the exchange rate on a day-to-day basis 'because of the insufficiency of foreign exchange' (Uganda, 1982a: 2). Since the currency was not allowed to depreciate sufficiently to clear the market, excess demand for foreign exchange persisted. To satisfy non-official needs and reduce parallel market dealings in foreign currency, while at the same time preserving a favourable rate for 'strategic' imports, a dual exchange rate system was adopted in August 1982. The use of dual exchange rates was discouraged by the IMF, which, with the three stand-by arrangements and purchases from its compensatory financing facility, was one of the main backers of the reform programme during Obote II. However, the government saw the dual exchange-rate system as a necessary interim measure to relieve the pressure of managing limited foreign exchange resources at a time of low institutional capacities.

Figure 4.1: *Official, Window 2 and Parallel Exchange Rates 1981–86 (UShs/$)*

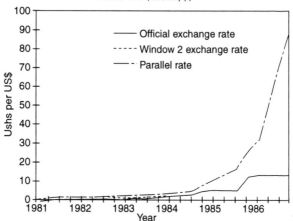

Note: the 1987 reforms removed two zeros from the Ugandan currency; all rates are expressed in the new Uganda shillings used after that date.
Source: Appendix 4B and Henstridge (1995).

The dual exchange rate system and control at the Bank of Uganda indicated that the government had not given up its traditional protection of importers and import-substituting industries. Thus though the international terms of trade improved by about 27 per cent from 1981 to 1982, the domestic price ratio between exportables and importables (P_x/P_m) fell by 15 per cent (Figure 4.2). This shows that the protection of domestic producers of importables actually increased during the dual exchange rate experiment. Thus initially the rapid currency depreciation was not necessarily accompanied by trade liberalisation. The situation was reversed in 1983, with falling international terms of trade but a rising domestic price ratio between

exportables and importables, as traditional exports were moved from
Window 1 to Window 2.

Figure 4.2: *Relative Prices 1981–86*

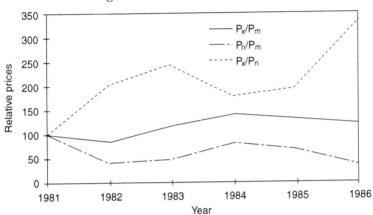

Note: P_x/P_m is the ratio of exportable to importable goods prices in
domestic currency; P_n/P_m is the ratio of non-tradable to importable
goods prices; P_x/P_n is the ratio of exportable to non-tradable goods
prices. Export prices are for products, while the remaining ones are
GDP deflators and thus for value added, with relative prices in 1981
set equal to 1.
P_x: exportable prices. Robusta coffee producer prices are used as a
proxy for exportable prices.
P_m: importable prices. The GDP deflator for domestic manufacturing
is used as a proxy for the prices of import substitutes.
P_n: non-tradable prices. The GDP deflator for utilities, construction,
retail and wholesale, transport and community services is used as a
proxy.

Sources: Uganda (1990c), *Statistical Bulletin* No GDP/2, *Gross Domestic
Product of Uganda 1981–1989*; Uganda (1995b), *Background to the Budget
1995–1996*; World Bank (various years), *World Development Report*.

There had been a total of 92 weekly auctions at Window 2 by mid-1984, with the currency depreciating rapidly, nearing the parallel (*kibanda*) rate of about 350 shillings per dollar (3.5 shillings in new currency). The Bank of Uganda had also allowed the priority exchange rate at Window 1 to converge towards the rate at Window 2. In June 1984, the two official rates were merged administratively into a single 'door', and a general foreign-exchange auction began. It was officially stated (Uganda, 1994: 4) that 'foreign exchange had become a matter which will not be of concern and frustration to the people of Uganda', but there was still a long way to go before an equilibrium exchange rate would be reached.

The government had sizeable budget deficits during 1981–83, necessitating domestic borrowing, essentially from the central bank. Credit to government expanded over 100 per cent in 1981 and by about 20 per cent per year in the following two years (see Table 4.1), contributing directly, via increased currency in circulation (M0), to growth of the money supply (M1).[2] This, together with the removal of price controls on most items, raised average annual inflation to over 40 per cent during this period. The bank deposit interest rate was allowed to rise from 3.5 per cent to 5 per cent in 1981, but real interest rates remained extremely negative, and domestic savings remained insignificant.

There was a fairly rapid recovery in 1982 and 1983, but in 1984, despite improvement in the international terms of trade, it came to a halt. There were two main factors behind the setback. First, escalating guerilla activity pushed government expenditure beyond planned limits. The discipline shown earlier in meeting IMF performance targets was now clearly lacking. The foreign exchange auction was under increasing pressure, and the shilling continued to lose value. Second, the 'fourth parliament' was drawing to an end and government was already gearing up for the coming elections; among measures taken during this time, definitely outside the IMF/World Bank mode, was a four-fold increase in public sector wages. Credit to the government increased by 70 per cent in 1984, while money supply expanded by 127 per cent; inflation (the GDP deflator) was 76 per cent and non-tradables prices rose by 227 per cent. The ratio of exportable (mainly coffee) prices to non-tradable prices fell by over 28 per cent

Table 4.1: *Economic Performance Indicators 1981–1986 (index 1960=100)*

	1981	1982	1983	1984	1985	1986
GDP growth (%)	4.0	5.7	7.4	-8.5	2.0	0.3
GDP per capita index (1960=100)	65	67	70	62	61	60
Gross domestic investment/GDP (%)	5	9	7	7	8	8
Gross domestic savings/GDP (%)	0	0	2	6	7	5
Export/GDP (%)	–	9	8	9	9	9
Terms of trade (1960=100)	86	85	88	109	107	122
Net foreign direct investment (US$ million)	–	0	0.7	0	30.0	29.0
Total external debt (US$ million)	717	882.1	1014.9	1077.4	1238.8	1422.1
Real manufacturing wages (index)	100	108	115	153	135	117
Inflation (GDP deflator)	55	34	44	76	154	135
Money supply (M1) (growth %)	103	5	46	127	140	174
Domestic credit (growth %)	104	35	38	65	114	112
Credit to government (growth %)	109	16	25	70	115	74
Interest, bank deposit rate	5	9	13	18	18	28
Interest, lending rate	6	15	16	24	24	38
Population (millions)	13.4	138	14.1	14.5	14.8	15.2

Sources: Uganda (various years), *Background to the Budget*; World Bank (1989b), *World Tables 1988–89*; Bank of Uganda (1986), *Annual Report 1985*; IMF (various years), *International Financial Statistics*; World Bank (1988), *Towards Stabilisation and Economic Recovery*; Uganda (1990c), *Statistical Bulletin No GDP/2 Gross Domestic Product of Uganda 1981 –1989*); *World Data 1995*.

from 1983 (Figure 4.2), indicating a deteriorating cost structure in the export sector, especially the increasing cost of transport. As domestic pressures increased, the government decided to abandon the IMF programme, most noticeably by reversing exchange rate policies. A year later, Obote had for a second time lost power to his military.

The period beginning with the collapse of the IMF's stand-by arrangements in mid-1984 saw a steep deterioration in economic performance. The earlier opening up of the economy had, ironically, made it more vulnerable to trade-related disturbances when the controls returned. The tightening of the foreign exchange system in 1985, as arms purchases competed with consumer imports, made it difficult to procure inputs and spares, reversing the earlier revival of the import-substituting sector. The rural economy was devastated by civil strife and the collapse of the local administration: in key producer areas the agricultural work force was displaced and rural property was destroyed on an unprecedented scale. The country seemed headed for a sharp increase in mass poverty (Bank of Uganda, 1986, p.15). The looting that accompanied the fall of Obote II in 1985 led to shortages of consumer goods and petrol. Domestic terms of trade fell by nine per cent, mainly reflecting negative shifts in the international terms of trade. Credit to the government rose by 115 per cent — partly in response to the new government's need for finances to secure its delicate military and political position — and money supply rose by 140 per cent. The military claimed up to 30 per cent of government expenditure in 1985 (Bank of Uganda, 1986). Inflation went up to 154 per cent. Rapid price increases in the importable sector were not fully compensated for by producer-price increases in agriculture, so a large part of the coffee harvest was again smuggled out of the country (see Figure 4.3).

In power, the NRM went through an initial period of indecisiveness as it tried to define an economic policy that would attract external support but remain faithful to the radical ideas of its leadership.[3] There was considerable discomfort with the notion of subjecting the economy to 'market forces', whereas state intervention and control were still very much part of the thinking of the day. This thinking was exemplified by a revaluation of the shilling at a time

Figure 4.3: *Relative Commodity Prices 1981–86*

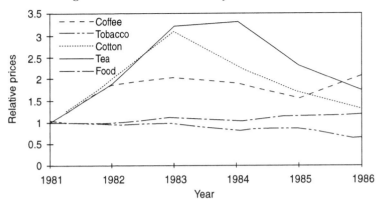

Source: Uganda (various years), *Background to the Budget.*

when the parallel rate was several times the official ones. In a press release, three months after assuming power (Uganda, 1986) the new government abolished the dual exchange-rate system, where the shilling had depreciated to 5000 shillings to the dollar (50 shillings in new currency) at Window 2 (but without clearing the market). Instead the government adopted the earlier priority (Window 1) rate of 1400 shillings per dollar (14 shillings in new currency). There was strong belief at the time that this would 'boost the buying power of the shilling', and also act as a nominal anchor, holding down domestic prices (see, for instance, Malik, 1995). While emergency war expenditures and the need to repair industries and other infrastructure continued, this measure allowed increased rent-seeking activities by, and premiums to, those lucky enough to have access to official allocations of foreign currency. The gap between the official and parallel exchange rates widened further (Figure 4.1). The government reverted to rationing with a priority list of imports including sugar, salt, soap, petroleum, scholastic materials, and agricultural inputs and spares.[4] Little thought was given to the administrative effort necessary to ensure compliance. When these 'essential' imports arrived in the country, the government was faced with the problem of distribution. Initially, the village resistance councils (RC1s) were enthusiastically thought to be the natural distribution points, but the logistics proved too complex for consumer goods other than sugar and salt. It was clear that another approach was needed. Nevertheless, in the first budget speech of the NRM presented in August, 1986, Professor P.S. Mulema, the Finance Minister, still found the IMF's 'pre-occupation with demand management' an inappropriate way to address Uganda's economic crisis (see also Loxley, 1989).

A mini coffee boom again helped improve the price of exportables relative to non-tradables, but there were also increases in the relative prices of importables as fixed exchange rates and rationing were re-adopted. Thus, in spite of a 21 per cent increase in the international terms of trade, the domestic terms of trade actually fell in 1986. Protection of the importable sector had thus increased sharply during the first year of the NRM government.

3. Production and Trade Performance

During the period of the first reforms, 1981–83, GDP grew at an average rate of 6 per cent; this was the first period with per capita income growth since the mid-1970s (Table 4.2). At the sectoral level, there was improvement across the board: monetary agriculture, mainly cash crops and food production, expanded rapidly, at 4 and 7 per cent, respectively. Of course, part of the increase in registered production may have merely been increased 'visibility' as producers brought their produce back into the formal marketing channels with the improvement of real producer prices. The prices of exportables (mainly coffee and tea) compared with non-tradables rose steadily from 1981 to 1983 (Figure 4.2), partly as a result of the rapid depreciation of the shilling, which enabled increases in producer prices without loss of government revenue. This gave export production a competitive edge versus non-tradables (Table 4.3). However, in 1984 there was a dramatic decline in agricultural production as the civil war intensified in southern Uganda and the positive effects of improvements in relative prices wore off. In 1984

Table 4.2: *Real Sectoral Outputs and GDP, 1981–86* (1981=100)

Year	1981	1982	1983	1984	1985	1986
Monetary agriculture	100	102.0	106.2	91.3	97.1	96.4
Non-monetary agriculture	100	108.4	119.5	109.8	109.8	112.4
Community services	100	103.8	107.6	112.5	116.6	120.8
Manufacturing	100	116.0	125.6	121.6	109.7	105.9
GDP per capita	100	103.1	107.5	95.6	94.9	93.4

Sources: Uganda (1990c), Gross *Domestic Product of Uganda 1981-1989*; Uganda, *Key Economics Indicators*, 6th issue, July 1991; Uganda (1995b), *Background to the Budget 1995/96*.

Table 4.3: *Indices of Agricultural Production, 1981–86 (1981 = 100)*

Year	1981	1982	1983	1984	1985	1986
Coffee	100	170.9	161.4	142.3	159.0	147.0
Cotton	100	124.4	243.9	297.6	397.6	107.3
Tobacco	100	600	1600	2000	1500	900
Tea	100	152.9	182.4	305.9	329.4	194.1
Bananas	100	111.8	109.9	105.9	109.6	111.3
Maize	100	114.9	120.8	98.8	103.5	94.2
Beans	100	98.8	130.8	122.9	111.3	111.3
Livestock	100	99.5	98.5	90.2	82.6	75.8

Sources: Uganda (1990e), *Background to the Budget* 1990–91; Uganda (1992) *Background to the Budget 1992–93*

Table 4.4: *Balance of Payments Statistics 1982–86 (millions of US$)*

	1982	1983	1984	1985	1986
Exports	347.1	367.7	407.9	379.0	406.7
Imports	−422.0	−428.1	−342.2	−204.1	−476.0
Trade balance	−74.9	−60.4	65.7	114.9	−69.3
Services net	−102.3	−115.4	−44.0	−98.9	−143.5
Unrequited transfers	107.3	103.5	85.4	61.0	208.7
Current account	−69.9	−72.3	107.1	77.0	−4.2
Capital account	14.6	27.7	−88.3	−27.4	51.1
Net changes in arrears	22.4	8.3	−77.3	17.3	44.3
Overall	−32.9	−36.3	−58.5	66.9	91.2

Note: arrears are included in the overall balance. Increases in net arrears (+), decreases (–). The net overall balance comprises changes in gross reserves, the net position vis a vis the IMF, and other (including errors and omissions).

Sources: Uganda, *Key Economic Indicators*, 3rd issue, October 1990, and 6th issue, July 1991.

alone, monetary agriculture fell by 14 per cent, and subsistence agriculture by 8 per cent.

Exports were gradually improving from 1982 to 1984 (Table 4.4), mainly thanks to increased coffee production (or reduced smuggling) in response to better prices for farmers. This, along with higher grants from abroad, helped pay for increased imports and debt servicing. Improvement in the availability of imported intermediates was a major factor in the dramatic turnaround of the manufacturing sector. In the budget speech for 1983, Obote declared (Uganda, 1983): 'To a very large extent, we have healed the wounds of the 1970s'. Evidence for this claim included the disappearance of queues for essential goods as price controls eased; eradication of *'magendo'*, the all-pervasive parallel markets of the 1970s and early 1980s; elimination of allocation committees; food abundance; and adequate transport.[5] However, the recovery was short-lived. Imports fell in 1984 in response to the hardening exchange regime. The government was also under obligation to service US$77 million of IMF debt. The collapse of Obote II then disrupted transport services, perhaps explaining the fall of imports to US$204 million in 1985. However, since exports were almost double this amount, it is plausible that some of the export earnings were simply retained abroad, waiting for resolution of the power struggle in Kampala. But availability of foreign exchange did help the Military Council, which replaced Obote, to resist the National Resistance Army's (now known as the Uganda People's Defence Forces (UPDF)) initial onslaught and preserve a semblance of government in Kampala. In 1986 transfers from Libya amounting to over US$200 million helped ameliorate some of the NRM's immediate foreign exchange needs, purchasing essential goods and services before donor aid could come on stream.

4. Summary and Conclusions

The Obote II government (1980–85) was faced with difficult tasks — restoring the functions of government, putting in place lasting incentives for producers, especially smallholders, and recreating distortion-free markets for goods and services — all with very limited financial and human resources. Furthermore, these reforms were devised in a politically-charged atmosphere,[6] and were often reversed in a bid to gain short-term political advantage (Mudoola, 1993). Other pressures included guerilla activity, with its nucleus in one of the most important coffee-producing areas. Breaking out after the contested 1980 election results, the rebellion plagued Obote II to the very end. Thus, despite Obote's efforts,[7] and substantial donor support, the reforms of the early 1980s did not lead to economic stability; they only began to falter when the civil war escalated.

Like the governments that immediately followed Amin, the military regime that replaced Obote II was vulnerable from the outset. Museveni's National Resistance Army had cut off the western parts of the country, while peace talks in Nairobi between the new military government and the NRM were not going particularly well. Worse still, under the threat of increasing insurgency, the new Military Council failed to put together a viable coalition of civilian politicians in its support; security matters overshadowed all attempts at reform.

Though the speed and ease with which the NRM took Kampala in early 1986 surprised everyone, it was soon apparent that the preparation of the new leaders with regard to economic management was inadequate. In a general climate of shortages, the new government instituted price controls and even sought to lower prices for certain key items such as sugar. While well-meaning, and certainly building short-term political capital, these were not the policies to encourage investment or increased donor assistance. The NRM's initial policies had mainly supported the import-substituting sector and, by default, the urban consumers. The rural-urban terms of trade fell, partly because of the preservation of an unfavourable exchange rate which reduced the incomes of coffee farmers. It is thus evidence of the government's flexibility, but also lack of a clear initial strategy, that these policies were abandoned in less than a year.

Owing to lack of domestic political stability, the reforms of the first half of the 1980s failed to take root. Governments were too pre-occupied with preserving their hold on power to give much attention to the detailed work that effective adjustment demands, or to take the necessary steps to attract international capital. It was only when a degree of domestic peace returned towards the end of the 1980s that the reform process was able to begin in earnest.

Notes

1. The *Background to the Budget 1981/82* (Uganda, 1981c) assessed the task as follows (p. 2): 'The task will require a willingness of a free and determined people to meet any challenge and bear any hardship without panic in order to pull the country out of a decade of economic quagmire'.
2. Money supply growth was particularly out of control in 1981, but was within IMF projections the following two years.

3. Museveni's NRM took power in January 1986. As an umbrella organisation, the NRM embraces a broad spectrum of economic and political philosophies. There was thus considerable infighting especially with regard to economic policy. It seems, however, that the liberal policies advocated by people in the Ministry of Finance and Economic Planning have prevailed. Even then, the policies initially emphasised devaluation and aggregate demand management as opposed to measures that directly increased export earnings and capital inflows. Mwega (1995) argues, in a study of Kenya, that inclusion of the latter two is crucial to successful trade liberalisation.

4. As an indicator of the priority initially given to foreign exchange allocation, a ministerial committee was set up to supervise it, headed by the Prime Minister.

5. As his own Minister of Finance, Obote also painted a favourable picture of the economy in the budget speech for 1984, which he called 'The National Will for Recovery and Development'. Given the performance of the first years of Obote II, his enthusiasm was perhaps understandable.

6. The naming of the Army Chief of Staff to the post of chairman of the Coffee Marketing Board, at the time two of the most demanding jobs in the country, provides an example of the difficult policy choices of the time. It seemed politically expedient to let the biggest user of foreign exchange, the army, control its immediate source, coffee.

7. The documents issued by Obote II in the early 1980s overemphasised recovery at the expense, in retrospect, of political work: see for instance the following budget speeches and communications from the chair by Milton Obote made in the period 1981 to 1985: *First Step to Recovery* (April, 1981); *The Challenge of Recovery* (March, 1982); *Programme for Recovery* (June, 1982); *Climbing to Recovery* (June, 1983); *Platform for Recovery* (March, 1983); *Responsibility and Recovery* (March, 1984); *The National Will for Recovery and Development* (June, 1984); *Mandate for Recovery and Development* (April, 1985); *Redeeming the Promise of Recovery for Development* (June, 1985). See also Ingham (1994) for an eloquent interpretation of Obote's complex career.

8. See Bevan *et al.* (1990) for a more detailed formulation of the model.
9. We assume here that the non-tradable sector is less labour intensive than the exportable sector.

Appendix 4A: Analytical Framework

In analyses of economic adjustment, changes in the real exchange rate are of interest because, while the nominal exchange rate is often politically determined, the real rate is endogenous. The real exchange rate measures the extent to which the government has been able to bring about a change in domestic relative prices, and thus potentially in sectoral production. With the small country assumption (the terms of trade given) exportables and importables can be grouped together into a composite category, tradables. The real exchange rate can be defined as the ratio of the prices of tradable, and non-tradable, P_t/P_n.

In Uganda, however, there have also been a number of trade interventions, so the standard concept of the real exchange rate does not apply. If trade policy varies, tradables no longer form a Hicksian composite; one must treat the prices of exportables (P_x), importables (P_m), and non-tradables (P_n) separately. This gives us three relative prices, two of which are independent.[8]

The domestic price of exportables is determined by world market prices (P_x^*), the exchange rate, and export subsidies or taxes. The domestic price of importables is similarly determined by world market prices, the exchange rate, import controls and tariffs. A trade-liberalisation, which could be in the form of a devaluation accompanied by increases in producer prices, or reduced export levies, or lower tariffs or more liberal quotas — leads to an increase in the ratio of domestic relative prices for exportables and importables, P_x/P_m, (called the domestic terms of trade), while higher tariffs or stricter quotas lead to a fall. The difference between the domestic terms of trade and the international terms of trade, P_x^*/P_m^*, is thus due to trade restrictions and the incentive structure.

To estimate the impacts of adjustment policies, we need to measure changes in the domestic terms of trade (P_x/P_m), as well as changes in the relative prices of non-tradables to importables (P_n/P_m), and also that of exportables to non-tradables (P_x/P_n). Prices for non-tradables are determined by domestic demand — which is a function of fiscal and monetary policies — and supply. Monetisation of the government deficit via the central bank increases P_n. The relative prices P_n/P_m and P_x/P_n are thus functions of fiscal and monetary policies, world market prices, exchange rate, and trade restrictions.

Changes in these relative prices are important transmission mechanisms for the effects of economic adjustment at the sectoral and micro levels. The classification of commodities in national accounts is not usually according to these categories, however, so a number of proxies have been derived as indicated in the footnotes of Figures 4.2 and 6.2.

To analyse the effects of adjustment on the earnings of different socioeconomic groups, one needs to consider how factor markets are affected. This theoretical outline is based on standard equilibrium analysis, with an initial assumption of full factor mobility. Let us assume — which is realistic for Uganda — that exportables are labour-intensive, whereas importables are capital-intensive.

A negative terms-of-trade shock, which is due to higher import prices, implies higher capital rentals in the importable sector: there will be resource reallocation out of exportables, that is, from the labour-intensive sector, into importable and non-tradable[9] sectors. This would tend to depress wages; such a negative terms-of-trade shock thus hurts labour-selling households. If, instead, we were to assume that capital is sector specific and cannot be reallocated, then the effect on labour earnings will be ambiguous (at least in the short run). Capital owners in the importable sector will definitely gain, while those in the exportable will definitely lose. If the sector-specific factor is land, which is the case in smallholder agriculture, it is not possible to reallocate it even in the long run. Since the income of coffee-growing peasants (in the export sector) is made up of both labour income and capital/land income, smallholders would lose from a negative terms-of-trade shock both as labourers and as land-owners.

Devaluation is a possible adjustment policy for dealing with such a negative terms-of-trade shock. In the mobile-factor case, the effect relative to the pre-adjustment situation (for a country such as Uganda dominated by a labour-intensive exportable-good sector) would be to raise wages and lower capital rentals. If we assume capital (or land) to be sector-specific, owners of land or capital in the exportables sector will gain; smallholders may thus gain both as labourers and as land-owners.

This analysis assumes functioning markets and individuals who stick to 'the rules of the game'. However, there have been a number of adaptations to the economic crisis in Uganda, some of which might not fit into the above scheme. Civil wars have destroyed some of the rural infrastructure, so that produce in remote regions finds it difficult to reach the towns; and with the decline of the civil service corruption, has increased. The presence of such rigidities and imperfections in the system implies that some impacts and responses might be perverse. We thus try as much as possible to take into account, at both the government and household levels, the implications for adjustment of the specific characteristics of the market structures.

Appendix 4B: Official Exchange Rate 1981–1996

Table 4B.1: *Quarterly Figures for the Official Exchange Rate[1]*
1981–1996

Year	I	II	III	IV
1981[2]	0.079	0.768	0.87	0.856
1982[3]	0.858	0.942	0.991 (3)	1.048 (2.4)
1983	1.17 (2.36)	1.39 (2.9)	1.763 (2.71)	2.338 (3.025)
1984[4]	2.74 (3.20)	3.07	4	5.52
1985	5.79	6	6	12.75

cont ...

Table 4B.1 cont ...

Year	I	II	III	IV
1986[5]	14	14 (50)	14	14
1987[6]	14	60	60	60
1988	60	60	150	165
1989	200	200	200	340
1990[7]	375	379	440	540
1991	620	700	850	915
1992	1160	1166	1185	1213
1993	1218	1199	1181	1146
1994	1079	963	921	930
1995	927	980	1000	1025
1996	1017	1059	1090	1100

Notes:

[1] Ushs per US$. In the second quarter of 1987, government embarked on an Economic Recovery Programme (ERP) which included reform and devaluation of the currency. For ease of interpretation, we have changed all earlier rates into 'new' Uganda shillings (1 new shilling = 100 old shillings).

[2] The shilling was floated in June 1981

[3] Window 1 and window 2 instituted in August 1982 (non-priority rate in brackets)

[4] Window 1 and window 2 were merged in June 1984

[5] The auction was officially replaced in the 3rd quarter of 1986 by a fixed rate

[6] 1987 saw a monetary reform coupled with a large devaluation

[7] Private exchange bureaux were introduced in 1990.

Source: Uganda (various years), *Background to the Budget.*

Chapter 5: Fully-Fledged Liberalisation (1987–)

1. Introduction

Officiating at the opening of Parliament in April 1987, Museveni spent some time reviewing the achievements of the NRM during its fourteen months in power. After a detailed account of the successes, the President posed the following rhetorical question (Uganda, 1987: 7): 'If there has been some success, why then is the cost of living very high?'. He blamed the problem on corruption and the 'lack of capable and devoted cadres'. A further answer, which underlay his address a month later during presentation of the Economic Recovery Programme (ERP), was the general lack of incentives in the Ugandan economy. The ERP marked a break from earlier vacillation, setting forward a more clear-cut strategy for economic recovery. While the focus was on economic stabilisation, policies ranged from restructuring of the parastatals to civil-service reform. Their main purpose was to create incentives that would boost individual initiative, encourage institutional rehabilitation, and improve the efficiency of government.

The basis for the change in direction lay not so much in ideological conviction as in pragmatism in the face of tough economic realities. The change allowed access to substantial amounts of foreign exchange,[1] which enabled resumption of economic activity, especially the increased production of consumer goods, without subjecting the population to harsher conditions than had already been experienced. The change was so sudden, and had such wide-ranging implications, that concerns were raised about 'ownership' of the new programme,[2] and its sustainability. For instance, in implementing reforms, an overall concern for policy-makers and donors alike was how to increase economic efficiency. Would this be best achieved by recourse to market forces, or by refining state controls? Theory suggests that the best way to arrive at optimal price levels for goods and services, capital, labour, and foreign exchange is via a free interplay between supply and demand; but how was this to be done in the extremely conflict-prone situation of Uganda in the 1980s? For example, while foreign-exchange controls might have created distortions and encouraged rent-seeking activities, they also ensured certain loyalties crucial for political survival. The tension between economic theory and political practice was thus a recurring theme in the 1980s and 1990s (Uganda, 1981a, 1989a; Mayanja-Nkangi, 1994).

Having newly emerged from economic and political chaos, Uganda in the late 1980s had serious problems of programme sequencing, with the government caught in something of a vicious circle. For example, while improving internal security was crucial for creating a peaceful environment for production, imports of ammunition competed with imports of raw materials for industry. There was also the contradiction of the public sector declared in all policy statements to be ill-equipped, poorly-run, and corrupt, yet expected to spearhead the adjustment effort. How would an unreformed public sector manage reform in the rest of the economy? Many of the reforms also presupposed a functioning financial sector, and yet the country's financial institutions themselves, including the Bank of Uganda, were still weak, and rampant inflation hindered the pace of policy and institutional reform. Failure to resolve these dilemmas delayed many ambitious initiatives, such as civil service reform, eradication of corruption, and a new Investment Code; the latter was only completed in 1990, and introduced in early 1991, although much of the Economic Recovery Programme of 1987 had been based on expected increased foreign investment (which did not materialise).

Still, policy-makers embarked on broad corrective measures, supported by a variety of financial packages from the international community. The country's capacity to generate its own resources remained weak; dependence on external aid and loans increased in the face of adverse terms-of-trade movements and continued civil strife in parts of the country.

2. IMF and World Bank Strategies for Reform

IMF and World Bank assistance to Uganda, together with aid from other Western donors, were crucial to the country's stabilisation, adjustment, and recovery. Such assistance typically comes with associated conditions.[3] None of the donor institutions has a unique set of conditions, they overlap. The World Bank's programmes focused on two broad areas: public-sector reform, including overhaul of public expenditures, tax reform, and reform of the civil service; and trade reform, including liberalisation of commodity marketing and reform of tariffs and non-tariff barriers. The IMF focused more on monetary and financial sector reforms, as well as external indebtedness.

The World Bank's conditions in the public area related to the need to increase expenditures on economic and social infrastructure — such as road maintenance, agricultural research, health, and education (mainly at the primary level) — by reducing military expenditures and subsidies to parastatals. Far-ranging institutional reform was necessary to revive the administrative and regulatory institutions and procedures without which the adjustment effort would achieve little. An effective budgetary system had to be developed and the tax system restructured, rationalised and simplified to increase the tax effort; improved tax institutions were necessary, and a system of enforceable sanctions for defaulters. As part of civil-service reform, there was need for an accurate enumeration of public-sector employees and reduction of their number in line with the government's capacity to pay them. Government ministries had to rationalise their functions and privatise some of their activities. Urban and rural district authorities had to be revived and their financial independence restored to improve their efficiency, while avoiding duplication with the central government.

With regard to parastatals, divestiture was said to be the highest priority. Structures and machinery in the parastatal sector were not being properly maintained, and soft budget constraints were breeding inefficiency, since poor performance was never punished, while subsidies increased budget deficits and inflationary pressures. The World Bank suggested strongly that the government should concentrate less on direct involvement in production and distribution and more on creating a conducive environment for increased private initiative.

Thus the government should allow increased private participation in the marketing of traditional cash crops such as coffee, tea and cotton. Barter trade should be phased out as counter to the goal of trade liberalisation; besides, some ministries were using it to circumvent expenditure controls, which increased the budget deficit. Tariff reform was necessary. The number of different schedules had to be reduced because they encumbered administration preventing the rapid clearing of imports at ports of entry, while tariffs on imported inputs for export production had to be refunded. The elimination of quantitative import restrictions was also important and export licensing was discouraged in favour of automatically renewable export certificates.

The main IMF goal in monetary policy was to achieve a rapid reduction in inflation by removing of the link between deficit financing and credit creation. Increased professionalism in the financial sector was emphasised. The Bank of Uganda needed to have a well-designed system for managing the commercial banks, with sanctions, including closure, for failure to meet guidelines; there should also be a monthly reconciliation of the accounts of the government, including production of audited accounts for the central bank itself.[4]

The IMF also suggested that the stock of foreign debt on non-concessionary terms should be reduced: the government should accept loans only on concessionary terms, and should reschedule payments on existing debt. This became a point of contention when the government continued to receive loans on less than IDA-terms (i.e., less advantageous than the most concessionary terms) from the African Development Bank.

There was also a set of traditional IMF structural conditions, not unique to Uganda, meant to prevent the economy from sliding back into more controls and administrative allocations within the external payments system. Uganda was not to impose or intensify restrictions on its external transactions, nor to introduce multiple-currency practices, nor to intensify trade restrictions for balance-of-payments reasons. Increasing exports, including non-traditional products, was seen as the most viable way to reduce the import constraint and improve the balance of payments.

It was argued that the negative protection suffered by the agricultural sector over the years had to be redressed by a policy package that raised the real incomes of farmers. Privatisation of cotton ginneries in the early 1990s gave a much needed boost to the cotton sector; deregulation of coffee marketing was completed just in time to take advantage of the 1994–95 coffee boom. However, though re-establishment of functioning markets was essential for growth and development, success of reform strategies depended on how fast exchange-rate unification could be achieved. This would bring an end to the high implicit taxes on exports, the poor market access and loss of incentives suffered by producers of export commodities during the years of decline.

As elsewhere in Africa, privatisation of parastatals has been difficult to implement at anywhere near the speed demanded by donors. A major impediment has been the lack of indigenous individuals with both the finances and the technical know-how necessary to buy and run these often extensive business ventures (Killick and Commander, 1988). The alternative, increased foreign ownership of hitherto public assets, has yet to gain much appeal. The new Investment Code (Uganda, 1990a) legalised foreign investment, and thus foreign ownership, but there remains a strong belief within key pressure groups that state firms should not be sold cheaply to foreigners, if at all,[5] and that cheap credit should instead be made available to enable Africans to acquire some of the parastatals on sale (see also Mazrui, 1991).

As in other countries undertaking adjustment, questions have been raised in Uganda regarding social impacts. The politics of public-sector retrenchment was heated (though perhaps not much more so than in neighbouring countries). To minimise social disruption in an already sufficiently burdened country, it was argued by opponents of broad intervention that the public sector should be kept intact, funded by curbing corruption and switching expenditure from the military. There was fear that adjustment would primarily hit poor groups — for example 'group employees', who were officially contracted on very temporary terms, though some remained in the system up to retirement — but without real efficiency gains. Public-sector reforms were blamed for destroying the morale of civil servants, and even for the corruption that was rampant in some government departments.

Identifying the most affected victims of adjustment in Uganda has been problematic (World Bank, 1992; UNICEF, 1994; ILO, 1995), partly because, unlike other African countries such as neighbouring Kenya and Tanzania, Uganda also had to address the effects of a long civil war. Was it the highly educated in the public sector who suddenly had to look for jobs outside government? Or the slum dwellers and the very poor in the villages? With World Bank assistance, the Programme for the Alleviation of Poverty and the Social Costs of Adjustment (PAPSCA) was set up in 1989 (Uganda, 1989b; Okune, not dated). War widows,[6] people from politically destabilised regions and AIDS orphans — not groups we would normally consider directly affected by adjustment measures — were included among those to receive assistance.

To provide a broader base for the poverty alleviation effort, the government, using its own funds, started a project called *entandikwa* — the beginning — to promote income-generating small-scale enterprises for the urban and rural poor. However, there is little precedent in the area of broad-based poverty alleviation, and therefore little praxis to fall back on. By mid-1995, the project had already come under considerable pressure from country-wide demands for financial assistance. Given the size of the poverty problem and the limited resources available, the programme might degenerate into simple political patronage.

3. Preliminary Reforms in the Late 1980s

In implementing the 1987 reforms, the government substantially devalued the shilling, introducing new currency notes 'with two zeros knocked off'; imposed a 30 per cent conversion tax on financial assets, bank balances, and cash holdings;[7] and committed itself to regular review of the exchange rate. The currency depreciated from

14 to 60 new shillings to the US dollar, reducing the gap between the official and parallel rates but failing to eliminate it entirely (Figure 5.1). It was evidence of the size of the earlier premiums, but also of the laborious paperwork related to accessing Bank of Uganda funds, that not all the foreign exchange available was purchased.

To expedite purchase of intermediate inputs and spare parts, an Open General Licensing (OGL) system was started, funded by donor balance-of-payments support. An OGL list was set up, initially including 25 firms and 8 products, and administered by the Bank of Uganda; a continuous supply of foreign exchange was guaranteed. To be included on the list, industries had to be deemed capable of a rapid increase in output of consumer goods, to reduce excess demand while contributing to government revenue via excise and sales taxes (Bank of Uganda, 1988).

Figure 5.1: *Official and Parallel Exchange Rates 1987–95 (Ushs per US$)*

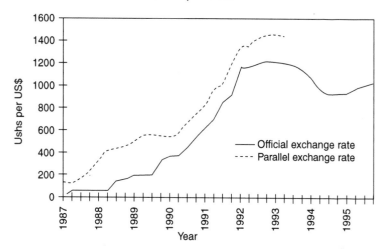

Sources: Appendix 4B, Kayizzi-Mugerwa (1994)

The OGL was intended as a temporary measure. There was still little attempt to reform tariff structures or relax other import restrictions to encourage competition and more efficient production. Indeed, the firms on the OGL list had likely depended on import controls for survival, perhaps even enjoying virtual monopolies, like most parastatals. These would not necessarily be the firms that would thrive in the competitive environment that the 1987 reforms were trying to resuscitate.[8]

The government also needed to increase men and equipment in the military to contain armed insurgency in parts of the country. This was somewhat easier than during Obote II, since the civil war this time was confined to areas far-removed from the major urban centres, and thus without severe direct impact on economic activities. Closure of the Kenya border after clashes in November 1987[9] reduced the flow of imports — notably consumer goods in the critical month of December — and, thereby, government revenue. Hosting the Preferential Trade Area heads-of-state meeting in Kampala in December 1987, and the related need for urgent infrastructure repairs, increased government expenditures, worsening the fiscal deficit.[10] Money supply continued to expand in 1987 in response to a net increase in credit to the government, with unfavourable impact on inflation: Prices grew by 224 per cent (Table 5.1).

Thus, close to a year after the drastic devaluation and reforms of May, 1987, the discretionary element remained strong, as shown in the belief that the government could pick winners in strategic sectors through foreign-exchange (OGL) allocations for essential imports. Little real progress had been made in exchange-rate reform, and still less in the fight against inflation. This inertia is consistent with the experience of many countries in the initial phases of adjustment. As Calvo and Veigh (1992: 12) have noted for Latin America, a region with a longer experience of attempted economic reforms, 'a history of failed stabilisations makes the public highly sceptical of any new attempts', and lack of credibility itself can then become a major further impediment to economic stabilisation (see also Dornbusch, 1991). In Uganda's case, continuing war in the north, delays in aid disbursements, and failure to reduce money creation made it difficult for the government to establish credibility. In spite of high inflation, the exchange rate remained fixed at 60 shillings to the US dollar; as

Table 5.1: Indicators of Economic Performance 1984–96 (index and %)

	1987	1988	1989	1990	1991	1992	1993	1994	1995	1996
GDP growth (%)	6.7	7.1	6.4	5.5	5.2	4.5	6.3	10.1	8.7	7.0
GDP per capita index (1960=100)	62	65	67	69	70	71	73	78	82	85
Fixed capital formation/GDP (%)	12	11	11	14	15	15	16	14	17	–
Gross domestic savings/GDP (%)	0	1	-2	1	1	1	2	6	7	–
Export/GDP (%)	9	8	7	7	8	7	8	11	11	–
Terms of trade (1960=100)	72	78	60	47	47	35	42	50	–	–
Net foreign direct investment (US$ million)	28.0	10.0	13.0	5.5	1.0	2.0	4.0	5.0	–	–
Total external debt (US$ million)	1940.4	1974.4	2253.5	2668.7	2877.1	3032.0	3055.5	–	–	–
Real manufacturing wages (1987=100)[1]	100	126	163	194	211	232	294	405	513	–
Inflation (GDP deflator)	225	164	73	27	32	60	1	16	3	–
Money supply (M1) (growth %)	167	118	93	40	64	16	38	37	15	–
Domestic credit (growth %)	116	95	189	58	64	23	-6	-1	-13	–
Credit to government (growth %)[2]	42	145	-13	42	551	-1	*	*	*	*
Interest, bank savings rate	23	23	33	32	30	32	12	6	3	–
Interest, lending rate	30	40	50	36	37	33	20	22	19	–
Population (million)	15.6	16.0	16.4	16.8	17.2	17.6	18.1	18.6	19.2	19.8

Table 5.1 cont ...

[1] Derived from annual wage bill for selected manufacturing industries.

[2] Since the claims of the banking system on government are becoming increasingly negative, it is not meaningful to compute percentage changes 1993–1996.

Sources: Uganda (1996), *Background to the Budget 1996/97*; Uganda, *Key Economic Indicators 24th Issue,* January 1996; IMF (various issues), *International Financial Statistics*; World Bank (1995); *World Data 1995.*

the currency became overvalued, parallel foreign-exchange markets expanded.

Coffee prices fell sharply in 1987 and 1988, and Uganda got an export quota much smaller than its production. While the international terms of trade fell, policy-makers increased producer prices, which was made possible by the devaluation. This helped to preserve the relative incomes of coffee producers, but there was then concern about the large volume of coffee production — improvement in domestic prices was blamed for a coffee glut in 1988.

To tackle the adverse impact of the falling coffee prices, two further devaluations were undertaken, in July and December 1988, changing the exchange rate from 60 to 165 Ushs to the US dollar, and reducing the parallel-market premium for foreign exchange from 650 to 100 per cent. Devaluations were accompanied by further price liberalisation and increases in interest rates. Taxes were raised, especially income tax deposits,[11] and the Ministry of Finance started a computerisation programme to improve fiscal planning; as a result of these efforts, budget discipline improved and the growth of domestic credit was contained.

In December 1988 OGL was supplemented by the Special Import Programme (SIP), which made foreign exchange available to all importers of goods on a positive list;[12] individuals and companies with private access to foreign exchange were also now allowed to import goods on a 'no-forex-required' basis. Thanks to aid disbursements, imports were not constrained by the low export earnings. Higher imports helped preserve capacity utilisation in manufacturing, and also enabled rehabilitation work to proceed on roads and other infrastructure.

Even as the reforms were beginning to have some positive results, coffee prices weakened further with the collapse of the International Coffee Agreement in July 1989; the Uganda coffee market lost more than half its value in a matter of months. Thus declining coffee prices were the major destabilising factor in the first years of the NRM administration (Ssemogerere, 1990).[13] Having committed itself to a market-clearing exchange rate, the government responded to the collapse of coffee prices with further devaluations.[14] The need to contain political dissent, via expansion of the cabinet and the army, began to take precedence over fiscal prudence. By 1989 the government had 48 ministers with 60 deputies, and the military had doubled to 100,000.[15] As political and military demands increased, it was also difficult to keep the focus on reform and the practical problems of improving revenue collection remained enormous. Broadening the tax base during 1988/89 made only a modest impact, and the weak state of the civil service made prospects for real improvements in revenue collection small, as large sums in both tax and tariff revenues were still being lost to corruption. Excluding grants, the budget deficit was now over 6 per cent of GDP, compared to the 3.4 per cent envisaged in the IMF's Extended Structural Adjustment Facility projections (Murinde, 1993).

And yet even in the face of these difficulties, the end of the 1980s showed some movement towards stability. Part of the improvement was obviously due to the restoration of peace in the country — a 'peace premium' after the long crisis period, consisting of increased production enabled by the return of peasants to their farms and of other producers to their normal activities (Collier and Gunning, 1995)[16] — and to the positive international response to Uganda's need for aid, something of a 'sympathy premium'. The increase in aid flows and project-related loans compensated for the fall in coffee income, while policy reforms helped revive economic activity. There was rapid rehabilitation of some key industries, along with the main communications network, and improvement in incentives led to a modest but visible increase in the flow of basic services. Thus, starting from a low base, there was a notable turnaround in economic growth in the first years of the NRM administration. Though broad money exceeded its target, the government still managed to meet the inflation target, thanks partly to improved food supply, and by 1990 real interest rates had become positive.

4. Deepening Reforms in the 1990s

By the early 1990s Uganda had reached a turning point, both politically and economically. Politically, the volume of treason cases before the courts embarrassed the government and the number of detentions without trial was still large, but in the northern and northeastern parts of the country the long-lived insurgency was largely contained; the government was no longer in a position to neglect demands from various groups, including foreign donors, for political reforms. Ugandan courts dismissed a number of sensational treason cases, setting the accused free, and pressures from advocates of multiparty democracy increased. Work on a new constitution — which had begun in March, 1989 — progressed slowly, hampered by lack of funds, but the effort put into making and debating the new constitution signalled the serious intention of the NRM government to leave a mark on the future of Uganda.[17]

Efforts were re-directed to winning hearts. With support from a cross-section of donors, a major rehabilitation programme for northern and northeastern Uganda was launched in July 1992.[18] At the same time, plans were made to reduce military expenditures and personnel; henceforth the armed forces were to resume a defensive posture *vis-à-vis* the country's borders, as opposed to their controversial role in maintaining internal security. This reversed what had become normal military turnover in Uganda — one set of soldiers driving out another, in a form of internal conquest. However, though the military has been a major drain on state coffers, its retrenchment was initially not received with broad acclaim; the prospect of unemployed ex-soldiers was viewed anxiously by the population. But in the event, the soldiers were laid off in an orderly manner, perhaps for the first time since World War II; former combatants returned to their villages, bringing with them new better organisational ideas and even some capital for investment (Brett, 1995).[19] Other signs of a more relaxed mood included encouragement of the traditional rulers from the defunct kingdoms of southern and western Uganda to repossess their palaces and other properties, and to resume their roles as cultural heads; the heir to the Buganda throne criss-crossed his kingdom to be, while in the smaller kingdoms royal baptisms once again commanded much pageantry, leaving pundits in disarray.[20]

Economically, a degree of stability had been achieved by 1990, but events soon exposed the fragility of the Ugandan economy, putting the government's commitment to reform to the test. As usual, disturbances originated from a combination of 'external' and domestic causes: severe drought, low coffee prices, and stranded reforms. In the face of the drought and depressed foreign-exchange earnings, the statutory safeguards provided by the 'old' Bank of Uganda Act failed to prevent the central bank from extending large amounts of credit to the government (Malik, 1995). An aid interruption for a few months in 1991 led to sharp depreciation of the shilling at the new foreign exchange bureaux (more below), and ultimately in the official exchange rate (see Figure 5.1). In many other African countries — notably Zambia, Kenya, and Tanzania — such difficulties led to collapse of the reform programme altogether and to the need for even more comprehensive policy changes when the countries eventually returned to the IMF/World Bank for assistance. In Uganda, the reform programme remained largely on track, thanks to the determination of key policy-makers.

Quick and unusual steps were taken to rectify the macroeconomic setbacks. In what was basically a victory of the reformers over the deficit spenders, the Ministry of Planning took over the Ministry of Finance, with Joshua Mayanja-Nkangi as the new Minister of Finance and Economic Planning. Emmanuel Tumusiime-Mutebile, another of the key players in the reform process, became Secretary of the Treasury. Other drastic measures instituted in fiscal 1991/92 included adoption of a cash budget in March 1992, with expenditures tied to revenues on a monthly basis, and across-the-board reductions of fourth-quarter expenditures by more than 70 per cent. The measures bore fruit. The rate of inflation came down from an annual rate of 230 per cent at the beginning of 1992 to about 10 per cent in May, while the bureaux exchange rate stabilised at about Ushs 1250 to the US dollar. The power of restrictive fiscal policy was thus demonstrated, perhaps for the first time in Uganda. The return of the rains removed the threat of a food shortage, and by mid-1992 food supplies had improved sufficiently to put further downward pressure on prices. At the Paris Club meeting of May 1992, donors committed over US$ 800 million to the country. Though not all of it came through, and much of what did was offset by debt service, the commitment indicated increased confidence in the policy-makers' handling of the economy.

Following the stiff expenditure cuts of the last quarter of the previous fiscal year, the 1992/93 budget was awaited with some anxiety, but in the event it was very restrained. It demonstrated the government's increasing confidence in managing the economy under pressure, and reiterated the government's commitment to structural adjustment and economic liberalisation. There were six broad goals: to improve government efficiency; to widen the tax base; to generate growth of at least 5 per cent; to increase savings and investment; to maintain annualised inflation at no more than 15 per cent by June 1993 and thereby stabilise the exchange rate; and to increase foreign-exchange earnings and strengthen the balance of payments.

4.1. Public Sector Reforms and Decentralisation

A central problem was the low level of salaries and the poor distribution of non-salary benefits. In 1989, for example, the real salary of a permanent secretary was only 3 per cent of what it had been in early 1975; but senior civil servants had a wide range of fringe benefits, such as cheap or even free housing, which had more weight in the remuneration package than the salary itself. Even then, incomes were often too low to support a family. The effects of low incomes on the civil service included poor discipline and absenteeism, low efficiency, and increasing corruption.

The low level of remuneration in the public service also affected the operations of donor agencies. To get their projects executed, donors used various types of incentive payments including field and travel allowances, free transport or transport allowances, free meals or food baskets, free housing or housing allowances, study tours and fellowships for study abroad plus various topping-up arrangements called 'responsibility and performance allowances'. The level of allowances was substantial; at the end of the 1980s the highest reached 230,000 Ushs per month (then close to US$1000). In one project, as much as 40 per cent of the budget was used for salary supplements to the local staff (World Bank, 1989a). It was also common for government officers to take leave from their normal jobs and be re-hired within donor-funded projects at higher salary. Though this response on the part of donors was understandable, it had some negative side effects, such as increasing competition between donors and the government for the best people. It also introduced frictions within the bureaucracy as relatively junior staff in projects within ministries earned many times more than top civil servants. From the donors' point of view it was probably valid to argue that money spent on allowances to the local staff was, on the margin, more effective than adding expatriate staff. However, given the diverse contractual forms thereby introduced in the labour market, the various incentives created potential barriers to future wage policy harmonisation.

The government tried to raise public-sector salaries as part of the Economic Recovery Programme of 1987, but since increases were financed by printing money, there were simultaneous price increases and, therefore, little or no increase in real earnings. To augment public-sector wages, which were only 10 per cent of subsistence level, the government planned to increase the wage share in non-debt recurrent expenditure, though improvements were contingent on a successful retrenchment of public-sector employees. At the beginning of the 1990s there were some 320,000 people employed in the public sector, about 40 per cent in general government, as many in teaching, and the rest in district administration, urban authorities, and the security forces (Uganda, 1989d). In June 1992 the long-awaited public retrenchment programme was finally launched; 5000 civil servants were laid off in mid-1992. Though reform of the public sector is generally recognised as a prerequisite for successful adjustment, it has of course been very controversial throughout Africa (Kanbur, 1995). The announcement of reform measures has been accompanied by serious riots in many countries and even threat of violent regime changes. In Uganda, however, the civil service as an institution had been destroyed; the capacity to resist reform was extremely low. This was not the first time the government reduced its work force either; thousands of casual workers had been laid off in the past. However, with expulsion of highly educated and highly placed individuals in government, the debate finally made headlines. Given the level of remuneration in the public sector, one would have assumed that employees would have taken every opportunity to exit from government service. However, the first retrenchment exercise was not exactly voluntary. There was much debate in Kampala and the general feeling was that the retrenchment had been badly executed. To avoid the bad blood that would have resulted from expulsions induced at the department level, all retrenched government officers received letters from the permanent secretary and the head of the civil service, including instructions from the President for their dismissal. But of those retrenched from the Kampala City Council in the initial round, the majority seemed to be from outside Kampala, indicating that the exercise was far from neutral. Newspapers claimed in fact that in many cases it was efficient and hard-working individuals who had been retrenched, while lazy ones and 'drunkards' were spared. Nevertheless, there were further retrenchments, including the military;[21] and by March 1995, the civil service had been reduced by over 50 per cent, to less than 150,000.

In retrospect, the retrenchments were smoother than anticipated, lacking the bitter recriminations that were feared beforehand, perhaps because many public-sector workers already had a foot in the informal sector, helping them to manage the transition. However, the reduction has yet to translate into substantial real wage improvements;[22] even after the retrenchments the civil service wage-bill was still larger, relative to GDP, than in the 1960s.

While retrenchment was a relatively quick process, re-professionalisation, retraining and re-equipping of the civil service would take time. In an assessment of Uganda's labour market, the ILO (1995) argued that in the past too much emphasis had been put on education for the attainment of national goals, such as political unity, and too little on personal career development. Now modern human-resource management methods have been introduced, and there have been changes in the national curricula to encourage new approaches to work including self-employment in the private sector.

As an extension of its reform agenda, the government embarked on a process of administrative and fiscal decentralisation in 1993/94 (see Uganda, 1994); 13 districts obtained a vote of their own in the central government budget, a provision which was subsequently converted to block grants, partly based on the levels of district expenditures on priority areas identified by the government. While unconditional grants based on size and need are also sent to each district, the government has borrowed a leaf from its own experience with the international financial institutions and has introduced 'conditional grants', which only accrue to districts which meet performance criteria, 'minimum national standards', in areas such as primary health care, primary education, and the provision of basic infrastructure. These *ex post* rewards will not in any way stop individual districts from undertaking their own initiatives, so long as they contribute to the long-run goals of the district councils, which in turn will be held accountable to the electorate. During 1995/96, the government decentralised the last districts, making all 39 managers of their own affairs.

Decentralisation has become a popular component of policy approaches in developing countries (Collins and Grèen, 1994). It is thought to increase responsiveness to local needs by enhancing rural access to policy-makers, facilitating community participation in decision making and thus increasing access to public goods and services. These changes are believed to soften resistance to change, ultimately promoting national unity; decentralisation is also said to incorporate 'market surrogate' properties, which fit in well with liberalisation in the rest of the economy.

It is an interesting administrative reform which is being embarked on with considerable enthusiasm. It is possible that decentralisation will increase the overall revenue effort,[23] but the difficulties of policy implementation at the district level have historically been substantial (Brett, 1993 and 1994). Many districts have very little experience in spending money. In 1992/93, for example, only 24 per cent of total public expenditures were undertaken by local authorities, and only

5 per cent of revenues were raised locally. Control mechanisms during the transition phase are weak; and the mechanism for resource delivery from the centre has also caused concern, since in the past money was often diverted. The World Bank has devised an experimental tracking mechanism to ensure that resources get to the districts, and that they have the impact intended. Indications are that resources are getting to the lower levels, but are poorly planned for at that level.

Of revenue raised at the local level, graduated personal tax on imputed income — imposed on all males over 18, except students and those exempted on grounds of disability — accounted for 50–90 per cent. Females also paid tax if employed full-time or engaged in business. There were 24 different rates created by the Ministry of Local Government, with the actual rates in each case set by a Tax Assessment Committee appointed by the local district or urban council. Smallholders, often without much cash income, comprised the biggest group paying graduated tax; because of fluctuating harvests and prices, their taxes often related poorly to their actual incomes. Fees and licences were also important revenue sources at the local level, contributing 5–25 per cent; property taxes were not levied in the countryside, but had been reinstated in urban areas.

4.2. Fiscal Policies

Uganda's tax-collection system had been transformed since establishment in 1991 of the Uganda Revenue Authority (URA), with special wage packages for staff, and an anti-smuggling unit to ensure tax compliance at the borders. Still, the tax collections were relatively low: the ratio of tax revenue to GDP was only 11 per cent in Uganda,[24] compared with 25 per cent in Kenya and 15 per cent in Tanzania. To reduce inflationary pressures from deficit financing the government would limit its borrowing from the central bank. Donors financed parts of the budget through balance-of-payments support. Import-support funds were sold at auction to importers, with proceeds allocated directly to the budget; import-support funds generated up to 40 per cent of the total budget in the early 1990s.[25]

Uganda's fiscal deficit, excluding aid, had improved to about 7–8 per cent of GDP by 1995, but the IMF thought this still too high, and in an ESAF evaluation suggested a level of 4 per cent as more in line with Uganda's 'macroeconomic framework'. A value-added-tax (VAT) system was introduced in 1996, but many industrialists thought 17 per cent VAT was too high; Kenya had only 15 per cent, and with lower transport costs and better access to utilities, its production costs were already much lower than Uganda's, giving Kenya an advantage in both its own and Uganda's domestic markets. The government would begin to pay taxes on its own imports, both to discourage the government from preference for imported as opposed to domestic goods and to reduce corruption in government purchasing. But while tax revenues have thus increased, the budgetary process remains weak. Dependence on cash budgets leads to frequent supplementary allocations, in which more powerful ministries (such as defence) often get the resources they want, while projects in other ministries (such as health and education) are scaled down for lack of funds. In the early 1990s the government made some attempts to shift expenditures in favour of the social sectors, but military pressure shifted the balance back.[26]

With improvement in government finances, demands on the public budget from various special-interest groups have increased, adding to pressures arising from Museveni's election 'manifesto pledges', especially the promise to improve social services and eradicate poverty. Uganda's social sector, including health and education, has recovered slowly, and many critics have argued for more social expenditures, even via deficit financing if necessary.[27] This would not have worked, since it would very likely have bred hyper-inflation. Still, some increases in social expenditures might have been possible via changed priorities in the budget itself, for instance, less for the military.[28] Makerere University lecturers as well as doctors and other health workers at Mulago Hospital have continued their perennial demands for better wages and working conditions, using strikes and walkouts, while ministries have recruited new workers since the retrenchment of 1992, when the goal was to reduce staff at the centre in favour of the districts as decentralisation took hold. Half-way through fiscal 1996/97, the government wage bill was estimated to have exceeded by 60 billion its target of 160 billion shillings. In December 1996 members of parliament were even demanding tax-free motor vehicles for themselves; the Minister of Finance had to be very firm.

4.3. Financial, Monetary and Exchange-Rate Policies

The weak state of the financial sector was a major impediment to the reform process in the early 1990s (Harvey, 1992). Progress in reducing inflation had affected interest rates very little. By 1994 when inflation was down to 16 per cent,[29] average commercial bank deposit rates were only 6 per cent per annum, giving a real return of negative 10 per cent, which provided no incentive for savings. The following year inflation was down to 3 per cent, but lending rates were as high as 19 per cent, impeding capital formation: only highly profitable short-term projects were financed commercially. At that point the real cost of borrowing was higher than at any time for at least 14 years, though in those years funds were rationed. Non-performing assets of the commercial banks were apparently not the main cause of interest-rate inertia: After the Uganda Commercial Bank — by far the largest operator — got rid of its large bad-debt portfolio (close to US$70 million in the mid-1990s), lending rates did not change much. Banks in Uganda had not been very innovative in terms of consumer products, or introducing new managerial processes, including computerisation. They still depended on a small clientele of politicians and businessmen, while the remainder of the country was largely neglected.

Stabilisation made it possible for the authorities to embark on a number of initiatives, however. The Financial Institutions Act of 1993 made the Bank of Uganda an independent manager of monetary policy and supervisor of monetary institutions; its resource base was improved, partly thanks to an ambitious personnel recruitment drive and to technical assistance from the IMF;[30] and the act provided guidelines on its licencing of commercial banks, including their capital requirements and loan classification; with a rationalised accounting system, the Bank would be able to provide timely data on its own operations and those of the commercial banks.[31] However, in the absence of secondary markets for treasury bills and other instruments, it was not easy to define a credible monetary role for the Bank of Uganda (Malik, 1995). With foreign aid covering 40 per cent of recurrent expenditure, the independence of the central bank to resist pressure for deficit financing from the central government was not put to the test in the mid-1990s. Instead foreign-exchange liberalisation has been the second pillar of economic reform in Uganda, next to fiscal policy.

A significant step had been taken in 1990 when foreign exchange bureaux were introduced to legalise the black market (Kasekende and Ssemogerere, 1994). The bureaux bought and sold foreign exchange with no questions asked. While the gap between the bureau exchange rate and the official rate was reduced, convergence of the two rates proved elusive because of delays at the official auction and transaction costs. Participants had to first supply documents to their commercial banks, and their imports were then expected to arrive in the country after a specified period of time, but the main 'cost' was that documentation increased liability to pay duties and other taxes. Many importers therefore preferred the less cumbersome bureau market, while the Bank of Uganda was unable to sell off its weekly allotment of foreign exchange. The proceeds of the auction went directly to the government budget, so the slow BOU foreign-exchange sales (and at a lower rate than the bureaux) reduced revenue. Quicker procedures for encashing balance-of-payments support were sought, including speedier handling of paperwork at the Bank. A unified interbank foreign exchange market replaced the auction (Kasekende and Malik, 1993).

To exercise monetary control, the Bank had to watch exchange rate and inflation indices jointly to determine how much appreciation or depreciation was necessary for price stability, but this was not immediately possible, because while exchange-rate data were available daily, consumer price indices were only compiled monthly. For much of the adjustment period, therefore, the Bank did not have an exchange-rate target, its main concern being merely to smooth out exchange-rate fluctuations; a balanced budget was perhaps the nominal anchor at that time. This was abandoned in the early 1990s, however, when increased revenue including aid eventually resulted in a fiscal surplus, leaving two choices for nominal anchor: the exchange rate or the money supply. The volatility of the money supply during the subsequent period eliminated it as an anchor, however, leaving the exchange rate as the natural choice, and also the least troublesome to track.

Higher coffee prices and freer movement of foreign exchange after the abolition of the auction in 1993 led to huge inflows of foreign currency, with appreciation of the shilling and unfavourable impact on the profitability of coffee sales, which are denominated in US dollars. The strong shilling also had a negative impact on the government budget, because the amount of shillings realised from balance-of-payments support fell. However, the liberalised economic environment, including removal of import controls, helped the system to sterilise itself, via higher imports, without raising inflation. The Bank of Uganda also intervened on the foreign-exchange market to ensure that the shilling did not appreciate too much.

Subsequently, simultaneous increasing money supply, falling inflation, and steady exchange rate were somewhat puzzling (Mbire and Mackinnon, 1993). From 1994 to 1996, for example, broad money increased about 25 per cent annually, while inflation was below 10 per cent, indicating financial deepening. However, the ratio of demand and time deposits in banks to GDP remains small, implying that money is still held outside the banking system; there is even speculation that a considerable amount of Ugandan currency is circulating in neighbouring countries. However, Henstridge (1995: 339) has empirically estimated a money demand function for Uganda that forecasts out-of-period observations rather well. He suggests that, from a low level of monetisation, large percentage increases in money supply may be non-inflationary

> if there are increases in the transactions demand for money and if the achievement of price stability leads to an increase in the asset demand for money. So long as increases in money supply do not outstrip increases in the demand for money then there is no increase in inflation, and a virtuous circle enables the economy to re-monetise.

This seems a plausible description of Uganda in the mid-1990s.[32]

4.4. Privatisation, Investment, Trade, Aid, and Infrastructure

By end of 1995 the government had privatised assets worth about 110 billion shillings (about US$110 million) and it was planned that 85 per cent of all previously public enterprises would be in private hands by 1998. As in other African countries, however, privatisation has been difficult to implement. Initially the government was only willing to sell off loss-making enterprises, but not those which interested the private sector the most. And perhaps due to the lack of previous experience with mass privatisation, there was a general lack of transparency; the process was riddled with political interference and was very slow. The units responsible for privatisation at the Ministry of Finance also underwent frequent staff changes.

The most controversial issue is valuation of the companies to be privatised. Publicly-owned companies had consumed considerable public finance in investments, repairs, and services; to the public it seemed obvious that their value should be assessed accordingly. There were cries of outrage when companies were sold for a few million dollars when millions more had been spent on their rehabilitation. Another issue relates to the general dearth of potential buyers in the Ugandan economy. Following the expulsion of the Ugandan 'Asians' in the 1970s, few large-scale African businessmen emerged; thus, under competitive bidding twenty years later, African purchases were confined to small hotels and other service industries, while the bigger companies reverted to Asian ownership, causing some African resentment (see Mamdani, 1993). At a seminar on privatisation at one of the new universities in Uganda, speakers referred to it as a new form of 'foreignisation'; it was argued that Africans need to take part in the privatisation process in order to ensure its success and irreversibility. In response, a number of African businessmen have launched a venture capital fund in readiness for introduction of a stock exchange.

So far, privatisation has had only small direct benefits for the government. The government no longer needs to subsidise the privatised companies nor underwrite their foreign and domestic debts, but a substantial part of sales proceeds has gone towards cash compensation for retrenched workers. It is hoped that an expanding private sector will be able to generate higher tax revenues for the government, but privatisation is only a first step in efforts to establish a dynamic market economy. When Uganda completes its privatisation programme at the end of the 1990s, it will have been able to salvage less than 50 per cent of the productive capacity available in the formal sector at the beginning of the 1970s; new investment is thus also necessary for growth.

Creation of a one-stop investment clearing agency — the Uganda Investment Authority, where permits, incentives and other regulations are handled — has speeded up the investment process; by 1996 two thousand investment licences had been issued to domestic and foreign firms. However, despite favourable macroeconomic development, less investment has materialised than was expected, perhaps due to a combination of the reputation for lawlessness, which will take time to eradicate, inadequacy of the incentive system, and poor infrastructure.

The success of privatisation and the likelihood of new investments also depend heavily on the state of infrastructure services, such as electricity, roads, telecommunications,[33] and the availability of venture capital, and of course privatisation followed by investment can also influence the state of the services. The Uganda Electricity Board (UEB), the Uganda Posts and Telecommunications Corporation (UPTC), Uganda Airlines, and the commodity marketing parastatals were initially considered 'strategic', to be preserved in government ownership. The commodity marketing sector has now been completely liberalised (more on coffee below), but the most important service parastatals have been difficult to privatise. The amount of investment needed to keep the UEB running and to expand services clearly exceeded the government's capacity,[34] but the management of a multitude of public-sector goals, including rural electrification, industrialisation, and export to neighbouring countries, might be difficult after privatisation.

It is planned to divide the UPTC into two separate companies: Uganda Posts and Uganda Telecommunications. The government would then be in a position to privatise the telecommunications company, while preserving the posts. Meanwhile, the government has licensed a number of telecommunications companies; thereby making the market contestable (see Anas and Lee, 1988), in that there are competing suppliers of services and consumers are no longer captive to the UPTC.

Improving incentives for investment has been a key feature of policy in the 1990s; for example, to attract foreign investors, Uganda adopted a generous tax-holiday regime (up to 6 years for investments of at least US$50,000). This was criticised, however, because tax holidays were not related to the potential value added or employment to be generated by the firms, merely to the size of investment; tax holidays also tended to favour companies with shorter lead time, as opposed to long-term investment in, say, mining. The incentive structure was also biased against exports, as a World Bank (1995) analysis of Uganda's export potential shows. First, estimates showed that Uganda's import-substitution incentives had serious negative implications for export production; there was high effective protection of some domestic industries, which in turn implicitly taxed exports. The effective rate of protection for extra-regional competition in the domestic market was 93 per cent, while that within the Preferential Trade Area (PTA) was 64 per cent, but it was minus 16 per cent for exports outside the PTA. Domestic producers could thus charge up to twice as much for value-added on the domestic market as they could on the world market, which attracted resources away from export production. Second, petroleum surcharges and other fiscal measures taxed exports indirectly, via higher transport costs, reducing retained earnings which otherwise might have gone to investment. Third, aid inflows also tax exports by appreciating the currency and thereby reducing domestic profitability. Adam *et al.* (1994a, 1994b) argue that exporters should be compensated for temporary appreciation caused by periods of high aid inflows, perhaps through subsidised credit, depending on the use to which they are put. The appreciation can also be reduced if it is used to finance imports rather than being directed to non-tradables or to accelerated debt service — as in aid used to support recurrent expenditures.

From 1991 Uganda pursued a debt strategy aimed at getting maximum debt relief from the Paris Club, the writing-off or long-term rescheduling of non-OECD debt, commercial debt buyback, and strict limitations on new borrowing, except on the most concessional terms. The country pursued a mixed strategy with regard to bilateral creditors (see S.G. Warburg and Co., 1991; Kapoor, 1995): While some had their debts duly serviced — such as India, China, and North Korea with whom rescheduling had been agreed — others including Tanzania, Burundi, and the former Soviet Union were ignored.

To address some of the concerns above, the Ministry of Finance was preparing a Tax Code including all investment incentives, removing all exemptions, and giving domestic and foreign investors similar treatment. To promote exports the Bank of Uganda also started an Export Finance and Guarantee Scheme, but in the mid-1990s many exporters, especially of coffee, were still arranging their own financing with foreign institutions.

4.5. Coffee Policy

Changes in international coffee prices and resulting changes in foreign exchange earnings and government tax revenues have impacted strongly on Uganda's foreign exchange rate and fiscal position, so coffee is clearly a vital sector for government policy. The years of crisis and stagnation severely impacted coffee production itself as many a farmer turned to subsistence production instead; exchange rate and tax policies themselves had impacts, as did trade policies, depressing production and encouraging smuggling of coffee exports. Coffee marketing itself has also been highly problematic, contributing to all these problems.[35] So reform of coffee policy and recovery of the coffee sector have been central in Uganda's stabilisation and adjustment efforts. Besides liberalisation of trade and foreign exchange controls generally, coffee-related reforms have included privatisation of marketing and removal of export taxes to shift income back from government to the smallholders.

The Coffee Marketing Board (CMB) had all the shortcomings of the parastatal sector but none of the potential strengths given by its autonomous and strategic position in the coffee marketing. CMB's traditional dependence on a hierarchy of institutions, from the cooperative union down to the primary society, had long ceased to be an asset; insensitivity to farmer's needs at the union level and below had turned this infrastructure into a liability.[36] CMB had huge overhead costs and its storage facilities and processing plants were run down and in need of new investment, but its most serious problem was failure to pay farmers promptly. A smooth flow of coffee from the countryside depended on the availability of sufficient credit to pay farmers, but due to shortage of credit, and corruption, money sometimes took years to reach them, and when it did it was worth very little because of high inflation (Uganda Cooperative Alliance Ltd, 1989: 13; Kayizzi-Mugerwa, 1993). By the end of 1989, for instance, farmers in need of cash were often forced to sell their coffee at up to a 60 per cent discount on the official price, which itself was below the world price (Uganda Commercial Bank, 1989). To improve coffee deliveries, the government instructed the Bank of Uganda to take over the financing of the Coffee Marketing Board, which meant clearing its outstanding liabilities to commercial banks, cooperative unions, primary societies, and private processors. The Bank of Uganda also provided commercial banks with guarantees to ensure continued lending to the cooperative unions. Many of the unions were not creditworthy, and loan facilities at the Bank of Uganda were abused; coffee purchases improved, but not by much.

What was initially a very short-term measure to improve the flow of payments to farmers became a serious economic and administrative problem for the central bank and the government. Centralised coffee financing, via the expansion of reserve money, was increasing inflationary pressures and even corruption. The IMF and World Bank considered the central bank's involvement in coffee financing and related guarantees to commercial banks as a major policy slippage. To stop the abuse of crop finance, a number of stringent measures were introduced. Legislation was passed to regulate the various segments of the market, including sanctions for criminal activities, and government audit teams travelled to rural areas to verify bills from cooperative unions and private processors. A committee would be appointed to examine the whole of the coffee-marketing system. For a liberalising government, financing coffee purchases proved impossible to defend and responsibility for crop financing was eventually returned to the commercial banks. The government was learning that bureaucratic interventions were ill-suited for correcting credit and marketing imperfections, especially where appropriate institutions and personnel were lacking.[37]

The CMB's monopoly on coffee marketing was ended in 1990, with the government initially giving export licences to three unions; later many more unions and private companies received licences. From being exclusively borne by government and peasants, the risks of commodity trade became more evenly spread, with more than 100 registered coffee exporters by the mid-1990s. By 1996 CMB handled less than 10 per cent of coffee exports, with the rest in private hands; from 2000 employees in the mid-1980s it had fallen to below 200. Interest groups associated with CMB's monopoly, notably the politicians that sat on its board, lost the benefits of being attached to a foreign-exchange generating parastatal company, while competition among coffee-exporting companies provided farmers better market access and prompter payment. The government's own direct and implicit taxation of the coffee sector has been reduced in the new regime but not by as much as is often claimed. The switch to higher fuel taxation to compensate for reduced coffee taxes implies, since transport costs are important in the determination of the eventual price to the farmer, only a modest reduction in the tax incidence on coffee. Ironically, the collapse of coffee prices in the late 1980s helped trigger the liberalisation of coffee marketing; it would have been more difficult to reform the CMB during a boom, as it would have been possible for the company to show some profits even as efficiency was collapsing.[38]

The coffee boom of the 1970s found Uganda in deep economic and political problems, and thus the potential benefits largely passed it by, but the country was now better positioned to take advantage of the coffee boom of the 1990s. The economy was smaller, but the macroeconomic environment was less regulated; the bulk of restrictions were removed and the shilling was convertible. The new policy environment also made the rate of 'pass through' fairly rapid; since urban-rural linkages remained strong in most of Sub-Saharan Africa (Haggblade *et al.*, 1989), a considerable portion of the benefits accrued to urban dwellers. Part of rural income was transferred to urban areas via taxes and relative price shifts, as also happened in Kenya in the 1970s (Bigsten and Collier, 1995).

Managing the enlarged coffee-export receipts was a test of the new approach to economic management, and there were three main concerns (Sharer *et al.*, 1995). The first was that huge inflows of foreign exchange would lead to appreciation of the real exchange rate, worsening the competitiveness of Uganda's non-coffee exports. The second concern, with the huge inflow of coffee earnings into the country, was that the government revenue was bound to increase, either via indirect taxation or directly via coffee-tax receipts; experience from other countries has shown (see for instance Edwards, 1984; Bevan *et al.*, 1990) that it could be very difficult for a poor country to maintain fiscal discipline in the face of such a windfall.[39] The third concern regarded the possible behaviour of private economic agents, who could be expected to try to maximise the present value of their private portfolios, and might respond in perverse ways; thus the issue was how to handle the boom as to avoid destabilisation and guarantee long-term benefits, given that coffee booms are temporary and prices would eventually go back to their normal levels.

The World Bank (1995) estimated that the present value of the coffee boom was about 24 per cent of GDP. Though spread out over several years, this represented a substantial shock to the economy, which could support a permanent increase in spending of about 2.4 per cent of GDP, though for this to happen about 70 per cent of the windfall income would need to be saved. Even if this level of saving were possible, the portion undertaken by the private sector would initially be in financial assets, in Uganda mainly money, only gradually shifting over into real assets. From 1994 there was an increase in capital imports, indicating an increase in real investment. In the public sector, savings would have to take the form of budget surpluses, and as noted above, net savings of the government actually has actually increased significantly from the 1993/94 budget year.

By the mid-1990s, the government had managed to get its expenditures in line with available revenues, inclusive of aid. The government did not have a deficit to finance domestically, so the treasury bill market was being used largely to realise monetary objectives. This discipline might, however, be jeopardised by the revenue generated by the boom as happened in Kenya during the

1970s, but donor leverage on Kenya at the time was much lower than that on Uganda in the 1990s.

There was disagreement between the IMF and the World Bank on how Uganda should address the destabilising effects of increased coffee revenues. It was argued in an IMF review of the Ugandan economy (Sharer *et al.*, 1995) that the fiscal stance should be long-run sustainable based on the permanent income hypothesis, rather than reacting to temporary increases in revenues with higher consumption expenditures as a result. Both the IMF and the World Bank in fact agreed that increased savings should be a major component of the stabilisation measures, but failed to agree on who was to undertake the savings — the public or the private sector? The World Bank (1995) argued against taxing the private sector. Due to the incidence of import taxation discussed in Section 5.4.4, coffee producers were already exposed to a high implicit tax; besides, coffee farmers in Uganda are mostly poor and should be taxed lightly. Taxation could also lower profitability and lead to smuggling as in the 1970s; and finally, given the public sector's past record, the private sector was better placed to save and invest the windfall. For the World Bank, the questions thus concerned not only income distribution and the difficulty of enforcement, but also who would make the best use of the money. However, the government sided with the IMF, which argued for a coffee tax as the quickest means of mopping up extra liquidity in the market. This tax was not introduced until January, 1995, as there seemed to be little currency appreciation, or even inflation.[40] Subsequently, there was movement towards the World Bank position, especially regarding the attractive income distributional argument. Farmers would be richer without the coffee tax, while the government would receive its revenue via the normal system of taxation. In response to complaints from exporters, the level of coffee taxation was reduced in the budget for 1995/96; and abolished completely the following year.

4.6. Land Reform and Resource Husbandry

The importance of agriculture in the economy put land reform high on the priority list (Agricultural Policy Committee, 1989). Uganda has two basic systems of land tenure: traditional tenure, which is common throughout the country but most concentrated in the north, does not recognise individual ownership of land; and freehold tenure, which was established by the colonial government, mainly in western Uganda. Mailo land tenure, another form of freehold, was established 1900. In 1975, Amin introduced a Land Decree which turned all freehold land into public land; former owners were given 99-year leases. However, though the decree remained on the statute books, and was thus a source of insecurity, few of its stipulations were ever implemented.

In a bid to establish a uniform land tenure system, which could command support from most of the country, the government set up a committee to draft a Land Bill to abolish traditional and leasing systems and replace them with freehold. All land would become publicly owned, under the Uganda Land Commission, but land transactions would be directly between buyer and seller, in a free market. To avert fears of alienation, there would continue to be restrictions on the acquisition of land by foreigners. Conflicts would be resolved by land adjudication committees at sub-district levels. The proposals were presented at varied fora throughout the country, but the goal of land reform has not been achieved.

To reduce pressure on densely populated areas, such as Kigezi in southwestern Uganda, the government undertook controversial resettlement schemes. In one, individuals were moved to Kibaale district in western Uganda; the settlers were later blamed for decimating Kibaale forest and game reserve corridor as they cleared land for their new homes. In other areas of the country protected forest reserves have been exploited by neighbouring populations for firewood and other forest products, and some sections have been turned into farms. Uganda's temperate climate and adequate rainfall are able to support several harvests a year, and its rich land, water, and other natural resources make its medium- to long-run prospects encouraging, but the environment is vulnerable: in southwestern Uganda land-scarcity has led to overexploitation and there are signs of serious land degradation. There has also been extensive reclamation of wetlands, leading to the drying up of rivers and the decline of water levels in lakes.[41] To bring an awareness of environmental issues into policies and legislation, the government established a National Environmental Action Programme run by a secretariat in the Ministry of Natural Resources. The 1994 Environment Management Bill focused on measures to increase agricultural productivity via use of improved technology, and land reform, but the need to generate income has generally been more pressing than environmental concerns.

5. Economic Performance under Full Liberalisation

5.1. Output

The basic purpose of all these reforms was to create a conducive macroeconomic and investment climate and thus raise output. So what was the impact on production? In spite of policy difficulties, GDP growth was over 6 per cent in 1987 (Table 5.1), the best since 1980 with the single exception of 1983. Though inadequate, even the initial reforms under the NRM had some positive impacts on production. There was a temporary slow-down in manufacturing activity after the May 1987 reforms, but a strong recovery was underway by the end of the year, largely a result of quick rehabilitation and restoration of capacities in key industries. Nevertheless, in a 1988 manpower and employment survey (Uganda, 1989a), 88 per cent of the manufacturing firms still utilised less than 20 per cent of installed capacity, and only 10 per cent used more than 60 per cent, so the sector was clearly recovering from a very low base. The relative prices for importables relative to non-tradables also rose during the second half of the 1980s (see Figure 5.2), indicating an improved competitive edge for manufactures in the domestic markets.

Manufacturing has benefited from liberalisation of the foreign-exchange market, enabling it to source intermediate imports, and to replace old and dysfunctional equipment without being subjected to controls. The sector responded favourably to the adjustment policies and improved relative prices; production averaged over 10 per cent annual growth from 1987 through 1995 (Table 5.2). Textile product-

Figure 5.2: *Relative Prices 1987–94*

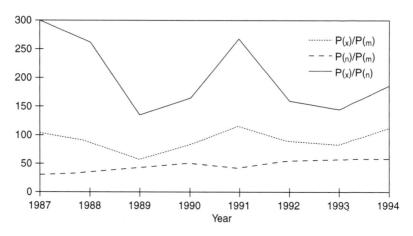

Sources and definitions: See Figure 4.2.

Figure 5.3: *Relative Commodity Prices 1987–94*

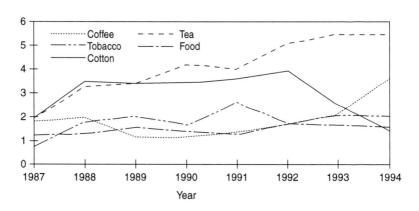

Note: Prices are estimated relative to the GDP deflator, with relative prices in 1981 set equal to 1.
Sources: See Figure 4.3.

Table 5.2: *Real Sectoral Outputs and GDP, 1987–95 (1987=100)*

Year	1987	1988	1989	1990	1991	1992	1993	1994	1995
Monetary agriculture	100	106.8	113.0	121.4	127.6	134.0	142.9	154.9	164.7
Non-monetary agriculture	100	106.0	112.1	113.6	113.7	114.5	118.2	123.7	126.7
Government	100	106.3	113.7	123.5	134.4	146.3	156.1	166.7	177.2
Manufacturing	100	116.1	129.6	136.5	152.8	164.8	178.4	218.5	256.2
GDP per capita	100	104.1	107.7	110.4	112.9	113.9	117.4	124.7	132.2

Source: Uganda (1995b, 1996a), *Background to the Budget 1995/96 and 1996/97.*

ion, however, was hampered by slow rehabilitation of the cotton sector, its main supplier of raw materials, and only improved to about a third of the production level in the late 1960s.

Though privatisation only started to gather momentum in the early 1990s, the impact on manufacturing has been substantial. The example of Hima Cement in western Uganda is illustrative. The company was privatised at the end of 1994, after a long period of low capacity utilisation — its power sources were ineffective, and its machinery was in a poor state of repair. By 1996 it had increased cement production to 600 metric tonnes per day, a 500 per cent increase from 1994, with plans to more than double output again by the end of 1997, employment has almost doubled. The soft drinks and breweries sub-sectors have also seen a rapid recovery. However, many still clamour for government protection: 'We need to get the scale of production that will allow us to compete with imports', they say, that is with those from Kenya (UMA, 1996).

Agricultural production also expanded quite satisfactorily after 1987, thanks to the return of relative peace, favourable weather generally — despite droughts 1991 and 1993 — and improvements in infrastructure, which increased access to markets. The prices of agricultural products also grew more rapidly than the general price level during the period 1987–94, with particularly strong increases for tea and for coffee after 1990. The cotton prices crashed after 1992. Lower coffee prices from 1988 to 1992 were partly the result of infrequent adjustment of the controlled domestic producer prices (see Figure 5.3).

Output fluctuated with the weather, with droughts having negative impacts on food supplies, but the long-term trend was upwards (Table 5.3). Non-traditional exports, such as maize and, to some extent, beans, were boosted by high demand in neighbouring countries, notably Kenya, and purchases by UN agencies for relief efforts in Rwanda. Food production generally had not fallen as much as cash crops due to a large subsistence component; while it was necessary to grow food to survive, it was often unprofitable or outright impossible to grow cash crops.[42] Coffee is the main cash crop and production was initially improved by a better supply of inputs, streamlined crop finance and road repairs, which eased transport. Tea is a plantation crop as opposed to coffee where small-holders are the main producers. Next to sugar, rehabilitation of tea production has demanded more capital input than have other sectors. Privatisation helped speed up rehabilitation, with 70 per cent of the estates back in production by the end of 1994.

Cotton used to be a very important export crop, but its recovery has been slow. The prolonged wars in the main cotton producing areas in the north and northeast led to a fall in output. Failure of cotton to establish itself as cash crop of last resort, like coffee, might in part explain its decline in Uganda.[43] In a study of Senegal, Goetz (1992) showed that for cash and food crops to co-exist demands the existence of sufficient inputs on the farm to enable existing technology to be used on either type of crop in a non-competing manner during at least part of the year. This condition would not easily be fulfilled for cotton production, as planting and harvesting could easily take up all available labour. In contrast, tobacco production rose strongly after 1987, with the return of Ugandan refugees to West Nile, the main tobacco producing area.[44]

The government grew by more than three quarters from 1987 to 1995 (Table 5.2), about twice as fast as during 1981–85. Defence and debt servicing continued to account for the bulk of government expenditure. The higher growth was at least initially largely aid driven, since tax revenue, especially from coffee exports, had contracted; the coffee-boom of the mid-1990s, however, improved the situation.

5.2. Investment and Savings

In spite of the reduction in economic distortions during the period of economic reforms, due to the liberalisation of investment- and trade-licensing requirements, improved access to foreign exchange and improvements in the tax structure, the private-sector response was weak. Though many incentives were introduced via the Uganda Investment Authority, the private sector's share in investment did not expand. Investments in plant and machinery are crucial for growth (see Collier and Gunning, 1991), and they were lacking. It was feared that the economy had reached a low investment steady state (Sharer *et al.*, 1995). Though the country's image had improved, foreign inv-

Table 5.3: Quantity Indices of Agricultural Production, 1987–95 (1987=100)

Year	1987	1988	1989	1990	1991	1992	1993	1994	1995
Coffee	100.0	90.5	101.2	72.1	88.2	66.0	86.5	118.7	93.5
Cotton	100.0	60.6	67.4	10.6	227.1	218.9	231.2	111.6	67.1
Tobacco	100.0	217.4	284.7	273.6	423.4	550.7	426.9	539.4	564.3
Tea	100.0	100.0	132.7	200.1	252.8	270.7	350.9	383.5	361.5
Bananas	100.0	103.6	106.1	111.1	114.5	110.9	116.8	120.8	127.9
Maize	100.0	123.2	174.8	167.6	158.0	182.9	225.2	238.1	255.5
Beans	100.0	113.0	130.1	128.4	124.2	130.3	143.1	126.4	129.4
Livestock	100.0	108.5	111.0	114.8	118.8	120.1	124.6	118.5	121.4

Sources: Uganda (various years) *Background to the Budget*; Uganda (1996b), *Statistical Abstract 1996*; Uganda, *Key Economic Indicators*, January 1966.

estors were still cautious. To make up for the investment gap, it was necessary to encourage domestic investors in various ways (see World Trade Organisation, 1995); in any case, the true test of a business environment is in the domestic response.

With the onset of privatisation since 1990, investment as a ratio of GDP has averaged 16 per cent, reaching 20 per cent in 1996, which is still below the levels of the high-growth economies of East Asia, but quite a turn-around from the poor performance of the 1980s. In the mid-1990s the private sector accounted for about 65 per cent of fixed capital formation, up from 50 per cent in the late 1980s, which is especially significant, since public investment also increased in the 1990s.

5.3 Trade

Like the government budget, Uganda's balance of payments (Table 5.4) is also heavily influenced by coffee prices and donor aid.[45] The value of exports was below US$200 million in 1993, it had doubled in 1994 due to the coffee boom and changed little in 1995. The volume of non-coffee exports has continued to grow since introduction of the ERP, from US$10 million in 1987 to almost US$150 million in 1995. Non-traditional exports include a number of food items, such as vegetables, beans, simsim, maize, and fish, plus hides and skins, vanilla and timber. Given its ability to raise at least two harvests a year of rain-fed crops, agriculture is clearly an area where Uganda has a comparative advantage. The expansion of non-traditional exports has encouraged the development of infrastructure for their handling, storage, and transport. Handling of export cargo has been out-franchised to private businesses, and cold-storage facilities are under construction at Entebbe Airport to preserve increased tonnage of fruit, flowers, and other perishable products.

While exports remained low for most of the reform period, increased aid inflows enabled the country to import above export capacity. Imports have been high (exceeding US$1 billion in 1995), and the services account has been consistently negative, but unrequited inflows have ensured that the overall balance of payments was positive in 1992–95. This enabled the Bank of Uganda to build up

Table 5.4: *Balance of Payments Statistics 1987–95 (millions of US$)*

Year	1987	1988	1989	1990	1991	1992	1993	1994	1995
Exports	333.7	272.9	251.6	177.8	173.7	151.2	183.7	440.9	548.9
Imports	-634.5	-627.4	-659.1	-617.6	-478.8	-513.3	-626.7	-672.2	-866.7
Trade balance	-300.8	-354.6	-407.6	-439.8	-301.1	-362.1	-443.0	-231.3	-317.8
Services net	-113.6	-126.9	-131.6	-116.5	-197.6	-189.6	-167.3	-315.4	-428.6
Unrequited transfers	244.6	287.3	332.0	293	328.4	423.3	494.2	476.2	566.3
Current account	-169.8	-194.1	-207.2	-263.3	-170.3	-199.4	-116.2	-70.5	-180.1
Capital account	142.3	54.7	243.4	177.5	34.9	-70.7	-84.2	36.1	48.3
Net changes in arrears	19.1	142.0	-41.5						
Overall	-8.5	2.6	-5.4	-85.8	-135.4	-190.2	-200.4	-26.9	-131.8

Note: arrears are included in the overall balance. Increases in net arrears (+), decreases (–). Net changes in arrears were excluded as a separate item after 1989. The net overall balance comprises changes in gross reserves, the net position *vis-à-vis* the IMF and other (including errors and omissions).

Source: Uganda (1990), *Key Economic Indicators*, 3rd issue, October 1990 and 6th issue, July 1991. Bank of Uganda, *Quarterly Economic Report* Oct–Dec 1993.

its foreign exchange reserves, which by mid-1966 reached more than four-month's worth of imports (about US$500 million). Debt servicing, however, has continued to be a major debit item. Foreign assistance has been crucial to Uganda's economic rehabilitation and performance; aid inflows increased rapidly after the NRM took power in 1986. In 1985 the aid inflow was only US$180 million, whereas by 1990 it was US$631 million (OECD, Development Cooperation Directorate Database, 1993). The high marks for performance that Uganda eventually got from both the IMF and the World Bank made it relatively easy to get aid, but also to increase Uganda's indebtedness; the eagerness of donors to give money to Uganda perhaps also reflected their frustration with other countries in the region which would otherwise have competed for the same money.

Since 1987 the IMF has lent money to Uganda under both a Structural Adjustment Facility and an Extended Structural Adjustment Facility; both types of loans had an initial interest rate of 0.5 per cent and a repayment period of 10 years, with a 5.5 year grace period. The initial burden of these loans was small, but once repayment of the principal started the burden became heavy. The World Bank at first lent money to Uganda on hard terms, but later only gave soft window loans to the country under the International Development Agency (IDA). IDA loans have a service charge of only 0.75 per cent, with a ten-year grace period and a repayment period of 35–40 years. Those loans thus have a very large grant element, and are basically conditional grants. The African Development Bank continued to lend money to Uganda on hard terms long after the World Bank had declared the country an IDA-only borrower, but with adoption of a new credit policy at the ADB in 1995, Uganda, along with the bulk of African countries, could only borrow from the ADB's soft window, the African Development Fund. ADF loans, like the IDA, carry a 0.75 per cent service charge and a ten-year grace period, but a repayment period of 50 years.

Inadequate institutional capacities, especially in the line ministries and at the Bank of Uganda, were partly to blame for problems of aid absorption; poor coordination among donors, applying widely varying demands and procedures, also contributed to the slow pace of project implementation and utilisation of disbursed funds.

Responding to these inefficiencies, some donors instead used substantial sums from their aid budgets to pay down Uganda's debt under the IDA's 'fifth dimension' scheme.[46]

There were substantial commercial debt buybacks in 1993 and several debt reschedulings by the Paris Club. Total debt remained essentially constant throughout 1993 and at about US$2.6 billion (about 75 per cent of GDP), but there was a shift towards a higher proportion of concessional debt, with longer maturities and lower average interest rates, and there was a significant reduction in arrears. In 1994 there was a large increase in the debt (to about US$3.2 billion) due to large loans from the multilateral agencies. At the Paris Club meeting of February, 1995, pre-cutoff debt to the Paris Club was reduced by 67 per cent; since this was the highest possible write-off, Uganda graduated from the Paris Club.[47] Relative to exports, the country remained one of the most indebted in the world (even though the coffee boom of 1994–95 had reduced the debt service ratio to 25 per cent), but the debt burden looks somewhat smaller when related to GDP since exports from Uganda were still very low. The debt restructuring efforts did little to alleviate the debts owed to multilaterals, which constituted 73 per cent of total debt in 1994, of which the World Bank, IMF and African Development Bank accounted for 94 per cent (Martin, 1994).[48]

6. Changes in Economic Structure

Starting from a pre-independence base (index) of 100 in 1960, GDP per capita reached a high of 112 in 1969 (Table 2.1), then fell steadily throughout the 1970s to a momentary low of 84 in 1980 (Table 3.1), then fell further in the mid-1980s to 60 in 1986 (Table 4.1). From there it has crawled steadily back up to 85 in 1996 (Table 5.1). Thus, GDP per capita is now worse than at independence, and much worse than at the high of 112 in 1969. Nevertheless, the recent reform period bears comparisons with the immediate post-independence period because they are the only two periods of sustained growth the country has had since independence. Current demands in the areas of poverty eradication, provision of social services, and decentralisation of authority are familiar from the policy statements of the 1960s (see Uganda, 1966a; Uganda, 1972b), as are emphases on modernisation in agriculture and manufacturing.

Following a three-year recession, the rebound of 1963 was exceptionally strong, with increased investment and employment, both spearheaded by the public sector. Expansion reached a peak in 1969 with growth of 12 per cent. The 1960s saw marked improvement in welfare for some urban groups, as well as generally the rural areas (Knight, 1967), as a result of increasing earnings in the formal sector, better producer prices in agriculture, and extension of modern infrastructure and services to the countryside. The prosperity of the post-independence years was too brief to enable a firm conclusion whether it was the product of effective policies, or more of favourable weather and improved terms-of-trade. Nevertheless, there was clearly a sharp contrast between the vibrant economy of the 1960s and the economy of the early 1980s on the verge of ruin.

The period from 1987 onwards is somewhat similar to that which followed independence in 1962. Both had high average growth rates.[49] 1987 marked a trend break, with the economy returning to per capita income growth after the long crisis period, thanks to substantial inflows of donor aid and the positive impact of adjustment on production, especially in manufacturing and services.

The recovery started from a low base. Capacity utilisation in manufacturing had fallen below 10 per cent, while in agriculture portions of the cash crop sector, such as tea and coffee, had partly gone to bush. It was not until the end of the 1980s that the economy was stabilised, and the government could turn to long-term economic issues, including poverty alleviation. In this section, we compare changes in economic structure during the two periods.

Export diversification is one of the main strategies adopted in Uganda's recent reform efforts. Table 5.5 shows export shares for 1969, when commodity prices (especially coffee) boomed, and for 1995, another year of good coffee prices. Coffee's share was 56 per cent of total exports in 1969, and 74 per cent in 1995; however, in the intervening years, coffee's share had sometimes reached 90 per cent. Better macroeconomic policies and exchange rate reforms meant that more of the higher revenues from improved coffee prices accrued directly to the farmer than in previous years. Thus in sections of coffee-growing southern Uganda, there were unmistakable signs of increased prosperity: new Chinese-made bicycles became a common item in most households, while farmers were re-roofing their houses with corrugated iron sheets. The experience was thus different from that of the late 1970s, when the bulk of proceeds from the coffee boom of those years went mainly to urban-based bureaucrats and to coffee smugglers.

Cotton production went into decline during the years of economic chaos, falling from 18 per cent of total exports in 1969 to only 1.4 per cent in 1995. Rehabilitation efforts since 1987 have had mixed results (Table 5.3). Tea has undergone a somewhat more rapid recovery. In contrast to both coffee and cotton, which are grown by smallholders, tea is an estate crop. It has been boosted by increased investment, generated partly by the privatisation programme and partly by the return of plantations to their original Asian owners. They have rehabilitated their estates, hired new managers, and in some cases revived the out-grower schemes, under which smallholders also grow tea for delivery to the estate's processing plant. Copper production, and thus exports, ceased in the 1970s, putting an end to the only sizeable industry in western Uganda.

Table 5.6 shows sectoral GDP shares at important dates from 1962 to 1995. At independence in 1962, monetary agriculture contributed about 30 per cent of total GDP, slightly less than half of modern sector GDP. The remainder was overwhelmingly subsistence agriculture, so agriculture as a whole accounted for about 60 per cent of total GDP. Nine years later (1971), just before the sharp decline began, the share of modern sector agriculture had fallen to 22 per cent, while the total share of all modern sectors had increased slightly. Manufacturing, commerce, government, transport and communication and other services had increased. The share of government had increased most, from 4.7 to 7.5 per cent.

By 1980, after a decade of civil strife and chaotic management, monetary GDP had contracted more than 30 per cent in absolute terms; monetary agriculture had fallen by about 20 per cent, but since it had shrunk less than GDP as a whole (partly because of relative price shifts in favour of agriculture), its share of GDP increased to over thirty per cent. Manufacturing, at 4 per cent of a much-reduced GDP, had become relatively insignificant, while electricity and water, construction, and transport and commun-ications construction, had come almost to a standstill. As a share of GDP general government fell by almost half during the 1970s: in spite of high military expenditures, the government was dwindling as the base for taxation in the modern sector shrank. With the decline of the modern sector, the subsistence sector increased to well over 40 per cent of GDP; since most of that was subsistence agriculture, agriculture as a whole accounted for about 75 per cent of GDP.

Table 5.5: *Principal Merchandise Exports in 1969 and 1995 (%)*

Crop	1969	1995
Coffee	55.8	73.7
Cotton	18.0	1.4
Copper	8.6	0
Tea	6.7	1.6
Tobacco	1.2	1.5
Sugar	1.3	0
Other	8.4	21.8

Sources: Uganda (various years), *Background to the Budget*

In 1987 the share of agriculture, including subsistence, was still above 60 per cent; the economy was more dependent on agriculture and non-monetary production than it had been at independence. Manufacturing had recovered slightly since 1980, but its share in GDP was still smaller than at independence. General government was smaller than it had been in 1980, reflecting both low activity and extremely low wages and salaries; 'other services', including health and education, had started to expand with the reforms, however. Construction and commerce were at record levels, while transport and communication had picked up substantially as well.

Table 5.6: *Sectoral GDP Shares at Current Prices, 1962–95 (per cent)*

	1962	1971	1980	1987	1995
Modern agriculture	29.7	22	32.4	25.1	25.8
Mining	1.7	1.5	0	0.1	0.3
Manufacturing	6.3	8.7	4.3	5.0	6.7
Electricity and water	1.6	1.2	0.1	0.4	1.1
Construction	2.5	1.3	0.1	3.0	6.2
Commerce	9.3	12.5	9.6	15.5	12.7
Transport and communication	3.7	4.7	0.5	3.0	4.2
General government	4.7	7.5	3.9	2.2	4.3
Other services, incl. education and health	9.6	10.5	4.8	7.4	12.6
Monetary GDP	68.9	70	55.7	61.6	73.9
Non-monetary GDP	31.1	30	44.3	38.4	26.1
Total GDP	100	100	100	100	100

Source: Uganda (1966c), *Statistical Abstract 1965*; World Bank (1988); Uganda (1996a), *Background to the Budget 1996/97.*

By 1995 the subsistence sector had shrunk to a record low (26%), while the share of monetary agriculture had increased, partly due to the coffee boom. The share of every monetary sector except commerce increased over 1987, including a sizeable increase in construction and a substantial increase in 'other services' including education and health. There is considerable similarity between the Ugandan economy of today and that of the first decade of independence, which perhaps suggests that a basis for growth has been recreated. The policy environment, with no controls on foreign exchange or trade, has become much more liberal than during the import-substitution strategy of the 1960s, so internationally-competitive production has improved.

Figure 5.4: *Average Sectoral and GDP Growth Rates, 1962–71 and 1987–95*

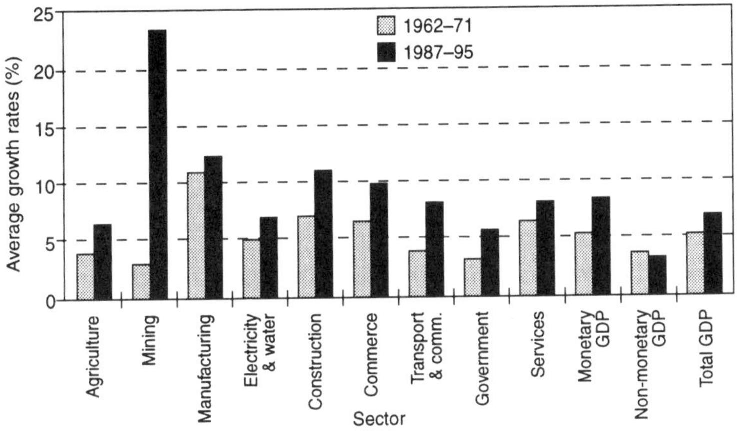

Sources: Uganda, *Background to the Budget* (various issues).

Average sectoral and GDP growth rates for the periods 1962–71 and 1987–95 are compared in Figure 5.4; both periods had per capita income growth. GDP growth in the post-independence period averaged 5 per cent, somewhat higher most recently (6.7 per cent),[50] substantially exceeding that for Sub-Saharan Africa as a whole. Generally speaking, both periods showed balanced growth in all sectors. Reflecting the higher overall growth, the latter period had higher growth in every sector, except subsistence. Average agricultural growth increased between the periods from 4 to 6.4 per cent. The cessation of operations at Kilembe mines brought mining to a virtual standstill in the 1970s; recent high growth is a reflection of the extremely low base in 1987. Recent exploratory prospecting for oil in western Uganda and for gold in northern Uganda suggests a possible further expansion. The recent growth rate of manufacturing

(12.5 per cent) is even higher than in the 1960s, when it was thought to be impressive in regional terms (see Uganda, 1972b). If high rates of manufacturing growth persist, the sector will increase its share in GDP and in total employment, providing a firmer basis for future structural transformation than has so far been possible (see for instance Saha, 1991).

Employment creation was a major goal in the 1960s. The relatively rapid expansion of employment opportunities in that decade resulted from the growth of the public sector. The role of the private sector in employment creation diminished in the 1970s, especially after the expulsion of the Asians, who owned most of the small to medium size industries. The economic improvements of the current reform period have yet to have a strong impact on job creation, partly because the private sector had high levels of excess capacity. It has been necessary, in many cases, to reduce the workforce to levels that could be ensured adequate remuneration in order to improve work discipline and raise productivity. Thus, given public sector retrenchment, formal sector employment is still a very small part of total employment. The informal sector will have to provide the bulk of employment opportunities outside of agriculture (see ILO, 1995).

7. Concluding Remarks

By most accounts (see Sharer *et al.*, 1995), Uganda has now gone further than most African countries in stabilising its economy, and the traditional dependence on agriculture has been reduced somewhat as non-agricultural sectors have expanded, but the country's exposure to the vagaries of the weather and commodity price changes remains. Although the role of government changed in the 1990s, the public sector remains, in spite of the retrenchment, a major employer and generator of investment. On the other hand, industrial production has yet to assume a sizeable portion of the economy. An important change from the 1960s, and even more so compared with the crisis years, is the greater part played by markets in Uganda, and the emphasis on decentralisation of power. Rapid economic growth since 1987 had, by the mid-1990s, returned Uganda roughly to where it had been in the early 1970s, during the only other sustained period of growth since 1960 — an outcome which leads us to the hopeful conclusion that given effective policies there are no permanent 'basket cases'. The future now looks better for Uganda than it has for a long time, but it has not yet actually recovered from the long crisis period.

Uganda's economic growth since the late 1980s has been exceptional in two ways: first, it has been sustained for a long period; close to ten years. Since 1987, average growth has been only slightly less than 7 per cent, implying an average per capita growth rate of about 4 per cent per annum. The economy has almost doubled since 1986. Second, high growth has been accompanied by relatively low rates of inflation. Other differentiating features of the performance have been the ability of policy-makers, to withstand shocks; the boom and bust in coffee prices, over 1994–96, and the internal strife and political destabilisation that have affected large parts of Uganda.

In the mid-1990s, the Ugandan economy was beginning to show signs of institutional revival, expansion of production capacities and increased demand for infrastructure. This change was most evident in the manufacturing sector, where the privatisation of recent years has introduced new investment, new participants and increased competition. It was becoming clear, however, that institutional reform, notably that of the public sector, was lagging behind private sector expansion. The private sector was now having to contend with slow regulatory mechanisms and the limited infrastructure. Still, these are the concerns of a growing economy and not of one in total disarray as when the reforms began in 1987.

Notes

1. Support was received from the IMF, the World Bank and other donors.
2. Even as the government embarked on the implementation of these IMF and World Bank-supported policies, some anti-IMF and World Bank statements persisted, notably from the NRM Secretariat and the government newspaper, *The New Vision*.

These declined over time as positive results of the reforms began to emerge.

3. The examples given here are general enough to provide the main thrust of IMF/World Bank conditionalities in Uganda for the entire period of adjustment, though they were specifically tied to the World Bank's Economic Recovery Programme and the IMF's Enhanced Structural Adjustment Facility, both from 1990.

4. For private-sector credit to be effectively allocated, improve-ment of the financial sector is essential. The impact of credit to the private sector has been limited so far, however, not because of the financial sector itself but because of the lack of sound borrowers.

5. The proposed sale to a British company of Nytil Jinja, a producer of textiles, for only about US$5 million was opposed by local government leaders at the end of 1994; it was believed that the company's assets, including houses for workers and executives, were worth more (see for instance Abraham Odeke, in *The New Vision*, 14 September, 1995). The government was not insensitive to the charge that incentives to foreign investors — notably tax holidays — were too generous; adjustments were announced in the budget speech for 1995/96 to level the playing field for domestic investors.

6. Targeting problems related to social intervention can be illustrated by the case of war widows in northern Uganda. An NGO based in Lira was contracted to set up a programme that was strictly for widows; women who found a new husband risked losing support. Since many of the widows were young, the programme became something of an impediment to a return to normal life.

7. It has been suggested that the conversion tax worsened Uganda's already low level of monetisation arising from the public's distrust of financial institutions after the long period of economic chaos (Sharer *et al.*, 1995).

8. In a survey conducted by the BOU, only 20 per cent of the firms on the OGL list indicated that they had or could obtain sufficient funds to purchase the foreign exchange allotted them; the rest had little or nothing. That 80 per cent of the companies had no

secure source of credit limited the impact of the OGL programme.

9. The guerilla movement's assumption of power in Uganda caused unease in Kenya, which had tried, without success, to broker a power-sharing arrangement between the warring factions. In the eyes of Kenyan leaders, Museveni had set a dangerous precedent.

10. However, the government was able to rehabilitate hotels (such as the Sheraton) and some accompanying facilities with the help of barter trade, mainly in coffee. The hosting of this meeting was in the main a morale-boosting gesture.

11. This system was abolished in 1995 as an example of the return to normalcy.

12. Importers could now buy foreign currency without controls and on a first-come first-served basis, but at a rate higher than the basic official one. This presaged the introduction of foreign exchange bureaux in 1990, where foreign currency was sold at market rates.

13. Just as growing guerilla insurgency of the early 1980s was the most important obstacle to economic stabilisation during Obote II.

14. Besides adjusting to repeated negative coffee-price shocks, frequent devaluations in Uganda were also the result of a lack of success in fiscal and credit policies and lingering monetary disequilibria; failure to accompany the devaluations of 1987–89 with monetary restraint made it difficult to lower inflation or stimulate exports (Bigsten and Kayizzi-Mugerwa, 1993). It has been argued (see Morris, 1989; Elbadawi, 1990; Henstridge, 1994b) that the devaluations *per se* had no serious impact on domestic inflation, since for all practical purposes the economy was operating on the parallel exchange rate (except for oil, where the lower official rate implied a substantial subsidy to oil consumers). But an investigation of the inflation-devaluation-inflation hypothesis in Nicaragua — a country richer than Uganda but with surprisingly similar pre-adjustment conditions — Gibson (1991) argued that while 'inflation is not caused by

devaluation, it is caused by the piling on of coincident policies which rob devaluation of its power'.

15. Gertzel (1990, p.207) has noted that, though costly, Museveni's creation of an enlarged National Resistance Army (NRA) from largely regional armies was a significant achievement. It turned the NRA into 'the state's official armed force', thereby preventing fragmentation.

16. Much like structural adjustment, the return of more peaceful conditions had positive impacts on relative prices, private portfolios, and incomes; on the other hand, those who had shifted into activities which benefited from the state of chaos (such as smuggling) lost a substantial part of their livelihood with the return of peace; see also Collier (1994).

17. During 1986–95, the National Resistance Council also passed a total of 113 statutes and 73 resolutions, an unprecedented amount of legislation, much of it important in laying legal and institutional foundations for economic growth and development; see also Uganda Constitutional Commission (1991).

18. The Northern Uganda Rehabilitation Programme, covering the districts of Arua, Nebbi, Moyo, Gulu, Kitgum, Lira, Apac, Kumi, Soroti and Pallisa, was run from the office of the Prime Minister. Since this post was occupied by a politician from northern Uganda, the programme was seen as a pacification measure. There were complaints, however, that the repair of infrastructure was doing less to reduce poverty in these areas than would, say, the restocking of cattle.

19. All retrenched soldiers were given a resettlement package, which included at least US$400 and iron sheets for constructing a house.

20. Relations between the Kabaka (king) of Buganda and the central government have greatly influenced the political history of Uganda; there was real fear, therefore, that the resurrection of a prestigious Kabakaship might distract the NRM from its decentralising mission. However, fear of a resurgent Buganda is far from justified: The prestige of Mengo, the Buganda capital, derived from the relatively rich Baganda peasantry, spread out in the vast reaches of the kingdom, but poverty has since struck this group beyond recognition. Ultimately, whoever succeeds in

returning this group to prosperity will have a powerful constituency.

21. As a more homogeneous sector, the impact of retrenchment in the military has been clearer, with resources freed for other uses, for example expansion of the civilian police force.

22. Government planned to raise its minimum wage to 70,000 Ushs, about US$70, by the 1996/97 financial year and to eventually monetise all benefits and allowances. The government no longer provides housing to civil servants, having sold off most of its houses (see Uganda, 1995a).

23. Decentralisation is also often embraced in the belief that it would generate resources at the local level. After 1989, six new districts have been established in Uganda, Kalangala, Kibaale, Kisoro, Ntungamo, Rukungiri and Pallisa. In early 1997 another six districts were created, namely Sembabule, Busia, Katakwi, Nakasongola, Koboko and Bukholi. See also Uganda (1987a).

24. Taxes on fuels and other imports generated the bulk of tax revenue, while the substantial budget deficit was covered by grants and loans as in earlier years. The activities of the anti-smuggling unit were halted for a while during the 1996 elections, but this led to a sharp revenue decline from loss of custom's duties, as more traders chose to avoid taxation by smuggling in goods instead.

25. Such a high dependence on foreign financing was not without its problems. The earlier expenditure overshooting was partly blamed on this over-reliance on external resources. Commenting on the 1992/93 budget presentation, Museveni (who had chaired the gathering) wondered pointedly whether Uganda was 'a country or a colony'.

26. The government has defined a number of priorities: primary education, primary health care, road maintenance, agricultural extension services, and security; but since peace is the foundation for economic development, and more resources were needed to put an end to the northern war, and other security threats, the military was claiming close to 30 per cent of total expenditure in the first half of fiscal 1996/97, while the Finance Minister claimed to be 45 billion shillings short, due to the war. (Despite the

appearance of peace in the southern parts of the country, the war had flared up again in the north as efforts towards a political solution failed.) Government troops had been fighting rebels of the Lords Resistance Army in the north since the 1980s, and, in 1996, the government was re-recruiting some of the soldiers it had laid off a few years earlier.

27. In the current form of delivery, with the bulk of health and education expenditures allocated to urban hospitals and higher levels of education, these public services still primarily benefit the middle classes anyway, not the poor who need it the most. As noted by Tumusiime-Mutebile (1990b: 7), 'very little government money gets anywhere near the poor'.

28. Some of the grounds for this criticism are illustrated by the government's establishment of a National Enterprise Corporation (NEC) for the military. NEC was a very ambitious project with sub-projects covering most areas of economic activity. Much of its rapid expansion was partly thanks to government support. Expansion of this organisation seemed contrary to the thrust of the adjustment programme which was aimed at getting the economy away from subsidised and inefficient state industries. Though, perhaps, doomed to fail from the outset, creating businesses for the armed forces also reflected the government's desire to reduce military expenditure.

29. Inflation reached its lowest annualised level of –2.4 per cent in June 1993; besides the cash budget and another good harvest, the government began paying off its loans from the Bank of Uganda, continuing tight liquidity in the economy, and there were also increased purchases of imports reducing the amount of shillings among the public.

30. The central bank was also to be recapitalised with 60 billion shillings.

31. As the supervisor of monetary institutions, the BOU was forced to take over two leading 'indigenous banks', the Nile Bank and Sembule Bank, in 1995. The two banks were similar to the 'political' banks of neighbouring Kenya, with owners and borrowers coming from a small circle of politicians and well-connected businessmen, thereby risking the accumulation of non-

performing assets. At the end of 1996, the central bank lent the two banks a total of US$6 million to restore them to solvency.

32. Uganda (1993: 12) provided some details. The demobilisation of soldiers meant the return of thousands of able-bodied individuals to the countryside, many of whom embarked on small-scale businesses using their retrenchment benefits. From their military isolation, ex-soldiers thus became part of the monetary economy, expanding the need for money.

33. It is estimated, that Uganda will need some 300,000 main lines by the turn of the decade.

34. The role of smaller power generating plants to supplement the main grid, especially in remote areas, is appreciated; among the bigger projects planned is a joint-venture between the Madhvani group and a Canadian company to build a dam on the Nile, with a capacity of over 350MW.

35. Many contracts (not necessarily written) are entered into by farmers and crop buyers in coffee marketing. Besides problems with the Coffee Marketing Board, lack of a framework to ensure compliance and irreversibility led to heavy financial losses for farmers, as well as the government.

36. Bunker (1991) has blamed the decline of the cooperative movement on central government interference. With the introduction of the Produce Marketing Act of 1968 and the Cooperative Statutes Act of 1970, the government became party to all organisational aspects of the movement, making it impossible to turn it into a truly democratic and representative institution. The new Cooperative Law of 1992 removed many of these incumbrances. Perhaps its most important provision is that a cooperative union will be forced into liquidation, when two-thirds of its capital is lost.

37. The Rural Farmers' Credit Scheme started by the Uganda Commercial Bank in 1987 is another example of policy initiatives that failed owing to corruption and poor capacity for implementation. Managers of the bank and politicians became the biggest borrowers in the scheme, contradicting all its objectives.

38. A failure to generate profits is, perhaps erroneously, used as the criterion for privatisation in the adjustment debate in Uganda. Thus an improvement in the profits of the Uganda Commercial Bank in 1995, after the removal of bad debts, was being given as a reason for it to remain in government ownership.

39. In neighbouring Kenya in the 1970s, a temporary increase in revenue led to spending levels that could not be sustained once the boom had subsided; the fear that something similar could happen in Uganda was fuelled by the fact that the NRM was going to fight a presidential election, following the promulgation of the new constitution. See for instance the article by James Kigozi in *The East African* of 9–15 October 1995, where fears were expressed that in the run-up to the elections, the cost of presidential pledges was rising beyond budgetary allocations.

40. There was considerable resistance to the tax which was 30 per cent on the part of the price that exceeded 1200 Ushs. To show its seriousness in the enforcement of the tax, the Uganda Revenue Authority ordered the closure of 14 exporting firms for non-compliance.

41. River Mayanja and Lake Wamala, in southern Uganda, have been affected by the destruction of the adjacent marshlands and the diversion of the small feeder streams.

42. The West Nile region, from which many peasants had fled to neighbouring southern Sudan to escape atrocities, was such an area.

43. In a study of cotton farming in Tanzania, Dercon (1993) found that the response to higher prices in cotton production was at the expense of food production. Conversely, improved food prices, even when cotton prices remained attractive, led to decreased production of the crop.

44. About 25 per cent of the population had taken refuge in Southern Sudan after the fall of Amin in 1978.

45. Besides the direct effects, increases in either one tends to appreciate the exchange rate, which makes expansion of non-traditional exports, such as manufactures, harder.

46. The fifth dimension is a mechanism developed in donor circles to enable borrower countries to continue assessing cheaper IDA

funds by having their obligations to the World Bank proper, in terms of interest payments and amortisation, taken care of by a donor or group of donors.

47. The 'cutoff' date for debts owed to the Paris Club is 1981. Since Uganda's debt only began to escalate afterwards, the impact on the debt stock was not that dramatic.

48. The 'fifth dimension' has been used extensively by donors such as Sweden to cover Uganda's interest payments on World Bank debt, thereby enabling continued flow of IDA resources. Since 1989 IDA has allocated part of the repayments on its loans under the fifth dimension to cover interest payments for countries in the Special Programme of Assistance for Africa. These credits were disbursed every year in proportion to the interest payments due to the World Bank, on condition that the recipient country was undertaking an adjustment programme, as well as servicing its debts to the World Bank group. Having met these conditions, Uganda benefited from the fifth dimension arrangements and as a result, direct World Bank debt shrunk and was scheduled to be completely repaid by 1998.

49. Another feature shared by the two periods is data availability. In 1966, for example, the Statistics Division at Entebbe undertook a census of agriculture, manufacturing and distribution, as well as food consumption surveys. After a long period of decline, the Statistics Division was refurbished in the late 1980s with donor assistance, enabling it to embark once again on major economic surveys.

50. The second period is inflated by the high 1994 figure of 9.5 per cent, largely explained by the coffee boom of that year.

Chapter 6: Income, Poverty, and Social Services

1. Introduction

In Uganda, the government's involvement in the provision of social services has been fairly extensive. In the 1960s, education and primary health care were given considerable emphasis; they were seen as instruments that would help reduce poverty, ignorance and disease in the countryside, thereby giving a boost to overall economic development.[1] Thus, partly with donor support, a rapid expansion of health and education services took place in the first years of independence, accompanied by broad private sector initiatives in both areas. However, high population growth, and the crises of the 1970s and after began to reduce the supply and quality of social services (Heyneman, 1979); increasing the difficulties of welfare improvement. The overriding problem has been the inability of the central and local governments to provide adequate resources. The institutions set up for training, regulation and research fell into disrepair while financial constraints reduced the levels of remuneration in the service sector to intolerable levels.

Furthermore, the provision of social services in Uganda has been plagued by an urban bias with services concentrated in the confines of the major urban centres; and by a shortage of both resources and personnel to modernise and adapt the institutions to the needs of the expanding population.

At the policy level, concern relates to where to focus the meagre resources — whether to provide a cheap or even free basic education to the broad masses or to concentrate more on the higher levels of education in order to improve manning capacity in government and the private sector (Opio-Odong, 1993). Similarly, while the government continued to emphasise the importance of primary health care, in reality the bulk of its health expenditure went to urban hospitals.

2. Changes in Real Incomes

The 1960s began with relative price stability, but inflation was becoming a serious problem by the end of the decade, as demand pressures in the economy grew. Over the period, high-income groups experienced only modest inflation levels (an average of 4 per cent) while low income groups experienced slightly higher inflation (close to 8 per cent). Food was an important factor in the CPI for low income groups, with upward swings during the drought years of the mid-1960s, while food prices impacted less on higher-income groups. Wages generally increased sufficiently to compensate for inflation, and the supply of social services in urban areas was good, with the bulk of health services supplied free of charge by the government. Indeed, if the budget surveys of the 1960s are good indicators, households spent only a very small portion of their incomes on health care.

Even workers in the lowest skill categories earned enough to meet most of their cash needs; among low-income groups in urban areas, regular employment was the main income source, comprising over 90 per cent of total income. Sale of produce and casual employment, though widely-spread even in the 1960s, made up only a small share of total income.

Table 6.1 shows weekly food and miscellaneous expenditures for a family of two adults and five children (aged 5–16 years) which resided in Kasubi on the outskirts of Kampala in 1990. While the head of this household described himself as a small trader, the family also had a small vegetable garden which helped supplement food supplies. The weekly consumer basket cost 10,730 Ushs in 1990, or roughly 42,920 per month. Using official retail prices from December 1971, we estimate that the comparable monthly expenditure in 1971 was only 260 Ushs; the price of this basket had gone up by a factor of 165 in the interval.

From Table 6.2 we can infer that, even given a single wage-earner in the household, a majority of wage-earning Kampala families might have been able to purchase this monthly consumption basket in 1971. In Masaka, Lango, and Kigezi, wages were much lower, but since the cost of living was also correspondingly lower upcountry, and with better possibilities for growing one's own food, wages were still relatively good.

Table 6.1: *Weekly Food and Sundry Expenditures for a Family of 7, April 1990 and Equivalent Expenditures, December 1971*

Item	Quantity	Cost 4/1990 Ushs	Cost 12/1971 Ushs
1. Matooke	30 kg	2400	16
2. Maize meal	5 kg	1000	6.5
3. Meat	1.5 kg	900	8
4. Sweet potatoes	20 kg	1000	6
5. Cassava	10 kg	700	3
6. Beans	5 kg	850	7.5
7. Groundnuts	1 kg	300	2
8. Tomatoes	2 kg	300	1
9. Onions	0.5 kg	300	1
10. Cabbages	3 kg	300	1
11. Sugar	2 kg	1200	3
12. Salt	1 kg	180	0.3
13. Milk	1 litre	250	0.7
14. Soap	1 bar	300	3
15. Charcoal	1/4 bag	250	4
16. Paraffin	2.5 litres	500	2
Total food and sundry		10730	65
Index		165	1

Sources: Data for 1990 are from a small survey on prices and basic needs undertaken in parallel to a larger socioeconomic survey (see Bigsten and Kayizzi-Mugerwa, 1992). Data for 1971 are from Uganda (1972c).

By 1990, real formal wages had declined markedly. At least 65 per cent of Kampala employees could not then afford the 42,990 Ushs monthly consumption basket, which the majority could afford in 1971. Table 6.3 and Figure 5.3 compare the distribution of earnings in 1971 and 1990. To take into account the 1990 cost of living, wages from 1971 were multiplied by the factor of 165 discussed in the previous paragraph. While in 1971 no one had a monthly wage income below 16,500 Ushs (in 1990 prices), only 44 per cent had such an income in 1990. This made it imperative, particularly for poor wage- dependent households, to find complementary sources of income. In 1971, 16 per cent had earnings at or above 165,000 Ushs per month, but in 1990 only 6 per cent. The distribution of income among employees also became more unequal (Figure 6.1)

Table 6.2: *Percentage Distribution of Monthly Wages by Level in Selected Regions of Uganda, 1971 (Ushs)*

Region	Up to 149	150– 299	300– 499	500– 1449	1500 and above
Kampala	4	53	17	15	11
Masaka	29	32	12	15	2
Lango	46	23	18	11	2
Kigezi	52	21	17	9	1

Note: The number of sampled wage employees in each region was: Kampala 70,300; Masaka 8,910; Lango 7,850; Kigezi 10,200. The former district of Lango is now split into two districts, Apac and Lira. In 1971, Ushs 7 was equal to 1 US dollar.

Source: Uganda (1972c).

Table 6.4 gives the structure of household expenditure for Kampala, Jinja, and Mbale for 1965 and 1992. The share of food expenditure for Kampala is only 2 per cent higher in 1992. Since the share of food normally goes up when incomes are falling, its near constancy may be an indication that, via various coping strategies, households managed to protect their income levels rather better than our income figures suggest.

Figure 6.1: *Lorenz Curves for Kampala Employees in 1971 and 1990*

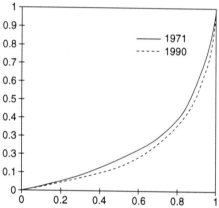

In the late 1980s, a typical civil servant earned some 5,000 Ushs per month, but surveys performed by the Statistics Department showed that the average level of household expenditure in Kampala was about thirteen times this level. Further, though school fees in Uganda were quite high relative to declared incomes, many urban families still managed to keep their children in school.[2] How was this possible?

There were a variety of options. Since many urban families retained contacts with rural areas, there was potential access to food from there, although lack of transport meant that only a small number of households could get food from the countryside on a regular basis, and in most towns everyone with access to a patch of land grew food. While food availability provided a level of security, however, multiple income-generating activities provided the cash income. For example, civil servants acted as brokers, using their positions to put together deals of various sorts; possession of an office provided a fixed address in town, access to a phone, and contacts; some borrowed money on the strength of their positions.[3] For the top echelons, foreign travel at government expense became a source of foreign exchange.

Table 6.3: *Distribution of Wage Earnings among Kampala Employees, 1971 and 1990*

Ushs per Month	Per cent Employees	
(1990 prices)	1971	1990
0–16499	0	43.7
16500–24749	4	13.6
24750–32999	24	7.3
33000–49499	29	9.6
49500–65999	10	8.3
66000–82499	7	4.3
82500–164499	10	7.6
165000–247499	5	2.6
247500–329999	6	1.0
330000–494999	3	1.6
495000+	2	0.3

Sources: Own survey, Bigsten, Kayizzi-Mugerwa (1992), Uganda (1972c).

People in government also still demand money for a wide range of services. You may have to pay to have your child registered at school, to receive treatment at hospitals, which are officially free, or even to keep your telephone connected. Over-invoicing became common, and there were even cases where payment was received for no work done or goods delivered. The 'supply of air', as this practice was known in Uganda, hampered many government programmes, disrupting the whole process of central tendering for goods and service. To combat corruption, the government revived the Public Accounts Committee and established an inspectorate of government, IGG. A 'leadership code' was also adopted by parliament to regulate the acquisition of assets by politicians while still in office.

Table 6.4: *Monthly Expenditure Patterns (per cent) in Kampala, Jinja and Mbale 1965/92*

Category	Kampala		Jinja		Mbale	
	1965	1992	1965	1992	1965	1992
Food	50.2	52.5	47.2	56.0	53.5	52.0
Beverages and tobacco	10.5	3.0	7.0	5.6	10.3	4.0
School fees	2.0	2.4	2.5	2.6	2.4	1.4
Medical care	1.0	1.7	1.7	2.0	1.0	1.0
Transport	1.8	3.4	3.2	3.0	1.9	4.5
Clothing	7.0	4.5	7.5	6.8	6.5	5.7
Other	27.5	32.5	30.9	24.0	24.4	31.4

Source: Uganda (1967a); Uganda (1993c).

But it was not just civil servants who had to devise survival mechanisms in Uganda's difficult economic situation. Two other groups, urban informal sector workers and smallholders, also had to adjust in various ways. Rural households should have benefited from the improvement in their terms of trade with the urban areas during the 1980s. With the improving economy, the number of households opting for subsistence was reduced. However, up until the coffee boom of the 1990s, increases in producer prices for coffee often remained on paper. Poor rural infrastructure and decline of the cooperative movement made it difficult for farmers to reach the market. For areas where access was better, administrative problems, including outright corruption, meant that farmers were not paid promptly for their crops. Rural areas close to roads leading to urban centres were of course best positioned to benefit from the ready market for their food produce.

3. Income Distribution and Poverty

The 1960s seemed to be the beginning of the period of sustained growth. Agriculture was gradually losing in importance to fast growing manufacturing and service sectors, while favourable terms of trade meant rapid increases in rural incomes and thus improvements in rural welfare. Eradication of poverty was a major goal in the 1960s. The government embarked on an 'incomes policy' (see for instance *The Third Five-Year Development Plan*, Uganda, 1972b)[4] to promote a more equitable distribution of income by influencing the level of wages, profits, and property incomes relative to each other, including the rural/urban income gap. This goal was to be attained through progressive taxes and free health care for the poor. To 'minimise the chance of their exploitation by employers' and ensure urban workers a minimum standard of living, the government periodically adjusted the statutory minimum wage in the various sectors of the economy. Price regulation was used to ensure the maintenance of purchasing power, so as not to defeat the purpose of minimum-wage legislation, while care was to be taken to ensure that producers were not discouraged.

Solid data on income distribution in Uganda in the 1960s are difficult to find. *The Third Five-Year Development Plan* used graduated tax assessment returns to estimate income inequality.[5] Rural and urban income distributions curves are shown in Figure 6.2. The rural sector had more even distribution in the lower income range, while the urban sector was more equal at the top; since the Lorenz curves cross, we cannot unequivocally determine where inequality was higher. On average, however, rural incomes were much lower than urban incomes — close to 60 per cent of rural taxpayers had annual incomes of 500 Ushs or less, but only 6 per cent of urban taxpayers.

Figure 6.2: *Distribution of Income Among Tax Payers 1969*

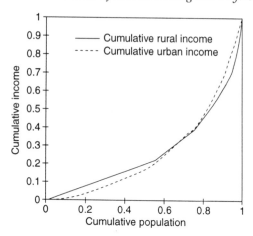

Source: Uganda (1972b) *Third Five-Year Development Plan 1971/2–1975/6*

Figure 6.3: *Distribution of Income Among Persons 1992–93*

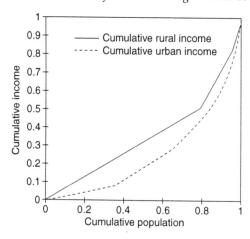

Note: household income was distributed on a per capita basis by number of persons.

Source: Uganda (1993a, b) *Report on the Integrated Household Survey 1992–93.*

There was also considerable inter-regional variation: in some rural areas in the north and southeast, 90 per cent of taxpayers had 500 Ushs or less. Even given the differences in living costs, these are very substantial differences.

The decline that began in the early 1970s reversed the progress of the 1960s. The modern sector was most hit. Though the public sector expanded in a bid to halt the growth of unemployment, resource pressures elsewhere in the economy led to high levels of inflation and reduced real incomes. A weakened macroeconomic environment, coupled with civil strife, led to vastly increased poverty. Figure 6.3 shows rural and urban income distributions curves for 1992–93. Incomes were now clearly more evenly distributed in the rural areas, at the top as well as in the lower income range, but poverty had become more widespread, in both rural and urban areas: about 75 per cent of urban monthly incomes were below 100,000 Ushs, while up to 95 per cent were below this in rural areas.

Direct poverty eradication has, in statements, been declared a top priority of the NRM government since 1986; however, instead emphasis has been on stabilisation and growth. Appleton and Mackinnon (1995) analysed the distribution of poverty in Uganda in 1992/93. After adjusting for urban-rural price differences, as well as household size, they defined a household to be poor if its expenditure level was in the bottom quartile; by this definition 27 per cent of rural households in the bottom 25 per cent (nationally) in terms of expenditure, while only 11 per cent of the urban households were in this category. With nearly 90 per cent of the population living in rural areas, poverty in Uganda was still overwhelmingly a rural phenomenon, but the relative well-being of urban Uganda was somewhat surprising (see also Kikafunda *et al.*, 1992). It could be because urban areas benefited more from rehabilitation of production capacities and the restoration of economic growth. The ability of urban households to find ingenious survival mechanisms also helps to explain the relatively low levels of open destitution in Kampala (see Appendix A). To evaluate the impact of adjustment policies on income distribution and poverty properly would require good comparative data from, say, 1986 and 1996; lacking that we will attempt to evaluate with the help of proxies. We can draw some inferences from changes in domestic terms of trade and consumption patterns. There was a slight fall in relative food prices in the 1990s, while the price of export crops, particularly coffee, went up considerably.[6] Consumption data shows that the poorest quartile were net buyers of food, so lower food prices were beneficial for them. Coffee accounted for 15 per cent of revenue for the poorest quartile in central rural Uganda, while it only accounted for 6 per cent for the best off, so coffee price improvements were distributionally beneficial,[7] while coffee tax introduced in 1995 was regressive; it was soon to be reduced and abolished.[8] Adjustment supported cash-crop production, while the related improvements of rural infrastructure, research and extension services also boosted food-crop production. The abolition of marketing monopolies also increased competition among coffee traders, the most positive outcome of which was prompt payment for deliveries.

Table 6.5 presents three indices of vulnerability and poverty for the various districts of Uganda: the percentage of the school-age population in school; the literacy rate; and the percentage of households in the bottom national expenditure quartile (larger than 25 indicates more poor households than the national average). Three districts had extreme levels of poverty, for example, Kotido and Moroto in Karamoja, as well as Kitgum, which was still affected by civil unrest. In Kotido and Moroto over 90 per cent of children in the school-age population were not in school, while literacy rates were down close to 10 per cent, compared to 51 per cent for the country as a whole, and 60 per cent for Africa (see United Nations, 1993). Many districts in other regions had much better indices, but even in some urban areas the indices were not particularly good: Jinja, the second largest town in Uganda, had 31 per cent of its school-age children not in school, not much better than the national average of 44 per cent; only Kampala got below 20 per cent. Should this failure of children to attend school be prolonged, there will be a huge human-capital gap between districts and for the country as a whole.

Table 6.5: *Household Vulnerability Indicators by District, 1990*
(per cent)

Region	District	Children out of School %[1]	Total Literacy Rate	Share of the Bottom National Expenditure Quartile[2]
Central	Kalangala	23	72	11.70
	Kampala	19	88	3.40
	Kiboga	34	55	19.10
	Luwero	27	59	26.90
	Masaka	36	62	20.50
	Mpigi	24	73	13.70
	Mubende	36	58	19.60
	Mukono	29	61	21.30
	Rakai	39	54	24.70
Eastern	Iganga	45	47	29.50
	Jinja	31	67	15.50
	Kamuli	50	41	42.60
	Kapchorwa	33	54	12.60
	Kumi	45	42	26.60
	Mbale	36	56	22.70
	Pallisa	48	47	31.30
	Soroti	38	47	37.30
	Tororo	45	53	28.60
Western	Bundibugyo	52	40	15.30
	Bushenyi	41	54	15.30
	Hoima	33	56	25.00
	Kabale	46	51	17.00
	Kabarole	47	49	15.20
	Kasese	45	50	22.80

cont ...

Table 6.5 cont ...

Region	District	Children out of School %[1]	Total Literacy Rate	Share of the Bottom National Expenditure Quartile[2]
Western	Kabale	46	51	17.00
	Kabarole	47	49	15.20
	Kasese	45	50	22.80
	Kibaale	45	51	21.00
	Kisoro	63	33	38.80
	Masindi	42	52	32.80
	Mbarara	43	52	6.80
	Rukungiri	40	57	26.20
Northern	Apac	45	53	24.80
	Arua	58	46	32.50
	Gulu	49	49	38.30
	Kitgum	53	39	63.50
	Kotido	92	12	67.60
	Lira	46	50	25.00
	Moroto	93	11	46.70
	Moyo	55	45	41.10
	Nebbi	58	47	45.20
	Average	44	51	25.00

[1] Refers to the school-age population only.
[2] Appleton and Mackinnon (1995) define a household as poor if its expenditure is in the bottom quartile.

Sources: Uganda National Council for Children (1994), Appleton and Mackinnon (1995), UNICEF (1994).

4. Education

Reading, writing, and arithmetic (the 3Rs) were popularised in Uganda at the turn of the century by rival Catholic and Protestant missionaries, and mission-built institutions remain at the core of the educational system. At the very top is Makerere University, followed by a number of schools and colleges. In 1963, barely a year after Independence, a commission on the future stressed the necessity of increasing opportunities for basic education in the country. Primary and secondary schools were built, in diverse parts of Uganda (Nsibambi, 1976; Odaet, 1990); in 1964 alone, 25 secondary schools were started or upgraded for government support. The government de-emphasised the role of missions in running educational institutions — the post of mission-school supervisor was abolished in 1963 (Uganda, 1965a) — in order to unify the system.

With the fall of government revenue in the 1970s, the state was no longer able to support and expand education. Much was left to private initiative, and many schools, of varying quality, were set up by individuals and groups. In areas which later underwent long periods of civil disturbance, many schools were destroyed; the donor-backed Northern Uganda Reconstruction Programme helped rehabilitate some schools, but the bulk of them remained in poor condition. In the mid-1990s education was still in deep crisis, though the slow process of recovery had begun, as in the rest of the economy. School supplies had improved but many schools still had outdated textbooks and other teaching materials.

With few opportunities for side incomes and a shortage of services in the countryside, rural schools find it difficult to recruit teachers. That schools continued to function through the chaotic period is largely thanks to the emergence of Parents and Teachers Associations (PTAs), which mobilised funds, topped up teachers' salaries and ensured continuity. However, studies in Zambia (Hoppers, 1989) and Malawi (Fuller, 1989) indicate that groups at the core of these communal efforts are often richer than average. There is thus fear of the evolution of a dual system of education, in which children of the affluent, with better PTA contributions and thus with better training at lower levels, find their way to better schools, while the rest make do with the largely makeshift offerings in the private sector or on a self-help basis.[9] The government has tried to curtail the influence of the PTAs, but lack of funds prevents it from establishing effective alternatives. Lack of funds also affects the quality of meal programmes, with poor schools, the majority in the countryside, skipping them altogether (Oundo and Burton, 1992).

Primary enrolment was 1.3 million in 1980, rising to 2.5 million in 1989 and 2.6 million in 1995 (45 per cent females). Enrolment then increased slightly. Since the return of relative peace the cost of primary education is largely met by the parents, and school fees have risen rapidly in the 1990s, up to 300,000 shillings per term at good schools in 1995; cheaper schools are so crowded that learning is impaired. In spite of the financial costs, about 75 per cent of all school-age children begin school, an equal number of boys and girls. But the ability of parents to send their children to school diminishes rapidly as children advance and school fees rise. When finances are tight, girls are the first to be taken out of school: by the fifth grade the enrolment is down to 60 per cent by seventh grade, 50 per cent; boys then outnumber girls 2 to 1. It has been estimated by UNICEF (1994) that of the cohort entering primary school in 1986, only 30 per cent reached the seventh grade by 1992; in contrast, 90 per cent of the 1975 cohort had done so by 1981.[10] There is also the problem of eradicating the large disparities in access to primary education: for instance while 90 per cent of children attended primary school in Kampala and surrounding areas in the late 1980s, only 24 per cent did in Moroto, in the north-western part of the country.

The government's tight resource constraints have made it difficult to respond adequately to these disparities. Hoping for a rapid economic recovery, in the 1987/88 budget speech (Uganda, 1987b) the government promised to meet a larger share of the costs of education, 50 per cent of primary and between 65–75 per cent of secondary, to reduce the financial pressure on parents, especially in rural areas. But the government was unable to meet these promises; while the principle of compulsory primary education was attractive, its financing demanded careful preparation. Policy-makers admitted that many families were in distress, but it was difficult to identify and assist those which genuinely could not afford to send their children to school.

In 1987, the government set up an Education Policy Review Commission to look at all aspects of the country's educational structure. In 1992, a government white paper on Implementation and Recommendations was released for general discussion, and was subsequently tabled in Parliament. From 1994/95 the government would allocate at least 20 per cent of its budget to education, compared with 11 per cent in 1993/94, and only 4 per cent in 1991/92. There would be increased emphasis on gender equity in education; with adequate facilities for girls in all schools. The cost of primary education would be lowered in stages, with the ambition of universal free primary education by the year 2010. And finally, primary school would be extended from 7 to 8 years, which would enable an increased emphasis on vocational education, to the benefit of those not able to continue.

In the run up to the 1996 election, Museveni promised that each household could have up to 4 children attend primary school free of charge beginning with the 1997 school year.[11] This was a strong commitment which the electorate took seriously; it is said that some parents delayed entry of their children into school, while others withdrew them from school to wait for free education. However, the fiscal implications of such radical reform are causing some anxiety, especially since the government has also vowed to abolish the special fees levied by the PTAs. PTAs often levied special fees, especially in urban areas, which were an important source of funding for many schools.[12] Up to 80 per cent of almost 4 million children in primary school would benefit, and a total of 14 billion shillings was budgeted for the exercise. The total cost is likely to be much higher, however, and the government has warned that parents will still be expected to provide uniforms and books for their children.

The removal of primary school fees for a large number of children was broadly welcomed. If it is well implemented and manages to cover a substantial portion of the population, it will mark something of a turning point: the government will be able to point to a tangible benefit for most Ugandan families, including the poorest. On the other hand, removal of fees at the lower levels implies that school fees will eventually have to be introduced at the institutions of higher learning, notably at Makerere University. For a long time the introduction of fees at the university level was politically difficult. However, with the advent of private universities in Uganda, it has become apparent that there is a broad willingness to pay for university education; Makerere itself introduced fees for privately sponsored students some years ago. More recently, all new 'government-sponsored' entrants to Makerere (for the 1996/97 academic year) were required to pay a registration fee of about US$50. The university students' council rightly saw this as the beginning of 'school fees' at Makerere.[13]

Following the relaxation of stipulations governing the offering of university degrees outside public institutions, there has been a boom in private tertiary education in recent years. Reflecting the structure of institutions at the lower levels, most of the new 'universities' are sponsored by religious establishments.[14] They are small and resource-starved — offering courses in the humanities and business with little attempt to enter the more demanding sciences and technical subjects — and it is still not clear what impact they will have on the country's educational infrastructure.

5. Health Care

In 1988 Uganda had a total of 81 hospitals, 122 health centres, and 870 other facilities; the government owned over half of the hospitals and most of the health centres and other facilities. The condition of Uganda's health institutions had deteriorated enormously in the 1970s and 1980s. By 1986 the public health budget, in real terms, was less than 10 per cent of that in the early 1970s. According to the World Bank (1992: 102), 'the absolute minimum recurrent expenditure necessary for effective primary and secondary health care is equivalent to about US$3–4 per capita per annum', but in 1990 the government was spending only about US$1.70 per capita, while Kenya was spending US$6 and Botswana US$29. The primary health care system collapsed in the 1980s, and mortality increased, particularly from diarrhoeal infections, malaria, and malnutrition.

Infant mortality in the second half of the 1980s was 120 per 1000, higher than the average for Sub-Saharan Africa (100). In Africa as a whole the median probability of dying by the fifth birthday fell from 0.228 in 1960 to 0.155 in 1985; in Uganda that had fallen below 0.2 by 1965, but rose again to above 0.2 by the late 1980s (Mackinnon, 1995: 2). In spite of Uganda being a country well endowed in protein-rich foods, a nutrition survey at that time revealed signs of malnutrition in 45 per cent of children under 5, compared to 28 per cent in Sub-Saharan Africa as a whole. If children suffer a nutritional setback in the second year, perhaps due to inappropriate weaning foods, it permanently reduces their height, and Uganda is found to compare poorly with other African countries in terms of stunting. The onslaught of AIDS put further strain on the already limited resources of the health sector (see Berkley, 1988; Macrae *et al.*, 1995).

Table 6.6: *Population per Hospital Bed by Area, 1971/1994*

Selected Area	1971	1994
Kampala	122	233
Masaka	800	1322
Mubende	1100	2926
Kamuli/Jinja/Iganga	704	2114
Kabarole/Kasese/Bundibugyo	917	1434
Kibale/Hoima/Masindi	667	1202
Arua/Nebbi/Moyo	641	983
Gulu/Kitgum	450	600
Kisoro/Kabale	714	1453
Bushenyi/Mbarara/Ntungamo	934	2850
Apac/Lira	826	1865

Source: Uganda (1972b); UNICEF (1994).

At over 200,000 people per hospital and 23,000 per physician, the needs of the population could not be met via the traditional delivery systems (Uganda, 1989c). Population per hospital bed had risen drastically and was still much higher in 1994 than in 1971 (see Table 6.6).

Kampala's main hospital, Mulago, is the teaching hospital for Makerere University and the main referral hospital for the rest of the country; it was barely limping along for much of the 1980s, due to too many patients and not enough equipment, drugs, or staff. Private initiative of course reduced some of the pressure: to make ends meet on the meagre civil service salaries, many government doctors opened small private clinics in and around Kampala, where they provided services in the evening and at weekends; quality was erratic,[15] however, and the health status did not significantly increase thereby (Kayizzi-Mugerwa, 1993).

The government made several attempts to revive the health services, but the supply of equipment and drugs in hospitals continued to be sporadic, and the morale of staff low. As much of Sub-Saharan Africa (Gilson, 1995), a major constraint on the provision of health services was the low level of salaries; resulting low morale led to negligence, absenteeism, and theft. As in education, there was also a wide disparity in the availability and quality of health services between urban and rural areas. To fill the vacuum left by the poor performance and inadequacy of government institutions, a number of private clinics were set up in urban areas. Rural households increasingly resorted to local herbs for treatment.

A Health Policy Review Commission set up by the NRM in 1986 completed its review in September 1987; the resulting National Health Policy emphasised that the health delivery system had to reach many more people (at that time it was reaching only 45 per cent of the population), it had to be affordable; and thus it had to be much more efficient. It was hoped that decentralisation would result in more services where most needed. A major immunisation programme reached more than 50 per cent of the school children since 1987, and seemed to have had some positive impact on infant mortality.[16]

The thrust of Uganda's health system has long been curative rather than preventive, and the availability of drugs has been crucial to its functioning. However, as in neighbouring Tanzania (Gilson *et al.*, 1993), there is a tendency to hurried diagnoses and improper prescriptions and a deterioration in resistance to certain diseases. Lack of a drug administration with a clear-cut licensing policy and poor guidelines for marketing of drugs, have also led to shortages of critical drugs. The Uganda Essential Drugs Management Programme, supported by a host of donors, alleviated the immediate shortage of key drugs in the late 1980s, but prospects remained precarious. Hospitals often only had prescriptions to offer out-patients, who had to find their own drugs. The situation has since improved, but in the mid-1990s drugs were still poorly administered; thefts and inadequate doses were frequent.[17]

In a bid to reduce the persistent shortages, policy-makers devised a number of cost-sharing schemes, such as that presented by the Health Ministry in the 1989/90 budget proposals (see Kaheru, 1990; Van der Heijden and Jitta, 1993; UNICEF, 1994). This, it was hoped, would allow higher pay for health-care workers, while reducing the burden on government, and in combination with decentralisation it would increase flexibility and innovation. A Task Force on Health Financing (Uganda, 1990a) also suggested that in the following 3–4 years, money collected via cost-sharing be retained locally and used to motivate staff. However, this fell through in the political process, partly due to the infighting between ministries. It is also possible that the government did not feel compelled to undertake unpopular reforms just then due to the extent of foreign financing; for example, in 1990/91 external funding of the health sector amounted to 61 per cent, 80 per cent of capital and 55 per cent of recurrent. Still, several local administrations introduced their own schemes to collect money, which they kept at the local level and used to improve wages for their staff. Work morale seemed to improve in rural areas where cost-sharing was introduced, notably in Arua in the West Nile area, but in the suburbs of Kampala, for example the Kasangati Clinic, cost sharing did not appear to improve performance in the early 1990s, though there was a short-term drop in patient load (UNICEF, 1994: 39). Availability of alternative income sources probably made Kampala health workers less responsive to increased incentive packages, which would probably need to be much higher before a change in work patterns would be observed.

Patients fear that cost-sharing will not eliminate the 'informal fees' they now pay to health-care workers, and that they will thus be charged twice. Kenya instituted a system of user fees intended to generate revenue without discouraging utilisation of necessary health care services or placing excessive burden on low-income households, but the Kenyan government had very little capacity to verify need and the programme failed to take off (Huber, 1993).

A new factor which has caused increasing concern is AIDS. Uganda is one of the most affected countries in Africa. Although AIDS itself is not the main cause of death in Uganda,[18] its impact rapidly extended beyond the health-care system, and is threatening to alter dramatically the structure and performance of the economy itself. The disease has caused an enormous strain on health-sector resources as more victims required assistance, and as patients with other diseases were threatened with being crowded out of the health-care system (Katabira, 1988). It is also disproportionately the young and well-educated adults who are most affected, causing the size and quality of labour input to fall, with negative impact on productivity (UNICEF, 1994). In some of the most affected regions, farms were abandoned with inevitable declines in agricultural production. In areas such as Rakai, reduced labour-supply could force smallholders to substitute away from labour-intensive cash crops and revert to subsistence production. Children are being withdrawn from school either due to lack of school fees or because their labour is needed by the afflicted families, thereby retarding human capital development. All these factors point to potentially serious increases in poverty and declines in welfare.

Some estimates put the number of orphans in Uganda at 2 million, of which about half are probably due to AIDS (UNICEF, 1994; UN Secretariat, 1995). In about half of the latter cases, the children were also not being cared for by the remaining parent, while in one-fifth of the cases, both parents were dead. Due to the long period of illness, AIDS victims often die penniless, leaving their children no financial support; lack of school fees, poor nutrition and exposure to disease added to the children's vulnerability. Children are often absorbed into the extended family network, though many of the people who step in to care for them are elderly. Orphanages were started, and in their own homes elderly women took care of the children with support from the community and NGOs, but the results have been uneven, and sometimes children have been left to fend for themselves.

A National AIDS Commission with a highly competent permanent secretariat was established in 1991; its agenda was not confined to health-sector matters alone, but included a broad-based approach to fighting the disease, including improvement of public awareness and the definition of a new national population policy taking into account the impact of the epidemic. Public awareness improved (UNICEF, 1994), and the infection rate stabilised and then started to fall in urban areas, though still rising in rural areas. UN assessments suggest that a large positive impact on the incidence of AIDS will take a long time to realise, however (UN Secretariat, 1995), and thus the disease will remain a formidable challenge to Uganda's economy and its resource-constrained public sector.

6. Summary and Conclusions

This chapter has looked at the challenges facing the social sector in Uganda in the era of adjustment. The main source of difficulty has been the low levels of government expenditure on social services in the face of a rapidly growing population and the erosion of the social infrastructure caused by the long period of instability. While no region of the country was left untouched, areas to the north and east of the country, where political disturbances persisted in the 1990s are most affected.

The education sector has gone through a difficult period. The burden of educating children especially in the lower grades has fallen increasingly on their parents. Thus, as in the case of large urban-based hospitals, which claim the bulk of the health sector allocation in the budget, tertiary education claims most of the money allotted to the education budget. However, equity and efficiency considerations demand that a more realistic approach to education access and financing be devised. Notably, that the cost structure be made more equitable between primary and tertiary education.

The collapse of the primary health care system led to the resurgence of diseases that had earlier been contained or, as the government argued above, 'confined to occasional incidence'. Furthermore, a considerable part of government expenditure on health services went to curative rather preventive measures, with public hospitals receiving the bulk of the money. But even given the substantial aid inflows, the total level of funding was inadequate to meet the health care needs of the urban and rural dwellers nor to ensure workers in the health sector an adequate remuneration. To cope, workers in the health sector demanded 'fees' from patients in a supposedly free health care system. Individuals who could not afford the fees withdrew from the system altogether, resorting to herbs or poorly prescribed medicines from Kampala's informal sector 'pharmacies'. However, since health and education sector interventions are ultimately directed at poverty reduction, the introduction of 'user fees' increases fears that the impact on the poor and the vulnerable groups will be adverse. Moreover, issues related to targeting and the control of the revenues generated in the scheme have featured prominently in the debate, again with concern that the poorest groups would not be able to benefit. What is clear is that in the absence of public funds, increased private funding of the social sector will be necessary to enable it to deliver an adequate supply of services. However, modalities still need to be worked out, not only to ensure the social sector's continued viability but also equity of access to health and education. It is with regard to this question of equity of access that the government's new initiative to broaden opportunities for primary education should be assessed.

In summary, three main issues arise with regard to the social sector and poverty. First, there is a serious shortage of skills, instruments and materials with which to improve the state of the social sectors. This makes the 'operationalisation' of the country's education and health strategies close to impossible. The ambition of a balanced national coverage of social provision in a bid to reduce poverty demands innovative approaches to financing, even including cost-sharing. Second, the delivery systems have been based on large structures — urban hospitals, boarding schools etc. — which are not suited to a fiscally constrained economy, with the bulk of the population living in the countryside. Moreover treatment in hospitals is often based on prescriptions, in a situation where prescription culture is poor. Similarly, education has not been good at enabling individuals to enhance their skills in urban and rural areas. Third, the ongoing decentralisation raises the issues of developing capacities at the local level for delivering social services and for fighting poverty.

Notes

1. A feel for Uganda's achievements in the health sector up to the early 1970s is given by the country's *Third National Development Plan* from 1972 (Uganda, 1972b: 301) where it is stated inter alia: 'Uganda enjoys a level of health services far superior to many other developing countries – with a total of well over 400 health units ... A number of once major health scourges such as smallpox, sleeping sickness, meningitis and certain venereal diseases have been reduced to only occasional incidence; while others such as tuberculosis, poliomyelitis, river blindness and leprosy are under control'. This favourable picture was to change drastically for the worse in subsequent decades. Thus while infant mortality decreased by 30 per cent between 1959 and 1969, it increased sharply between 1971 and 1993. With over 120 deaths per 1000 births, Uganda was one of the few countries in the world that experienced an increase in infant mortality in the 1990s.

2. A recent estimate by Lwanga-Ntale (1995: 66) puts the cost of education in good schools at Ushs 300,000 per term in 1994 (that is, close to US$1000 per year).

3. Part of the Uganda Commercial Bank's debt burden was due to a rapid increase in the volume of unsecured loans.

4. Development plans might have been long on strategy and short on results, but it is difficult to find better representations of the challenges facing them as perceived by the country policymakers, and the steps they sought to use to address them.

5. The *Third Five-Year Development Plan* (Uganda, 1972b: 93) advised that the data be interpreted with caution

    considering that they do not take into account such factors as differences in efficiency of tax administration, the relative size of the tax-exempt groups, the relative age and sex of the regional populations, and some variations in tax assessment methods.

6. The coffee boom certainly had a large impact on farm-gate prices, the part played by the return of peace and improved infrastructure in lowering transaction costs should not be underestimated.

7. The hardcore poor are largely subsistence farmers, however, and have not necessarily benefited from changes in rural-urban terms of trade brought on by the economic reforms (Lufumpa, 1995).

8. The World Bank (1995) advised that this had to be done as soon as the government's stabilisation motives were achieved.

9. According to the Minister of Education (see *The Weekly Topic* of 4 October 1989), almost half of the students who qualified for university had studied at one of the country's 21 leading schools (out of 400 offering the Higher School Certificate), the bulk of which is confined in and around Kampala; entry is rationed by performance on the primary-leaving exams, and often demands extra tuition or 'coaching', which is private and costs money on top of the regular school fees and PTA dues.

10. The drop-out rate at the basic levels of education increased markedly in the 1980s (see for instance UNICEF, 1989). This was not reduced by much in the 1990s.

11. In responding to demands for universal primary education, Museveni used the swimming analogy. A learner swims in the shallow end of the pool and only continues to the deep end when it seems safe.

12. There was also concern regarding how a household would be defined: in the event it included all household types in Uganda: monogamous, polygamous, and single-headed.

13. Resistance to school fees at Makerere has sometimes been based on the argument that it would discriminate against poor students

and the poorer regions of the country, but it has been difficult to devise workable methods of targeting the poor; food-for-work has failed miserably. One way to address the issue would be to send a support package directly to the district of origin of poor students, as part of the grant now received from the centre, and let the distribution be done at that level. This would be beneficial in two respects. It would reduce the effort of identifying the poor students, and it would fit well into the government's desire to relegate such decisions to the local level as part of its decentralisation plan.

14. They include: Mbale Muslim University; Martyrs University, at Nkozi (under the umbrella of the Catholic Church); The Christian University of East Africa (Church of Uganda/Protestant); Bugema University (Seventh-Day Adventist); Nkumba University; and Busoga University (while many others are being developed). Students at these universities paid up to 600,000 Ushs (close to US$600) per term in fees in 1994–95.

15. Hospitals and other institutions with their own sources of funds, such as those controlled by religious missions, still managed to offer good quality services at reasonable cost, though it was of course beyond the reach of the poor.

16. Another early achievement was the rehabilitation of the main health institutions, notably Mulago, with help from foreign donors; there was also a notable improvement in research capacity at Makerere University's medical school at Mulago Hospital, including establishment of the Child Health and Development Centre at Mulago, where multi-disciplinary research is undertaken; research on AIDS-related illnesses has also improved the flow of resources to Makerere's research community.

17. It is noteworthy, that the bulk of private health care is provided by workers employed by the government — the clinics being secondary activities.

18. Malaria, diarrhoea and infections of the upper pulmonary tract are still the main killers, though aids is responsible for about 50,000 deaths per year. However, since AIDS sufferers succumb

Chapter 7: Looking Ahead

1. Introduction

Having completed the debating and promulgation of the new constitution by October 1995, Uganda looked towards 1996 with much anticipation. There were to be elections for President and Parliament within less than two months of each other.[1] Paul Kawanga Ssemogerere, the leader of the Democratic Party and a man at the centre of Uganda's politics for decades, was Museveni's main opponent. Ssemogerere emphasised the need for fully-fledged democracy with 'real' parties, as opposed to the movement type of government favoured by Museveni; if elected, he promised political reconciliation and an end to the civil war.

In the end, Museveni's organisational skills, the power of incumbency, the general peace in the productive southern parts of the country, and some real achievements with regard to the economy, helped him win in May 1996. By the mid-1990s, the Ugandan economy, after a decade of economic reforms, was showing signs of institutional revival and expansion of production capacities. Changes were most evident in better policy coordination in key ministries, such as finance, and in the expansion of manufacturing, where privatisation has increased both investment and competition. However, to ensure that the achievements of liberalisation will not be eroded, the policies must be perceived as credible, that is, economic agents must believe that they will be maintained. The insecurity that continues to plague Uganda is thus a serious threat to long-term growth.

In something of a protest vote, the north voted overwhelmingly for Ssemogerere; for most of Museveni's ten years in power, northern Uganda has been politically destabilised, with insurgency affecting all aspects of life in Gulu and the surrounding districts, ravaging the infrastructure. The new parliament set up a committee of inquiry into the northern insurrection. Many politicians, businessmen, and lay people from the north and elsewhere were summoned to give

133

evidence. In a Consultative Group meeting in Paris in November 1996, donors also expressed concern and urged the government to resolve the conflict quickly.

But an even bigger political and security threat was the possibility of Zaire's implosion. Uganda shares 800 kilometres of border with Zaire, both ends of which were increasingly insecure. Uganda was also involved in diplomatic efforts to find solutions to other regional problems. It joined in imposing regionally-coordinated sanctions on the military regime in Burundi, and also participated in meetings on the Great Lakes region crisis in Nairobi in 1996.

The Ugandan economy is much stronger in the late 1990s than it was during the civil wars of the 1980s, and has been something of a buffer in a turbulent region. Still, there is concern that increased insecurity will deflect the government's focus from political and economic reform, and that in the military theatres gross abuses of human rights might reappear. Military expenditure had risen sharply by the end of 1996, and the government's pre-election promises of increased social expenditure will be difficult to meet. However, the liberalisation and privatisation programmes remained largely on track, mainly because the relatively prosperous southern parts of the country continue to enjoy rapid economic growth.

Since 1986 a considerable force in making and implementing economic policy in Uganda has been Museveni himself; many of the most crucial economic decisions were taken after his direct intervention. However, under the new constitution Parliament will exercise considerable power over economic policy; a standing committee on the economy is in place. Although Parliament as a whole seems well disposed to reform, some members have been critical of privatisation, while many have urged reduction or even a complete moratorium on debt repayment. While these might merely be the expected excesses of a largely new group of legislators, it is clear that policy-making will cease to be the private preserve of the Ministry of Finance and allied institutions. Inasmuch as this means more democracy, the development will probably be good for the country, though perhaps implying a slower pace of policy implementation, and in a different form, than has been the case in the past.

Despite a decade of stabilisation and adjustment under the NRM, the legacy of the long period of crisis and stagnation is that poverty remains a most pressing concern, even more so than in the 1960s. To address it will require developing markets and domestic capacities in the face of potential shocks and environmental concerns; despite the already large foreign debt, further foreign assistance will be required. We will discuss the issues in turn.

2. Addressing Poverty

Since poverty is widespread in Uganda, it is difficult to envisage a sufficiently broad system of transfers to address it. To help the hardcore poor who are subsistence farmers one must assist them to raise their productivity generally as well as improve their market access. However, given the high concentration of poverty in some districts, such as in northern Uganda, there is some scope for regional targeting. Poverty in these districts is partly the result of civil war, and it will be difficult to improve welfare in these areas substantially until there is sustained peace. Then it will be necessary to rebuild damaged infrastructure, increase public services, and encourage markets for goods and services.

There is a strong case for fiscal transfers to the poorest districts, such as those in Karamoja, and UNICEF was already operating at the district level in 1995. But decentralised allocation of resources to help the poor will require development of district-specific social indicators for guidance, and successful implementation will depend very much on capacity at district level to manage complex programmes, including direct delivery of services to the poor. Partly with these concerns in mind, the government is spearheading its decentralisation effort with training for district officers in budgeting, planning and project supervision.

A recent study of under-fives in Uganda (Jitta *et al.*, 1992) shows that malnutrition is widespread in both rural and urban areas of Uganda; some southern areas have worse indicators than the poorer north, indicating the insufficiency of some southern diets, especially the low level of protein intake. A strategy to address poverty in

Uganda must address four basic areas (Swedish Technical Mission, 1992; World Bank, 1995). Success will depend to a large extent on how well the needs of the poor are understood, including their likely responses to various interventions; thus research must be a key component of the poverty alleviation effort. The second is the enhancement of human capital via improvement of schools and health clinics at the district level, including adult education to raise the rates of literacy and numeracy.

To accomplish these goals and other future interventions effectively, there is need to increase institutional capacities by strengthening manpower and skills at all levels of government, but especially at the district level. Building institutional capacities also relates to the strengthening of laws and regulations governing individual property rights, land ownership and inheritance.

Finally, helping the poor to use their land, labour and capital productively is still the best way of addressing poverty. Poverty reduction will thus have to be based on a broad rural development agenda, supported by further macroeconomic reform accompanied by specific measures in support of agriculture. The sector needs better technologies, including enhanced crop varieties and improved soil productivity. Crops such as beans, sorghum, cassava and millet, which are grown in the poorer districts of Uganda, tend to withstand droughts and, as staples, command a broad market in East Africa, need to be developed further. Market access is a key element in the push for higher rural production, and this, in turn, will require much improved financial services to the rural sector.

3. Developing Markets and Domestic Capacities

In the 1960s, terms-of-trade shocks were softened to some extent by diversification of exports. In the 1970s and 1980s similar shocks were instead amplified by weak policy response, elongating the recessions. The long economic decline increased reliance on coffee exports, making Uganda more vulnerable to changes in its price. But Uganda will continue to depend on agricultural production for most of its exports, so crop diversification is an important part of export diversification efforts in the country's development policy. The government's reform programme has gone a long way toward reviving other traditional export crops such as tea and cotton, and staples such as maize and beans are being exported in increasingly large quantities; even the fish industry has begun to export to markets in the Far East. Future tasks include further cost effective diversification, raising productivity via enhanced technologies, and improving market access, especially through upgrading and extension of the infrastructure.

Land titling has been urged to improve the speed of land transactions and thus efficiency of use, and also to make title deeds available as collateral, but a comparative study of land tenure reform in East Africa (Pinckney and Kimuyu, 1994) argues that land titling is not as crucial to agricultural development as, say, market access. Thus the scarce resources used in reform measures could perhaps be better spent on improvements to rural roads and related infrastructure, in order to improve information flows and factor and product mobility in rural markets (see also Evans, 1994).

With close to 20 million people, Uganda would comprise a fairly large consumer market if rich, but the low purchasing power is already a constraint on the bigger manufacturing companies in Uganda. The market will eventually expand as average purchasing power rises, especially in the countryside, but to broaden it has become necessary again, after 20 years, to encourage broader East African cooperation, which could attract investment, tourism, and that could spur trade and industrial development; once established it could also serve as a basis for lasting regional security. Uganda would benefit as a transit route and even as an important supplier of food to an integrated regional market.

However, Kenya is much more industrialised than Tanzania and Uganda, and the fear of being overwhelmed by Kenyan firms is very much in the thinking of governments and businessmen. Thus closer cooperation will require a substantial policy coordination, not only with regard to taxation, tariffs and investment but also with respect to a broad range of political issues; the European Union provided a sum of up to US$30 million to support regional projects, and since the appointment of a Secretary General for the East African Secretariat at

Arusha, a number of joint projects have been undertaken between the three countries: in transport and communications there are projects for a common road legislation for the whole of East Africa, the mapping of Lake Victoria to ease maritime transportation, and meteorology and air transport. An East African ID card will also be introduced, making passports unnecessary within the region. In a bid to encourage regional investment, there are plans for East Africans to buy shares from each other's stock exchanges. These are small but important gestures that will help to re-establish the feeling of belonging to the East African region. While the earlier cooperation was spurred by governments and built around supra-national institutions, current developments have also involved the private sector to a greater extent.

Economic liberalisation has led to rapid changes in production structures which have, in turn, put demands on administrative and technical skills, as well as on socioeconomic infrastructure and markets. Outcomes will, to a large extent, be determined by the progress achieved in two important policy areas: market development, and political and administrative decentralisation.

A competitive atmosphere should be part and parcel of market development. However, in spite of the rapid pace of liberalisation, the bigger companies still possess considerable market power.[2] They are also in a position to influence government in setting tariffs on imports. In a recent interview (UMA, 1996) an industrialist had the following advice: 'Government should also institute measures to protect manufacturers against imports ... while locational disadvantages (especially in rural areas) should be considered by the government to encourage investment in the country'. Many manufacturers mention, almost as a threat, the importance of their tax contributions to government finances, which would be reduced by liberal import inflows. However, the government should listen to these arguments with some scepticism, with its eyes firmly focused on enhancing the efficiency of the economy.

Another important aspect of market development in Uganda relates to the enhancement of administrative and technical skills.[3] It is quite likely that the training pursued in the years of control was not adequate to ensure the management and professional needs of the privatised companies. This is especially true in the area of technical training, technological competence and entrepreneurial development. Uganda still has an inadequate capacity to adopt and absorb imported technologies, resulting in sub-optimal utilisation of available capacities. There is thus need, via training, to create an environment which is conducive to technological absorption and innovation. It is important, therefore, to assess the impact of the current education system on the output of skills required for industrial development.

Finally, markets will not be able to develop in Uganda without the supportive role of fully developed financial markets. As noted above, the reform of the financial sector has proved to be one of the most demanding interventions so far. While the economic variables are quite well streamlined, financial institutions remain weak. As discussed earlier, the financial sector still suffers from the overhang of a bad loan portfolio accumulated in the 1970s and 1980s; the quality of the borrowers, many of them politicians and soldiers, was bad in the past. The farmer-owned Cooperative Bank has been laden with debt for decades, even after the infusion of capital by USAID in the 1990s the bank cannot meet the central bank's capital adequacy requirements. To do so, it might have to cede control to individuals outside of the cooperative sector, depriving farmers of a bank which they think of as having their interests at heart.

It would thus be erroneous to argue that the financial sector in Uganda is overbanked, especially in the view of the absence of facilities in the rural areas. However, the bank sector needs to strengthen its capital base and adhere to strict capital adequacy requirements and exposure ratios; these factors also indicate the need for better managerial training. Above all, the sector must desist from insider or politically motivated lending.

In light of the weaknesses of the financial sector, it is surprising that the government considers a stock exchange market to be of high priority. A functioning banking sector is a prerequisite for a successful stock exchange market (the reverse is not true). Thus, reforming, upgrading and strengthening financial and accounting procedures of business enterprises and banks, in order to increase their efficiency, are also important steps to take.

Tanzanian experience has shown (see Gilson, 1995) that another key element for successful local management of financial and other resources was independence. To survive, districts in Tanzania were often compelled to establish formal line relationships with the centre, thereby counteracting the very essence of decentralisation. However, Uganda's experiment emphasised a high level of political decentralisation from the outset, so its outcomes may be different.

For a number of districts, the gap between expenditure and revenue will remain large, and closing it will require a well-developed system of transfers, as well as the possibility of borrowing. The system of block grants implies that the local councils will have the final say on the distribution of the money, so the local decision making powers will be greatly enhanced; in keeping with what donors are advocating — the control of development programmes by citizens, through their representatives, at the various levels of government (see Swedish Technical Mission, 1992). Thus, allowed to run its course, the decentralisation process should lead to a real regime shift. However, given the diversity of endowments at the district level, it is instructive to note the impact of this administrative change on communities that are at a remove from Kampala and which traditionally had only been able to generate modest resources from their own tax efforts. A considerable portion of the success would, in turn, depend on the ability of the people residing in the various districts to prevent resources from being lost to corruption.[4]

4. Foreign Assistance and Debt

Besides 'normal' development needs, Uganda continues to face a security threat in the north, AIDS throughout the country, burgeoning environmental problems, and acute poverty worsened by the years of chaos and decline. All of these problems can benefit greatly from foreign assistance, and Uganda has been a good and successful client, so it seems likely that aid to Uganda will continue to flow, though there would probably not be any significant increase in total aid volume. Having gone beyond the stage of emergency aid, and perhaps even that of rehabilitation, concern is now for appropriate use of available resources, and how to avoid becoming more aid dependent. As before, positive resource-enhancing effects of balance-of-payments support must not be allowed to damage the competitiveness of the export sector by causing unwarranted real appreciation. Since the inflow of aid must end eventually, it must not be allowed to induce resource shifts that will be difficult to reverse when it stops.[5]

Beyond that, countervalue funds supporting the budget should finance necessary expenditures, not substitute for government tax efforts or for needed expenditure cuts. Even when the government's retrenchment efforts are completed, however, the wage bill will still have to be increased to make operations effective, so overall costs will go up rather than down. Though increasing, government revenues will not be anywhere near those required to sustain expenditures for some time. To create a large tax base for the future, the government should perhaps use the resource inflows to lower current levels of taxation and thus broaden private-sector participation in the economy. There is thus still a good case for budgetary support from donors, though it could be made conditional on patterns of expenditures in the budget, such as the shares of education and health care or the regional distribution of resources within the decentralised programme.

There have also sometimes been absorption problems, and diverting aid money to resolving debt problems, as has been done by some donors, can ease access to multilateral resources. This approach could be broadened to include coordinated donor participation in future multilateral programmes, including debt buy-backs, or the commitment of untied balance of payments resources for debt service, but since regular World Bank debt is mostly paid off (see Chapter 5), this meant that future benefits from fifth-dimension arrangements would be limited. Introduction of a new credit policy at the ADB in 1995 put Uganda unambiguously among the group of countries which could only borrow on concessionary terms, that is, only from the ADF, but since over 40 African countries were designated ADF-only, those funds will be extremely scarce and rationed among applicants; competition among countries will result in small loans.

However, a fifth dimension-like mechanism to alleviate the burden of servicing ADB loans was being considered by the ADB in 1996.

For Uganda's debt situation to be sustainable, debt service obligations must be compatible with the country's repayment capacity, in terms of both foreign exchange and the budget. Since the chance is small of extensive write-offs beyond, those achieved at the Paris Club in 1995, maximisation of concessionality and the informal refinancing of debt service remains the best additional strategy (Martin, 1994).[6] Thanks to large IDA loans, there was a positive net transfer from the World Bank group to Uganda during the reform period, a trend that will most likely continue into the next century. It would be even better to use increased IDA transfers to replace the somewhat harder terms of IMF loans. However, to minimise the increase in the debt stock and in resulting debt service, inclusion of an element of bilateral grant co-financing in the new commitments would be desirable. This would ensure a positive net transfer from the international financial institutions and a gradual decrease in the debt service/export ratio, making it possible for Uganda to cover a larger share of its external commitments from its own resources.

Notes

1. Officially, about 20 billion shillings were spent on the presidential elections, with donors contributing 60 per cent.
2. The revival of manufacturing activity in Uganda is reflected in the fortunes of the Uganda Manufacturers Association (UMA), a body to contend with in the Uganda economy. UMA was established already in the 1960s, but was dormant for most of the 1970s and 1980s, as manufacturing declined, before its revival in 1988. UMA has organised a number of international shows and lobbies government on behalf of industry. However, strikes over VAT in 1996 indicated that the lower ranks of the business sector, notably the traders and middlemen, do not necessarily subscribe to the views of UMA, considering it to be too close to the incumbent powers.

3. As part of market development, the Uganda Private Sector Competitive Project (PSCP) was launched in early 1996, a joint venture of the Uganda private sector, the World Bank and the Uganda Government. The project is managed by the Private Sector Foundation which was itself started recently by the private sector. The goal of the project is to make the Uganda private sector more competitive, enabling it to attract investment and to engage in export markets. The Foundation provides advice to businesses, introduces Ugandan firms to business partners and supports the establishment of investment promotion services that are separate from the granting of licences and exemptions.

4. It has been argued in the Ugandan papers that if not checked, the rampant misappropriation of funds at the central level might spread to the decentralised administrations. They argued that this would in effect amount to the 'decentralisation of corruption'. In a study of India, Wade (1985) has noted that lack of management capacity hinders the realisation of the goals set at the local level, especially since these are set with little regard to available resources.

5. If the inflow is permanent, resources should reallocate to accommodate it.

6. Uganda's prospects for a large debt write-off under the new IMF/World Bank-led initiative for highly indebted poor countries are good. However, implementation has been slow.

Chapter 8: Concluding Remarks

This study has traced the history of the Ugandan economy from the eve of Independence to well beyond the mid-1990s, a period of more than thirty years, but with its analytical focus on the sustained period of political and economic restructuring embarked on after the NRM's assumption of power in 1986. The first years of Uganda's independence saw rapid economic growth, and by the early 1970s the country had built up an infrastructure and socioeconomic network that could sustain a functioning economy. But by the end of the 1970s, most of it under Idi Amin's regime, the economy had undergone one of the most rapid declines in Africa: per capita income had fallen by more than a third and the monetary sector was largely ruined. The post-Amin era was characterised by political instability, aborted reforms, and civil war.

Was Uganda before and during adjustment a typical African economy? The sequence of events that led to IMF/World Bank-type reform in Uganda — declining terms of trade, weak economic management, and internal strife — was in most respects similar to that in many other countries in Africa. However, in Uganda there were additionally displaced populations, armed insurgency, collapsed institutions of government, and dislocated infrastructure. Lacking adequate remuneration, government employees had 'privatised' the bulk of public services. Queues for essentials were building up, and there were signs of hyperinflation. Thus Uganda was exceptional because of the very poor conditions under which it had embarked on adjustment: the NRM government set out to establish a policy environment to support the economic recovery with very few resources or functioning institutions.

In evaluating Uganda's reform outcomes, it can be tempting to dwell more on inadequacies of the still fragile institutions and less on the positive changes in the broader economy brought about since the late 1980s. Ofcansky (1996) argues, for example, that 'No matter what policies the NRM or any other successor government adopts, the country will remain desperately poor and unstable for the foreseeable future'. That in the face of rampant violence, criminality and corruption, and limited government resources, the goals of 'achieving peace and prosperity are not realistic'; thus the policy-makers' role will be to minimise but not eliminate the causes of disorder. However, a singular achievement of the NRM was putting together, within a year after assuming power and in the face of internal political opposition, a fairly strong domestic consensus for adjustment. To recover from economic decline and civil war, sound and sustained economic management was essential; economic efficiency had to improve, including in the public sector; and the prices to farmers had to rise to stimulate output. Outcomes from the reform efforts provide reason for optimism.

Uganda's return to more peaceful conditions was important for the implementation of the reforms; the environment became more predictable and the credibility of policy-makers increased. The resulting once-and-for-all increase in production — notably of food — helped ameliorate the impact of shocks arising from reform measures. However, civil disturbances continued to prevent some areas, especially in northern Uganda, from sharing in the benefits of an expanding economy and the country as a whole from enjoying those of reduced military expenditure in favour of social expenditure. A switch to higher social outlays is necessary to address issues like infant mortality, which remains high throughout the country, even though similar countries have managed to lower theirs. Many preventable diseases are still widespread, and a new and serious scourge, AIDS, has surfaced. Thus there is a difficult social situation in Uganda, requiring various forms of public support, which in turn require more resources. A proliferation of NGO activities, especially in poverty alleviation has helped to close the resource gap, though with considerable duplication of effort and inadequate skill transfer.

In political terms, and more than other governments before it, the NRM has projected a pro-rural profile; indeed, it seemed that the government had found itself a natural constituency among the peasants. But nevertheless there have had to be realistic tradeoffs in economic management. For instance, in spite of improvements in the major roads, rural infrastructure remains inadequate. Farmers still find it difficult to take their produce to market without high costs.

Even in southern Uganda, lack of support services and credit has hindered some peasants from moving away from subsistence production and into cash crops. Kampala's bustling activity, partly a result of the expenditure of aid money, still contrasts starkly with the slow return of the market economy to the countryside, most especially in the north and east.

The policy dilemma in adverse times — with or without IMF/World Bank involvement — is how to be both efficient (balance the budget, improve conditions of service, reduce corruption, etc.) and compassionate (extend health care services, care for the displaced, educate the poor, etc.) while, at the same time — to make sure that state power does not slip away — ensuring a strong and effective military. Economic adjustment thus required many trade-offs. For example, in spite of the respectable growth rates, it was not possible to protect all social categories. Initial attempts to balance the budget illustrated other short-term trade-offs. The 'hard' sectors, such as military expenditure, continued to get the larger share of the resources, so improvements in government-financed education and health care were relatively slow. The significant expansion of these sectors during the reform-period was financed privately, so poor children often had inadequate access, or only inferior education. Retrenchment was a central element of public-sector reform, and the benefits of a trimmer public sector were not in doubt, but some of those retrenched certainly saw their incomes fall.

Access to adequate financial and human resources is important for the success of economic reform. The donor community provided substantial resources to both the recurrent and the development budget, helping the country withstand the terms-of-trade deterioration for most of the late 1980s, and later the spill-overs from civil strife in neighbouring countries. The level of donor dependence became high and will most likely remain so in the medium term, as the country takes steps to generate more of its own resources. The inflows have implied a higher level of indebtedness, while the associated conditionality led to some loss of domestic policy determination. Future inflows should be directed increasingly towards the private sector to encourage investment, create employment opportunities, and expand the tax base. However, while the attraction of foreign private capital will continue to be important, an indigenous process of capital formation is even more crucial for the sustenance of growth.

Although in the macroeconomic sphere considerable ground had been covered by the mid-1990s, more needed to be done in the area of institution building. It was evidence of Uganda's overall recovery that, from short-term issues of economic stabilization, its focus increasingly turned towards medium to long-term issues: producing legislation covering most areas of political and economic life, writing and debating a new constitution, resurrecting the royal families of southern Uganda, and decentralizing the administration. Policy-makers were thus able to combine far-reaching economic reforms with substantial, if somewhat controversial, political reform. The government was also divesting itself from business: a number of public enterprises were sold outright or put under private management by the mid-1990s.

The economic strategy adopted by Uganda, if consistently pursued, will lead to a situation in which markets and the private sector assume the bulk of economic activity. Nonetheless, the role of the state will in some respects become even more important than before: it will have to ensure that the economic actors play on level ground by improving the distribution of infrastructure, regulating goods and financial markets, and rationalizing the tax regime. This calls for institutions that are flexible and responsive to the needs of an increasingly complex economy. Related to this is the need to protect the interests of the poor and the vulnerable, as well as the environment itself. The creation of an efficient and dynamic economy is a long-term project, and Uganda is only now beginning to lay its foundations. The tension between domestic politics and economics will no doubt continue to affect the pace at which further reforms are implemented while adverse domestic and regional security developments will constrain the expansion of investments, and thereby growth. Still, Uganda has shown that it was possible to overcome one of Africa's severest socioeconomic declines through a willingness to change direction, nurturing the good-will of neighbours and the international community, and setting free the production capacities of the country.

Appendix A: Urban Responses: a Study of Kampala Households

1. Introduction

The main text looks at macroeconomic and sectoral impacts and to some extent distributional consequences. In this and the subsequent appendix we will look at economic adaptation at the household level: urban responses (specifically Kampala) in this Appendix, and rural responses (Masaka District) in Appendix B.

The population of Kampala has had three growth patterns. After Independence it expanded rapidly in response to the boom in urban employment opportunities. Then calamities befell the economy, particularly the modern sector, moderating rural-urban migration in the 1970s and early 1980s. With the return of relative peace in the latter half of the 1980s the city's population was once again expanding rapidly; it was estimated at 0.8 million at the end of the decade.[1]

The social costs of the decline were high. Development of urban infrastructure and services was not able to match demand: electricity, water, sewage and garbage collection systems were stretched to and beyond the limit. Slums closed in on the modern parts of the city.[2]

While the sharp economic reversal was recognised as the main source of the misery, and alleviation was desired as part of stabilisation and adjustment, the lack of current household-level data made all attempts at devising alleviation policies seem rather *ad hoc*. We undertook a socioeconomic survey in April/May 1990 (on which this and the next appendix are based), in order to begin to remedy this lack. Because fully-fledged liberalisation had not begun until 1987, this appendix thus portrays Kampala households in the early stages of economic adjustment. Its primary value is in its detailed description of urban household adaptation to severe economic decline, as well as to initial adjustment efforts. Income structures are estimated and analysed, including econometric estimation of the determinants of employment and earnings.

148

2. Aspects of Urban Responses

As in many other countries in the region,[3] relative incomes for wage-earners in Uganda developed very favourably in the late 1950s and 1960s: boosting wage incomes was part of a deliberate policy to reduce circulatory migration and create a stable urban working class (Knight, 1967); and the minimum wage, for instance, increased fourfold in real terms between 1957 and 1970. Consequently, in relation to their farming cousins in the country-side, wage-earners were sometimes referred to as a labour aristocracy.

The Amin years changed the picture completely. Problems began with the departure of the affluent class of Asian employers, skilled artisans and workers in 1972. Real minimum wages fell by 95 per cent between 1970 and 1980 (Jamal, 1987). The public sector seems to have been most hit. The bulk of the high-level labour force, 20 per cent of the formal sector (Uganda, 1967b), was in public service and teaching, but the relative position of this group deteriorated drastically in the 1970s. Civil service jobs were seen as a way to reduce unemployment, especially among the educated, so the number of employees soon exceeded the government's capacity to ensure them a decent wage. Some employees responded by taking up other jobs, leaving Kampala, or venturing into the informal sector (Chew, 1990; see also Vandemoortele, 1993). Many changed their diet and lifestyles and a number grew their own food, leading to a visible ruralisation of Kampala. The fluidity of wage employment caused a decline in efficiency in the formal sector. Though once a professional body of high repute, the civil service lost its capacity to implement government policy in the years of economic decline. But with continued regulation and control on the part of the government, *magendo* (rent-seeking activities) became prevalent in the 1980s.

There has always been an informal sector in the city; the expulsion of the Asian business class left a vacuum that was slowly filled by more small-scale businesses, generally financially constrained and based on household labour.[4] Even by 1990, the attraction of 'business' in Kampala said much more about the *status quo* elsewhere, especially in the public sector, than about its absolute lucrativeness. Stiff competition in the transport sector left margins crumbling at a time when the prices for petrol and spare parts were rising sharply. Easy entry led to even stiffer competition in food-selling. On the other hand, areas demanding substantial initial capital remained profitable, for example house-renting, small-scale manufacturing, and intermediate-goods delivery. Of course, Kampala's business sector also includes some parastatals, multinationals, indigenous and foreign-owned banks, and now a number of large but struggling private domestic ventures, embarked on in the age of economic liberalisation.

Farming had become a common activity within Kampala. The City Council had become more vigilant, fining those who encroached on public land, but apart from the city centre, most empty spaces were planted with perennial crops. The rural sector seemed to be overtaking the city, instead of the reverse. A wide variety of crops were grown: cereals, beans, fruits, and vegetables generated about half of the crop revenues in our sample, though consumption claimed about a third of the output; the majority of households thought that potatoes, cassava and yams were their most profitable crops. Apart from coffee, which was sold through middlemen, output was sold directly to the consumer. Bananas were also grown in many homes, most for own consumption. While some labour was hired, with high wages, labour costs on average still claimed 20 per cent of gross farm income. Most households tilled their own gardens; many children were reported to dig in the gardens and farms after school or during holidays. Little fertiliser was used, and few seeds were bought for planting.[5] Many homes had small poultry projects; pigs, cattle, etc., were kept at a distance, though cows were a common sight wandering near the city centre. Livestock production was about 30 per cent of total farm production in the city.

Kampala households thus responded to the decline by diversifying income sources in a bid to preserve living standards. The decline itself and the ceilings on resource availability, including human capital, were however crucial constraints on each household's ability to generate an adequate income.

A typical urban household is mainly a supplier of labour, but could also have a little land for farming and some capital in business activities. Though in most cases the latter would be informal, some households do own firms in the modern sector. We assume that decisions regarding the degree of participation in those activities are made by the household on the basis of utility maximisation subject to budget and resource constraints. Utility is derived from income and leisure; income is comprised of wages, capital rentals or profits, and remittances. Wealth in the form of capital or land is assumed to be sector-specific in the short run. Output in each activity is constrained by the available stocks of the factors of production.

Abstracting from differences in risk, the first order conditions with full labour mobility imply that the value of the marginal product is equal to the market wage across sectors. Labour input into the different activities is then a function of the fixed factors of production and the prices of goods and leisure. However, economic activities are associated with varying degrees of risk, risk-averse (probably poor) households avoid risky activities more than (perhaps better endowed) others.

It is useful to distinguish between tradable and non-tradable goods:[6] export commodities are tradable, whereas food, especially local staples, are considered non-tradable. Urban dwellers generally have, at most, only enough land for production of some food, though there is some coffee production in the less populated suburbs of Kampala. The bulk of modern industry output is potentially tradable, but due to the effects of the extensive trade controls in earlier decades it is still non-tradable in practice. Public-sector output and other services are non-tradable. Informal output produced by an array of largely non-taxed and often semi-legal activities, is non-tradable. One can thus identify five distinctive production sectors: food, cash-crop, formal-sector industry, formal-sector services, and informal. Only cash crops are tradable.

The crisis of the 1970s saw the destruction of infrastructure and capital stock and the departure of the traditional class of entrepreneurs causing a non-price negative supply shock primarily on the formal sector (i.e., both formal industry and formal services). The immediate short-term effect, assuming equilibrium before the shock, would have been a fall in formal sector productivity, output, and profits. Reduced demand for labour would then lead to an economy-wide decline in wages. Given the difficulty of laying off workers in the public and parastatal sectors, the wage decline there might be particularly severe.

What would happen to profits in other sectors? In tradable agriculture (cash crops), with an exogenously fixed product price, the rental would increase in response to the lower labour costs; and the sector would want to hire more labour. In practice, however, there have been large swings in real producer prices (primarily coffee).[7] Higher coffee prices would strengthen the expansionary effect, whereas lower coffee prices would reverse it. Profits in non-tradable food production and in the informal sector could either rise or fall, depending on the effect of the economic decline on aggregate demand relative to the lower labour costs; given the captive nature of the market created by the massive decline of the formal sector, and since informal activities are labour intensive, rentals could be high, at least in the short run. Since in non-tradable firms wages and rentals often accrue to the same household, one cannot, *a priori*, determine the net effect on the total returns.

In the long run, capital reallocates and rentals are equalised. In practice, this results largely from depreciation of the existing stock in some sectors and building up of new capital in others. In Uganda's case this adjustment was disabled by lack of both domestic and foreign savings in the 1970s and 1980s. The modest capital movements were mostly towards tradable agriculture, and possibly towards food production and the informal sector.

The analysis so far has used standard assumptions, with agents sticking to the rules of the game. Based on real variables, we implicitly assumed external balance. The government was mostly allotted a neutral stance, while in reality policy distortions have further complicated the picture. For instance, a negative economic shock decreases government revenue; the government may compensate for this for a while by cutting back on development expenditures and running down assets. The scope for domestic borrowing is very limited and not much money can be raised internationally. Then, within a relatively short period of time, the government may resort to printing money; an inflation tax is thus used to generate the required revenue, while the purchasing power of the public is further eroded. With high domestic inflation the exchange rate, if fixed, becomes seriously overvalued, the production of tradables is impaired, and the adjustments outlined above will be delayed.

There may also be other kinds of adaptation to the crisis. For example, given the sharp decline in formal sector wages, one could ask why Kampala workers were not on the streets,[8] why they had not quit the modern sector *en masse*? Was this political lethargy, engagement in other income-generating activities, or were they living off their rural cousins? In spite of low real wages, a public sector job might still be worth keeping, because the place of work is a potential base for coordination of external income-generating projects;[9] one can also imagine an increase in corruption in response to falling real wages, civil servants can impose property rights on government services, for example official stamps, permits, etc., and extract rents, in effect terminating the public-good character of these goods. Of course, the average employee would have little interest in subsidising the government, so effort will fall to equal remuneration, for example via increased absences from work or longer 'coffee breaks'.

Some households may also adjust by letting some members migrate to the rural areas, or they may obtain increased food remittances from the rural sector. Household members who have left the country may also remit money to members left behind.

With overall contraction of the economy, the end result for the typical household, even given diversification in income generation, would be a decline in living standards.[10] Wage-earners would be most affected, along with those individuals in the informal sector who supply the bulk of the wage earners' consumption basket.

3. The Kampala Survey

The survey, carried out during the months of April and May, 1990, in collaboration with Makerere University, covered the five main divisions of Kampala: Kawempe, Kampala Central, Nakawa, Makindye, and Rubaga. The survey was unprecedented in Uganda in the amount of detail devoted to each household's income structure and time-use.

We started by randomly picking 30 parishes (RC2s): 4 from Kawempe, 5 each from Makindye and Rubaga, 6 from Kampala Central, and 10 from Nakawa. Then we picked a sample village (RC1) at random from each parish.[11] For the interviews, 8 households were chosen at random from each village,[12] a total of 240 households; data for one household was lost, leaving 239. The smallest household had 1 member, the largest 20: In all, detailed data was collected for 1876 individuals, for an average household size of 7.8.[13]

Total income was made up of five categories: wages, allowances (in cash or in kind[14]), farm income (including the value of non-marketed output), business income and remittances. The recall period was in general one month, but 12 months was used for farm production; net annual farm income was then divided by 12. No information was obtained on transfers in kind (typically food) from the rural areas, nor on incomes from corrupt activities. Questions were also asked about access to, and the cost of education and health care, including changes in the availability of services since 1985.

Our survey had somewhat larger household sizes and higher levels of education than for others undertaken at about the same time (Bank of Uganda, 1989; Uganda, 1990b), perhaps a consequence of the sampling procedure. In any case, we believe that the sample represents a good and representative cross-section of Kampala households.

4. The Structure of Incomes in Kampala

How did Kampala residents make a living at the beginning of the 1990s after almost two decades of decline followed by beginning recovery? Formal urban employment was in government departments, parastatals, financial institutions, and retail and wholesale trades; the major industries were in Jinja, about 80 kilometres away. Kampala accounted for a quarter of the 380,000 individuals in the formal sector, which occupied 5.3 per cent of the total labour force.

Informal activities varied from vegetable growing — often illegally on public land (as was the case for a poor family residing at the

Institute of Teacher Education, Kyambogo) — to odd manual jobs, petty trade, prostitution, and even theft in Kiyaaye (literally 'home for the riff-raff') in Rubaga Division. For the elderly, widows, young single mothers, refugees from politically destabilised areas or households giving them refuge, life was difficult. Often the only source of income was an unlicensed stall by the road side to sell bananas, vegetables, and an occasional chicken. Some sub-let their already congested rooms, while others sold illicit brews.[15]

Groups doing measurably better were those that had taken advantage of the high cost of formal-sector services to provide labour-intensive services at low cost. In places like Kifuufu ('dusty alley'), in the centre of Kampala but off the main roads, one could buy a cheap but decent lunch; an even cheaper supper could be bought at dusk from the open-air kitchens (*Toninyira Mukange*) along the Kampala car and bus parks. Charcoal and firewood could be delivered to your door in most areas of the city, while frequent shortages due to breakdowns of the main water plant at Ggaba created a market for water, unfortunately not always drawn from hygienic sources. At Ntinda some civil servants were engaged in poultry-keeping; others owned taxis and prowled the streets of Kampala, giving their owners a sense of the middle class that their salaries did not. Many of the small kiosks, and even the bigger businesses in town, were owned by civil servants or parastatal employees.

Lastly, there was a small group of people who had done exceptionally well, ranging from businessmen who had withstood the succession of domestic crises to build extensive and lucrative businesses, to people in government with connections to the administrative and delivery systems of the many projects that had come with the beginnings of economic recovery. Kampala newspapers were full of reports of massive swindles and gross misuse of funds. Before the parallel exchange markets suddenly became legal in 1990, there was a burgeoning trade in foreign currencies and even in precious metals. While much was made of the fact that wages in government were very low, thus giving rise to corruption, the pervasiveness of the practices and the sums involved seem to point to other causes (Kayizzi-Mugerwa, 1989).

Appendix Table A1 shows the distribution of households by activity combination. About 26 per cent depended entirely on wage employment, while about half that depended on business alone; as one might expect in the city, less than 3 per cent depended only on farming. The remainder, over 50 per cent, had multiple income sources:[16] 25 per cent had both wage employment and business activity, while another 18 per cent combined wage employment, business and farming. We see that most households have incomes from more than one type of activity. Altogether, 79 per cent had wage income, 62 per cent had business income, and 34 per cent had farming income; 54 per cent also had allowances besides wages.

Appendix Table A1: *Distribution of Households by Activity Combination in Kampala, 1990*

Activity Combinations	Percentage of Households
Wage income only	26.3
Business income only	14.0
Farm income only	2.5
Wages and business income	25.2
Wages and farm income	8.8
Business and farm income	4.6
Wages, business and farm income	18.4

We have analysed the sample here in two different ways, first based on income quintiles, and second on the employment of the household head. The following sections will develop these analyses further.

Appendix Table A2: *Household Income Structures by Adult Equivalent Quintile* (Ushs/Month)

Type of income	Quintile 1	Quintile 2	Quintile 3	Quintile 4	Quintile 5	All
Wages	4258	7326	18748	20317	49363	20068
Allowances	1270	5896	19755	38790	96026	32477
Farming	-6307	2232	1544	17390	33269	9696
Business	1362	10106	17677	43021	213096	57286
Remittances received	1	458	1229	3942	250	1183
Income per adult-equiv.	102	4365	10822	21441	75220	22503
Adult-equiv.	5.7	6.1	5.5	5.8	5.7	5.7
Household size	7.8	8.3	7.5	7.8	7.8	7.8
% of total Income						
Wages	–	28	32	16	13	17
Allowances	–	23	34	31	24	27
Farming	–	9	3	14	8	8
Business	–	39	30	35	54	47
Remittances	–	2	2	3	0	1

Note: Quintile 1 includes individuals who declared large business or farm losses, which makes interpretation of this column difficult. At the time of the survey, 350 Ushs was equal to one US dollar.

4.1. Income Structure by Quintile

Appendix Table A2 shows household income structures by adult-equivalent quintile.[17] Quintile 1 consists of those households with the lowest incomes per adult-equivalent, quintile 5 of the highest. Average income in the first quintile was very low mainly due to a few cases with large reported losses in farming.

Business accounted for 47 per cent of total income. Outright wages were a small share of total income, on average 17 per cent, while employees' allowances were 27 per cent (so the total remuneration package of wages and allowances made up 44 per cent of total income). Although 34 per cent of households had farming income, it accounted for only 8 per cent of the total. Allowances had become an important part of remuneration policy, which explained to some extent why wage demands were not more militant.

29 per cent of the households remitted money to members living elsewhere, amounting to 9 per cent of total income on average; reverse flows of food (matooke, etc.) from the countryside were probably also not negligible. The urban sector's contribution to development in the countryside was thus rather limited.

The structure of incomes varied by quintile, but not by as much as one might expect. Wages and allowances constituted the largest share of income for the third quintile, followed by the second and fourth; the highest quintile had a below-average share of wages and allowances, even though in absolute terms its wages were almost triple the average, and more than double the fourth quintile. The highest reported wage income was 400,000, and the highest allowances 800,000. To enjoy this level of remuneration one had to either belong to the highest business echelons, or, if in government, to be involved in an externally-funded project. In general, high cash wages were confined to the private sector, but 'established' staff in the public sector were often furnished with houses with a high value on the open market.[18] Such a house could have a potential rental value many times the salary of its occupier. Incomes in the highest quintile were derived disproportionately from business, from which in absolute terms it received almost 4 times the average, and almost 5 times the business income of the fourth quintile.[19] This was thus the major differentiating category. To have a very high income, one almost had to engage in business. Business profits were an important income source for all groups. Some urban incomes were from farm production; the fourth and second quintiles had above-average shares, while the third was also lowest absolutely (not counting the first). The very poorest, apart from encroaching on public land, had little access to arable plots.

Although income diversification had increased dramatically during the previous two decades, it was also important earlier. A survey of Kampala employees in 1969 (Elliott, 1973: 30) showed that they were heavily involved in other activities such as shops, bars, taxis, rented rooms or market stalls. Those with high incomes (170 Ushs per month and above) derived 33 per cent of their income from such activities, 3 per cent from their *shamba* (farm), and 64 per cent from regular employment. The middle category (140–170 Ushs) received 9 per cent from other activities and the poorest category (less than 140 Ushs) only 2 per cent. The magnitude of informal activities was much smaller than today, but the structure was similar: it was mainly those with a strong foothold in the modern sector who could enter the most lucrative business activities. Business was less open to the poorly paid and the unemployed.

4.2. Income Structure by Socioeconomic Class

To get some feeling for income structures differentiated after socioeconomic class, we reorganised household incomes with respect to the type of employment of the head of household (Appendix Table A3). Though this demarcation might not seriously comprise economic classes, it was deemed superior to the use of other criteria.

Appendix Table A3 shows household income structures by five groups:[20] households with heads employed in the private sector, the public sector, those with heads primarily engaged in own businesses, or primarily engaged in farming, and a small 'other' category including those households with heads not otherwise engaged, such as pensioners. Most were public-sector households, followed by business and private-sector; very few were farming (6%) or other (3%). On average, private sector households had the highest income, followed by business and the public-sector households; all were in the range of 6–7 times the income of farm households, and 10 times the income of 'other' households. Because business households were the largest, their income per adult equivalent fell below that of both private- and public-sector employees; in income per adult equivalent, farm and 'other' households fell even further behind the leaders.

Appendix Table A3: *Income Structures by Socioeconomic Group*
(Ushs/Month)

Type of Income	Private Sector	Public Sector	Own Boss	Farming	Other
Wages	39632	22769	3834	4240	4250
Allowances	52708	44788	4727	13705	2500
Farming	9596	10279	10801	3762	4986
Business	40092	41672	113403	0	1125
Remittances	1017	876	2091	286	0
Per adult equiv.	41170	29122	26428	4770	2311
Total income	143045	120384	134856	21992	12862
Adult equiv.	5.3	5.8	6.2	5.9	4.7
Household size	7.3	7.9	8.5	7.9	5.9
% of households	25	38	28	6	3
% of total income					
Wages	28	21	3	19	33
Allowances	38	41	4	62	19
Farming	7	9	9	17	39
Business	29	38	94	0	9
Remittances	0.7	0.7	1.5	1	0

The structure of incomes varied considerably by socioeconomic group. In absolute terms, private-sector households had the highest share of wages in total income,[21] followed by public sector household and farm households, but the latter had the highest share of employee remuneration in total income. The ratio of all allowances to wages was also highest (more than triple) for farm households, about double for public-sector households; only 'other' households received less allowances than wages. Business house-holds had the smallest share of wages and allowances in total income,[22] and by far the highest share of business income followed by the public sector.[23] Households headed by farmers did not engage in business.

4.3. Summary

The share of wages in incomes was very low, though allowances compensated to some extent. Most households were engaged in multiple income-generating activities. We did not have any solid survey data from the period before the crisis, but it seemed clear from anecdotal evidence and comparisons with neighbouring countries, that there had been considerable income diversification, at least partly in a bid to reduce the risk of being trapped in low or no-income situations (see e.g. Bevan *et al.*, 1989), while very few households were engaged solely in business (14%), and still fewer solely in farming (2.5%), 57 per cent were engaged in some combination: increased engagement in farming in the urban sector was one of the most visible responses to the crisis. The extensive diversification was largely driven by shifts in the relative attractiveness of the different income-generating options.

Those who did best had ventured into business, though a foothold in modern wage-employment seemed essential for access to lucrative opportunities in the formal and informal business sectors. Households headed by public-sector employees seemed to have taken advantage of this fact in their business engagements.

5. Analysis of Income-Generation

5.1. Wages and Allowances

Appendix Table A4 shows the structure of wages and allowance by wage group. Women accounted for 36 per cent of all employees, ranging from a high of 47 per cent in the lowest income range to a

Appendix Table A4: *Structure of Wages and Allowances by Wage Group (Ushs/month)*

Wages	Up to 3000	3001– 5000	5001– 10000	10001– 20000	20001– 40000	40001– 80000	80000+
Sample %	24	23	23	15	7	6	2
Female %	47	42	31	33	24	22	14
Public employees %	49	54	50	29	48	39	43
Wages	2351	4314	7717	16577	26444	56000	202398
Allowances	9018	27896	27122	43816	38901	44294	223845
% of allowances:							
Medical	10	6	9	7	11	19	12
Education	5	1	1	1	0	4	0
Housing	2	30	20	18	30	42	39
Transport	13	13	27	13	15	11	37
Other	44	20	7	10	5	21	12
House	26	30	36	50	39	3	0
Total remuneration	11369	32210	34839	60393	68345	100294	426243

cont ...

Appendix Table A4 cont ...

Wages	Up to 3000	3001–5000	5001–10000	10001–20000	20001–40000	40001–80000	80000+
Wage/total (%)	21	13	22	27	43	56	47
Gap	−18855	−33885	−45947	−33967	−48199	−77527	52857
Gap/total (%)	−166	−105	−132	−56	−70	−77	+12

Sample size: 302

Note: to calculate the gap, that is the difference between total earnings and total expenditure, respondents were asked to estimate by how much total monthly expenditure exceeded the sum of wages and allowances (the latter includes an imputed value for housing provided by the employer).

low of 14 per cent in the highest range. The public sector accounts for 46 per cent of all employees,[24] slightly less in the upper income brackets, and particularly in the middle bracket. 70 per cent of employees earned less than 10,000 Ushs in cash wages, slightly below the weekly sum needed to purchase food for a family of seven. Wages accounted for only 20 per cent of total employee remuneration. Housing allowance or an employer-supplied house were the most important add-ons, but transport and medical allowances were also substantial. Average total remuneration for the bottom quarter was about 11,000 Ushs, while the top 2 per cent averaged 426,000 Ushs.

Respondents were asked to estimate the gap between their employee remuneration, and their expenditures. For the bottom 70 per cent, remuneration did not even cover half their expenditures:[25] only the top 2 per cent had a surplus.

5.2. Econometric Analysis of the Determinants of Employment and Remuneration

We estimated the probability of employment participation as a function of years in primary, secondary, or post-secondary education, age as a proxy for experience, age squared, sex, head of household or not, and total income of other household members. According to the classic human-capital theory of wage determination, each individual's pay is determined by her level of human capital, including education and total experience (here proxied by age). Analyses of Kenya by Bigsten (1984) and of Kenya and Tanzania by Knight and Sabot (1990) support use of this theory of wage determination in an African setting. Education and experience were found to be major determinants of earnings, and Knight and Sabot also showed that the higher the level of education, the more rapidly earnings rose with experience. Investments in schooling and experience were thus found to be complementary in their study, so we also tested for a multiplicative term between age and education, but obtained unsatisfactory parameter estimates, perhaps due to our use of age as a proxy for experience. Sex might affect earnings or the labour-supply decision directly, and household-head status might affect the desire to participate. 'Other household income' might also affect household members' labour-supply decisions, because there should be strong pressure to venture into the wage-labour market if other household income is small. We also introduced household size in order to see whether this would affect participation, especially that of women, but the variable was far from significant and was dropped.

Two other factors, which might affect earnings (but not the labour-supply decision) are public sector vs private sector employ-ment and the number of years with the current employer. Earnings might increase with seniority, because as employees acquire more firm-specific skills their value to the firm would increase.

Knight and Sabot established the existence of a filtering-down process in Kenya and Tanzania. The occupational attainment of recent cohorts was substantially smaller than that of earlier ones with the same education. The pressure of adjusting to the increased supply of educated labour thus mainly fell on new entrants into the labour market. This presupposed a relatively stable labour market such as that enabled by a large and functioning public sector, but given the chaotic state of the Ugandan economy, a long time in the labour market might be worth relatively little. Moreover, the public sector could hardly be considered a wage leader today. To test whether sectoral affiliation had an impact on earnings we introduced a dummy for public sector employment.

The explanatory variables used in our analysis are given below. The means and standard deviations of these variables are given in Appendix A1.

For the dependent variable we tried two different income definitions, namely wages and total remuneration (the sum of wages and allowances) per day. We restricted the analysis to those 15–64 years of age who were not disabled or students. Of the 1876 individuals in the survey 723 met these labour-force criteria (353 men and 370 women), and of these 41 per cent had wage income, 54 per cent of the men and 29 per cent of the women.

When we visited the households, we normally interviewed the head of household or another senior household member. If the other members were present, they were asked about their work, but if absent, we had to rely on the information from the informants we interviewed. In some cases the respondent might have been ignorant of the work of some member, or reluctant to disclose the information, so it is likely that some of those who were reported as not working actually did work. Some individuals might have also worked in wage employment only for some part of the year, but not in the month of our survey. In our data we, therefore, have both individuals who abstained from work as a matter of choice and others who failed to report work. We used a double-hurdle model in the analysis because it allows for a censored dependent variable, while at the same time correcting for the under-reporting outlined above.[26] The two 'hurdles' in this application are whether participation is correctly reported or not, and whether the individual wants to participate or not (see Appendix A2).

E1	years in primary school
E2	years in secondary school
E3	years at post-secondary institution
AGE	age (divided by 100) as a proxy for experience
AGE2	age (divided by 100) squared
SEX	dummy for male
GOV	dummy for government employed
LEP	number of years with current employer
INCOTHER	total income of other household members (divided by 10,000)
HEAD	dummy for head of household

The basic participation or sample selection equation (the probability of receiving a positive wage) was

(1)
$$d = f(E1, E2, E3, AGE, AGE2, SEX, HEAD, INCOTHER).$$

The behavioural wage determination equation was

(2) $\ln Y = g(E1, E2, E3, AGE, AGE2, SEX, GOV, LEP).$

We ran two versions of the model using the two measures of the dependent income variable, logs of wages and total remuneration (ln

EARN). The results were similar in most respects, although the level of significance and predictive power was slightly higher for total remuneration. Since total remuneration, including allowances, is the best measure of the reward to the worker, this alternative was thus used in all subsequent analysis.

Since the sex dummy was significant, implying that participation and wage-determination processes functioned differently for males and females, we split the sample into male and female groups.

Female participation (Appendix Table A5) was poorly explained by our equation. Only post-secondary education (*E3*) was significant at the 5 per cent level, and head of household (*HEAD*) at the 10 per cent level. The income of other members had no significant impact. Male participation (Appendix Table A6) was better explained by our equation: post-secondary education, head of household and other income were all statistically highly significant.

In the earnings equation for females only the *AGE* variable is significant at the 10 per cent level. In the male equation *AGE*, *AGE2*, and *E3* are all statistically significant. Our model explains earnings better for men than women.

To summarise, men were more likely to participate, and received somewhat higher remuneration. It may be that women are also more restricted in their choices due to other responsibilities in the home, but being head of household increased participation significantly for both women and men. Other income in the household had a significant negative effect on male participation, but not on female participation. Participation decisions were not age-related, though the incomes of men increased more significantly with age than those of women. This may be due to discrimination against women in the labour market.

The factors determining male participation and earnings differ from those for females, suggesting labour-market segmentation. Apart from university graduates, female employment was concentrated in the lower-wage categories. But the impact of education on income levels is not very clear-cut, probably as a result of the breakdown of the formal economy, especially the public sector. Public-sector employment (*GOV*) had a negative impact (though not a very significant one) on male earnings, while firm experience (*LEP*) had little discernible effect on earnings, probably as a result of the severe wage compression of recent years. With respect to the public sector, this suggests that individuals stay at their posts for reasons other than the incomes accruing, for example the impact of formal employment on business opportunities.

Appendix Table A5: *Employment Participation and Wage Determination for Females*

Variable	Parameter Estimate	Standard Deviation	t-value
Sample selection equation:			
Intercept	−0.9315	0.6499	−1.4333
E1	0.0199	0.0390	0.5107
E2	0.0644	0.0418	1.5884
E3	0.1407	0.0680	2.0710
AGE	0.6167	4.1807	0.1475
AGE2	−1.9750	6.1211	−0.3227
HEAD	0.5044	0.2949	1.7104
INCOTHER	−0.0001	0.0031	−0.0250
Behavioural equation:			
Intercept	3.1067	1.1348	2.7377
E1	0.0970	0.0679	1.4275
E2	0.0119	0.0653	0.1815
E3	0.0439	0.0927	0.4730
AGE	14.1888	7.7797	1.8238
AGE2	−15.1329	11.0854	−1.3651
GOV	−0.2133	0.2638	−0.8083
LEP	0.0180	0.2706	0.0667

Sigma = 1.1682; Log likelihood = −376.8

construction (brick making, building, repairs); informal trades and retailing (hawking, shoe-shine, kiosk or shop); services; and other (commissioners, dealerships). There is no clear distinction between formal and informal activities, given the thin line between the two in Uganda. Informal trades and retailing was the most common activity followed by 'other'. The remaining third of the sample was divided amongst the other 4 categories. Women owned 31 per cent of the businesses. They dominated the grain-related ones, and were well represented in cottage industry, informal trades and retailing, and 'other'; no female-owned businesses were in construction or services. Generally speaking, where women were represented, the average age of the owner was lower, as was the average years of education.

Profits per hour were high in grain-related business and services. High profits in grain-related business is difficult to explain, but beer brewing may be a profitable business. High profits in services may be explained by the high average education (15.3 years) of those engaged in the sector, which included lawyers, doctors and other professionals.

We estimated the probability of participation in business, for those in the labour force as defined above, as a probit function of *AGE*, *HEAD*, *GOV* for government-employee, *PRIV* for private-sector employee, and *E3* for post-secondary education. The results of this probit are reported in Appendix Table A8.

The probability of participation declines with age. Business is normally associated with ownership of assets, which tends to accumulate with age, but much business in Kampala was of the hawking type, demanding more physical stamina than capital. The probability of participation increased significantly if the individual was head of household; perhaps heads were under stronger pressure than non-heads to earn income for the household. We experimented with different configurations for education, but none of them provided any significant estimates. We dropped *E1* and *E2*, while retaining the somewhat more significant *E3*, but it did not increase the likelihood of participation significantly. Thus education by itself does not seem to increase participation, but it may be important for the profit levels achieved. Public-sector employment had a significant effect on the probability of business participation, while private emp-

Appendix Table A7: *Structure of Business Incomes by Main Business*

	Grain Processing Related	Cottage industry	Type of Business — Informal Trades: Construction and Retailing		Services	Other
% main business	5	13	8	39	7	28
% female owned	80	48	0	39	0	30
Profits (Ushs)	187175	14886	31733	47563	181769	91724
Days worked per month	18	20	20	23	22	20
Hours worked per day	6	6.7	8	8.5	6.3	7
Age of owner	31	33	42	35	44	43
Education of owner (years)	10.6	10	11.2	11.7	15.3	11
Profit per hour (Ushs)	1733	111	198	243	1312	655

n=180

Appendix Table A8: *Probit Estimate of Business Participation*

	Parameter Estimate	Standard Error	χ-square
Intercept	0.5850	0.2837	4.2511
AGE	−0.0158	0.0059	7.2329
HEAD	0.9474	0.1528	38.4491
GOV	0.8917	0.1896	22.1228
PRIV	−0.3567	0.1331	7.1776
E3	0.0120	0.1433	0.0071

loyment had a somewhat weaker negative effect. This is consistent with our suggestion that people hold on to government employment since it provides more and better opportunities for business; government employees may also be under greater pressure to supplement their meagre public-sector incomes.

5.4. Remittances

An important aspect of the support network in Uganda is remittances out of the urban sector. In our sample, 47 per cent of the households had children or spouses living elsewhere: of these 7 per cent were spouses and 10 per cent were in urban areas, mostly Kampala, but 90 per cent lived in the countryside. The poorer quintiles remitted larger quantities of money, relative to their incomes. To explore the determinants of remittances we ran a simple regression with total remittances-out as the dependent variable. The explanatory variables included the age and education of the head of household, total cash wage income of the household, total allowances, income from farming, profits from business activities, and number of persons in the household's labour force. Though some of the parameters were not very significant, incomes from farming had a strong positive impact on the level of remittances, as did allowances, whereas cash wages had a negative impact, and profits had no effect whatsoever. The parameters for household size and for age and education of the head were not statistically significant; thus remittances were not clearly correlated with household characteristics, but seemed to be a phenomenon steeped in tradition and circumstances spread across most household categories.

6. Changes Under Early Adjustment 1985–90

Obote was (for the second time) removed from office in 1985, the first year which showed clear signs of the beginning of economic recovery was 1990, when our survey was undertaken. We asked respondents in our sample about changes during the five-year period. Of the heads of household, 20 per cent had changed jobs (perhaps several times), often from own business to private sector employee, or to re-employment in the public sector, as prospects in the latter had improved. Informal business seemed to have been entered into irrespective of age and income categories.

The volume of land transactions had increased markedly during the period when other financial transactions were difficult or impossible, and land transactions thus enabled urban households to accumulate or reduce assets. Our sample households reported 60 land transactions during the period from 1985 to 1990, mostly purchases. Though undertaken by all income categories, richer groups spent much more money on land purchases than did poorer ones, but there were also many small purchases in the crowded parts of Kampala, partly as a way of preserving household savings from inflation. In comparison with the rural sector (see Appendix B) urbanites depended more on business incomes and loans for the finance to purchase land: 53 per cent mentioned business as the source of finance for their land purchase, 18 per cent wages, 20 per cent loans, and the rest sale of crops. More than half who sold land claimed that it was for their children's school fees, while the rest wanted to purchase livestock and/or start business. The average age of those selling (heads of household) was about 50, while buyers averaged less than 40; there is thus a life-cycle aspect to the observed transactions, with older heads dissaving, and younger ones accumulating assets. A similar pattern was evident in the construction of houses for own dwelling: 65 households had built houses, while another five had purchased houses. Given the difficulty of acquiring normal credit from banks during this period, the bulk of land and housing transactions in Kampala were undertaken either on a cash basis, or with loans acquired using political influence.

7. Summary and Conclusions

Given the sharp fall in living standards since the 1960s, only a handful of people in Kampala were satisfied with their lot in 1990, while some slum-dwellers continued to live in unspeakable misery. Income diversification has always been a form of insurance for resource-poor households in many countries. Though relative peace had returned to Uganda in 1990, the economy had not yet stabilised sufficiently to provide secure incomes, so it still constituted the main household response in the aftermath of economic decline.

The role of the informal sector, traditionally that of a pressure valve for urban unemployment, changed drastically; formal-sector employees also had to embark on informal activities to supplement their meagre wages. For many in the urban economy, the 'residue' sector thus became the main source of livelihood, a process which has become increasingly common in Africa (see Stren, 1992; Bigsten *et al.*, 1994).

Engagement in business was the main income differentiating factor in Kampala, most successfully exploited by those in wage employment, especially the public sector. But when modern-sector employees adapted by diversifying income sources, they were competing with the traditional informal-sector participants: incomes in the informal sector thus fell as more individuals embarked on similar activities. Modern formal-sector 'part-timers' in the informal sector may even have out-competed the rest, due to superior contact networks. The main casualty of the decline in Uganda was therefore the modern sector, especially the government. It underwent 'casualisation', as the income of those engaged in the sector and the quality of the services they provided declined. A policy dilemma then became how to restructure the public sector so that there was less encroachment on the sources of livelihood of the urban poor. A better paid civil service would restore morale and eventually reduce the need for side activities, but that would require public-sector lay-offs which would initially increase the pressure on the incomes of the poor engaged in informal activities.

What impact would adjustment policies have on Kampala as a whole? Relative-price changes and fiscal restraint were being used to boost the tradable sector of the economy, cash crops, and a profitable agricultural sector could halt the rural-urban drift, but, barring a return-to-the-land strategy, it was doubtful whether this alone could reduce the pressure on the informal sector, in the short run. The few import-substituting industries had rather limited capacity for expansion, as the trade regime was not yet sufficiently transformed to make them tradable. As the seat of government, Kampala was the main producer of modern-sector services, so fiscal restraint would have a negative impact on the city. Long-run changes would of course depend on how quickly resources were shifted across sectors in the rest of the economy.

Notes

1. Between 1969 and 1980, the population of Kampala grew on average by 2.9 per cent per year, while the country as a whole grew by 3.1 per cent (see Uganda, 1991). Between 1980 and 1991 Kampala grew at 4.9 per cent per year, the country at 2.5 per cent.
2. The New Vision newspaper of 16 May 1995, cited the Mayor of Kampala lamenting, 'Our city has already been turned into a slum'.
3. See Collier and Lal (1986) on Kenya
4. In Nairobi in contrast, the informal sector has become quite sophisticated, even sub-contracting (King and Aboudha, 1991) on public sector projects.
5. For a more favourable assessment of urban agricultural activities, see Maxwell (1995) and Maxwell and Zziwa (1990).

6. See, for instance, Hazari and Sgro (1991).
7. Coffee prices on the world market increased rapidly between 1975 and 1977, but then dropped back to much lower levels. The real price to peasants in Uganda, of course, also depended on the explicit and implicit taxation of coffee exports.
8. There have been some strikes in Uganda, notably a bank-worker's strike, but they have been small-scale and have had little apparent impact on policy.
9. For instance, many school administrators also owned or had an interest in the companies which supplied their schools with textbooks, chalk and paper.
10. There is evidence that Uganda has experienced a drastic change in nutrition patterns and standards since the early 1970s (see Herbert, 1987; and Ciantia, 1989). In the north and east, for instance, there has been a relative shift from labour-intensive crops like millet towards maize and matooke.
11. The parishes and villages are listed in Appendix A3.
12. As a stipulation from the authorities, enumerators had to report to the chairman of the village resistance council (RC1) before interviewing; in some cases, especially where village boundaries were doubtful, some intervention from the RC1 chairman in selecting respondents proved unavoidable.
13. The household was defined as all members living in the house at the time of the interview, including visitors who had stayed for more than two weeks and who shared meals.
14. Besides the traditional housing, medical and transport allowances, there were also 'responsibility' allowances, night allowances and even food allowances.
15. An article by N. Adyanget in *The New Vision*, 5 January 1994, was titled, 'Brewing Booms in City Suburbs'.
16. See Kayizzi-Mugerwa (1995a), for a comparison with the Gambia.
17. For simplicity a child under 15 was assumed equivalent to half an adult.
18. Information was collected about the value of housing benefits, but the reliability of this data is uncertain.
19. The highest reported monthly profit was 1,500,000 Ushs.

20. Other factors that might have given some feeling for socioeconomic class of the households were place of residence and education of level of the household head, but apart from the most affluent areas, place of residence was no longer a good indicator of social class in Kampala, due to the decline of many urban neighbourhoods and the general lack of housing; given the difficult labour market situation, education was also dismissed as a useful differentiating feature.

21. The private sector had been more responsive to wage demands than the public sector, so government had lost a number of good people to the private sector; in the early years of adjustment attempts were made to close the gap (largely through increased allowances), so the differences in total remuneration between private and public sectors was smaller than earlier.

22. Suggesting that other members of the household found employment in the head's business.

23. That public-sector households had a higher share of income from business than the private sector households probably reflects the looser control of employees in the public sector; unable to pay them 'a living wage', government had taken a soft line on work discipline.

24. This is an increase from 1971, when the public sector accounted for only 38 per cent (Uganda, 1972c).

25. This apparent break-up of the wage-earning class in Uganda was similar to the pattern in Tanzania (see also further below), but contrasted sharply with the situation in Kenya, where a distinct wage-earning class still existed (see for example Jamal and Weeks, 1993).

26. This model has been applied to many similar situations, see e.g. Cragg (1971). It has also been used in labour supply applications (e.g. Blundell *et al.*, 1987). Here we apply this approach to the issue of wage determination.

Appendix A1: Descriptive Statistics for Variables in the Earnings Function

| | Male | | Female | |
	Mean	Standard Deviation	Mean	Standard Deviation
E1	6.40	1.75	6.02	2.13
E2	3.01	2.53	2.03	2.31
E3	1.02	1.75	0.45	1.27
AGE	0.35	0.12	0.30	0.10
AGE2	0.13	0.09	0.10	0.07
GOV	0.32	0.47	0.14	0.35
LEP	0.37	0.59	0.17	0.41
INCOTHER	8.93	25.86	11.05	22.35
HEAD	0.58	0.49	0.08	0.26
EARN	1135.7	2871.5	508.0	912.0

Appendix A2: The Double-Hurdle Model

The double-hurdle model used in Section 5 is formulated as follows:

$$(1) \quad \begin{aligned} y_i^* &= x_{1i}\beta_1 + u_{1i} & u_{1i} &\sim N(0, \sigma_1^2) \\ d_i^* &= x_{2i}\beta_2 + u_{2i} & u_{2i} &\sim N(0,1) \end{aligned}$$

$$y_i = \begin{cases} Y_i^* & \text{if } d_i = 1 \text{ and } y_i^* > 0 \\ 0 & \text{if } d_i = 0 \text{ and } y_i^* > 0, \text{ or } y_{i*} \le 0 \end{cases}$$

$$d_i = \begin{cases} 1 & \text{if } d_i^* > 0 \\ 0 & \text{if } d_i^* \le 0 \end{cases}$$

y_i^* is an unobserved latent variable related to the observed variable y_i, which is the wage level. This is 0 if the individual is not working and y_i^* if working. d_i^* is a latent variable for the probability of a positive observation for person i. The observed variable d_i is equal to 1 if a positive wage is observed, that is, when the individual is working and is reported as working; and 0 otherwise. We assume that the sample selection equation can be estimated with a probit specification. The likelihood function for this type of model is shown in Blundell *et al.* (1987) and Flood (1988).

Appendix A3: Sample Parishes/Wards and Villages

---

1. Kampala Region (1st Round)	
Parish/Ward (RC II)	Village (RC I)

A. Kawempe Division

1.	Kawempe	Kawempe I Zone
2.	Komamboga	Katalemwa Zone
3.	Makerere II	Mukwenda Zone
4.	Mulago I	Upper Mawanda Road

B. Kampala Central Division

5.	Kagugube	Makerere Kivulu I
6.	Kamwokya I	Zone A
7.	Kisenyi I	Central
8.	Kololo III	Kitante
9.	Nakasero II	Flats Village
10.	Old Kampala	Zone IV

C. Nakawa Division

11.	Banda	B II
12.	Bugolobi	Village 3

---

cont ...

Appendix A3 cont ...

---

1. Kampala Region (1st Round)
Parish/Ward (RC II)   Village (RC I)

C. Nakawa Division cont ...

13.	Kiswa	Zone 5
14.	Kiwatule	Central
15.	Kyambogo	KI
16.	Kyanja	Kasanyi
17.	Mbuya II	Village 9
18.	Mutungo	Zone 13
19.	Naguru I	Village 27
20.	Ntinda	Village 6

D. Makindye Division

21.	Kibuye I	Nabisalu Zone
22.	Luukuli	Kizungu
23.	Makindye I	Lukuli
24.	Nsambya Central	Central Zone
25.	Salaama	Mulungu

E. Rubaga Division

26.	Lubya	Lugala
27.	Lungujja	Wakaliga
28.	Nakulabye	Suzana
29.	Namirembe	Kiyaaye
30.	Namirembe	Mengo Hospital

---

cont ...

Appendix A3 cont ...

---

2. Kampala Region (2nd Round)
Parish/Ward (RC II)   Village (RC I)

A. Kawempe Division
1.	Bwaise II	Nakamiro Zone
2.	Kikaaya	Kisoota Zone
3.	Mulago II	Bakery Area
4.	Wandegeya	Busia

B. Kampala Central Division
5.	Kamwokya II	Kisenyi I
6.	Kisenyi III	Kiguli
7.	Kololo I	Makenzievale
8.	Nakasero III	Nakivubo Road
9.	Nakasero IV	Luwum
10.	Nakivubo/Shauriyako	Shauriyako B

C. Nakawa Division
11.	Bukoto I	ED
12.	Bukoto II	Kalinabiri
13.	Butabika	Biina D
14.	Luzira	Agaati Village
15.	Luzira	Kamwanyi
16.	Luzira	Kasumba
17.	Mbuya I	Buyinja
18.	Naguru II	Bukoto Brown Flats 1–9
19.	Nakawa	Uganda Railways
20.	Nakawa Institutions	Posts

D. Makindye Division
21.	Bukasa	Muyenga B

---

cont ...

Appendix A3 cont ...

---

2. Kampala Region (2nd Round)

Parish/Ward (RC II)	Village (RC I)

D. Makindye Division cont ...

22.	Gaba Parish	Bunga Hill
23.	Kansanga	Wheeling Zone
24.	Kibuli	Lubowa
25.	Kibuye II	Kategura Zone

E. Rubaga Division

26.	Busega	Nabisasiro
27.	Kabowa	Suuna
28.	Kasubi	Kasubi III
29.	Rubaga	Wagaba
30.	Najjanankumbi I	Masiro

Appendix B: Rural Adaptation: Evidence from Masaka District

1. Introduction

Appendix 8A reported the responses of Kampala households to economic crisis and early adjustment. Here we report the responses of rural households, based on our 1990 survey. Masaka District is one of the major food and coffee producing areas of Uganda, and economically one of the most important districts in the south (Uganda, 1967a). It lies on the southern arm of a broad crescent bordering Lake Victoria. With good climate and fertile soil, it has long been Kampala's bread basket. The district headquarters, Masaka town (which was not sampled) is the third largest urban concentration in the country after Jinja and Kampala. Masaka is a gateway both to the western regions of the country and to Rwanda and Tanzania to the South.

In 1990 Masaka comprised five counties: Bukoto (including Masaka town), Kalungu, Bukomansimbi, Mawogoola and the Ssese Islands in Lake Victoria (see Appendix Table B1).

Economic decline from 1972 to 1986 disrupted traditional forms of rural livelihood in Uganda, lowering incomes from the sale of cash crops, such as coffee, and reducing remittances from relatives in urban areas. To generate more income it became necessary to reallocate household resources among the various available rural activities. Ability to do this, as well as the capacity to respond to the incentives in the government's IMF/World Bank-supported prog-rammes are functions of the household's endowments. Life-cycle considerations are also important determinants of a household's capacity to adjust, while the structure of the factor and goods markets constrains the household's ability to realise its desired allocation. Within farming, land can also be allocated to a variety of uses.

Appendix Table B2 shows land-use in Masaka. Keeping livestock was common in the district with substantial amounts of land set aside for grazing, leading to relatively higher incomes from livestock production than in other districts. Mawogoola is a sparsely populated area with savannah-like vegetation, mostly suitable for ranching, and the Ssese islanders have fishing as their main economic activity.

Appendix Table B1: *Masaka District:*
Administrative Divisions and Population Shares[1]

County	Sub-counties	Parishes	Population (%)	House-holds (%)	Sample Hh (%)[2]
Bukoto	9	60	52.4	57.5	66.0
Kalungu	6	30	20.0	17.2	14.5
Bukomansimbi	4	21	14.2	10.4	12.7
Mawogoola	3	12	12.3	12.7	6.8
Ssese Islands[3]	6	14	1.1	2.2	0

[1] According to the 1986/87 Agricultural Sector Survey, Masaka district population was about 800,000, comprising 132,000 households.

[2] The total number of households in our sample was 220.

[3] The islands have since been transferred to a new district, Kalangala.

Most of the land in the other three counties is used for crop production, primarily bananas; coffee's share was much smaller. Coffee's share of crop land in the district was 38 per cent in 1963 (Uganda, 1964: 41), but now only Kalungu had more than a fifth of its crop land in coffee, suggesting that there might have been some uprooting of coffee during the years of decline (Uganda, 1982b). 'Other crops' such as maize, beans, and cassava, had a substantial collective share reflecting the move away from coffee production in recent years, and an apparent desire to diversify the 'crop portfolio' to reduce the insecurity of earning a livelihood in the countryside,[1] similar to the multiplicity of income-generating schemes in Kampala (see Appendix A). Besides coffee, this fertile district grew no other significant cash crop; its relative prosperity was based on food production.

Appendix Table B2: *Masaka District: Land-Use by County 1986/87*
(hectares and per cent)

	Total Land			Use of Crop Land		
	Use (has)	Grazing (%)	Crops (%)	Coffee (%)	Bananas (%)	Other (%)
1. Bukomansimbi	68,689.2	34.0	66.0	16.0	45.0	39.0
2. Bukoto	221,843.6	43.5	56.5	17.5	36.0	48.5
3. Kalungu	97,462.4	43.2	56.8	26.2	45.0	28.8
4. Mawogoola	52,306.0	66.6	33.4	5.8	12.0	82.2
5. Ssese Islands	6,350.0	95.0	5.0	16.2	22.2	61.6

Source: Planning Department, Ministry of Animal Industry and Fisheries (1988), *Agricultural Sector Survey, 1986–87*

After describing the survey itself, the structure of rural income by activity type is analysed by quintile and age of household head. Then income-generating processes (activity types) are analysed by quintile, age of household head, and size of holding, plus econometric estimation of productivity; business income by main business, plus probit estimation of the likelihood of participation in business; and wage employment by wage group, plus probit estimates of participation in formal employment and in farm or estate employment. Finally, changes from 1985 to 1990 (the period of early adjustment) are reviewed.

2. Aspects of Rural Responses

2.1. Introduction

A number of recent studies have analysed household survival strategies in Africa (Cornia, 1987; Maliyamkono and Bagachwa, 1990; House, 1991) including Uganda (Jamal, 1987, 1988; Meagher, 1991; Bigsten and Kayizzi-Mugerwa, 1992, 1995; Kayizzi-Mugerwa, 1993; Nabuguzi, 1993). A pattern has emerged for Uganda. In urban areas, proximity to a market for goods and services without effective commercial or statutory controls has enabled households to adjust to economic decline by engaging in informal business, ranging from petty-trade activities demanding little or no capital — in the slums and at the fringes of urban centres — to large business ventures in central Kampala. Many urban households also grow food for their own needs, not infrequently with a small surplus for the market.

The economic bond between rural and urban households, as reflected by the level of remittances, is weaker today than in the 1960s; the impact of urban resource flows on economic activity in the rural areas has been reduced. How have rural households adjusted to economic decline and reduced urban remittances? So far, the evidence has been anecdotal.[2] Since the rural sector could always fall back on subsistence production, it has often been assumed that it was spared the worst ravages of the economic crisis (Helleiner, 1981). Moreover, since revitalisation of agriculture was one of the main goals of adjustment strategies in the 1980s, it was assumed that, as a result, the rural sector, experienced a net gain from increases in producer prices and improvements in rural infrastructure. But while peasants were encouraged to increase output, late payment for their produce,[3] rampant corruption in the cooperative unions, and poor access to markets (the rural infrastructure remains poor) dampened results. Perhaps the peasants had become less willing to invest in the potentially more lucrative but riskier cash crops, preferring safer food crops or a diversified insurance strategy.

2.2. Determinants of Rural Household Responses

To analyse the response of a typical semi-commercial rural household we formalise the choice problem that it faces by first assuming full information, perfect markets and the absence of risk, with product prices and the wage rate exogenously given, and the household constrained neither in the product nor the labour market.[4] Family labour and hired labour are assumed to be perfect substitutes (other purchased inputs are disregarded for the moment). In the short run, the amount of land and capital available to the household is given, as is its allocation among activities. The household is engaged in agricultural production, own business, and off-farm wage employment. It maximises a well-behaved quasi-concave utility function, with own-produced agricultural goods, market goods and services, and leisure as arguments, subject to time, cash-income and production-function constraints.

With given technology, wage, prices, land, and capital, the only endogenous variable is labour. Labour should be applied in agriculture or business up to the point where its value marginal product equals the market wage. Depending on the size of its time endowment, the household will either hire-in or hire-out labour. Due to differences in the initial allocation of capital to each activity and in its mobility, returns to capital in agriculture and business may not equalise in the short run. In reality, of course, agriculture itself is not a homogenous activity, but comprises many activities including food, cash-crop, and livestock production, among which labour should be allocated so as to equate its value marginal products; in the long run, land and capital should also reallocate among activities to equalise factor returns.

2.3. Introducing Imperfections and Risk

In Masaka there are various constraints which hinder the optimal allocation of labour, leading to differences in returns to labour. Lack of information and wage rigidities, leads to the access to formal employment being rationed. Given restrictions on factor mobility, differences among households in ownership of the complementary resources land and capital may also make wage equalisation impossible. Finally, family and hired labour may not be perfect substitutes; the resultant disparity in returns would have implications for both the hiring-in and hiring-out of labour.

But even if in the long run the households were able to reallocate their land among agricultural activities, inter-household differences in factor proportions might persist. To equalise factor returns between households, they must be able to compensate for differences in land-labour ratios by choosing among activities with sufficiently different factor intensities. However, if specialisation occurs before factor prices have been equalised, then factor price differences will persist. Poor access to credit made it difficult for smallholders to build up capital stocks. The modest increases were almost wholly financed directly through own savings. Socio-economic and state of nature variables such as access to markets, government services, and communications networks, plus weather patterns and land fertility were also key determinants of performance.

To ensure themselves a cash income in an insecure environment, households also increasingly engaged in multiple production; because of a lack of adequate infrastructure, corruption along the marketing channels, low producer prices, and lack of some (incentive) consumer goods, some households exited from cash-crop production altogether. Constraints in the generation of cash incomes led to barter (a less efficient form of exchange), and herbs were increasingly used to cure ailments. With these possibilities for exit, responses to market mechanisms were weakened.

2.4. Life-cycle Aspects

The ability of a household to generate income also depends on its demographic and life-cycle characteristics, including the size of the household and its labour force, and the age, sex and education of the head, the spouse, and others in the labour force. In their study of the evolution of a farmstead in Buganda over the life-cycle, Robertson and Hughes (1978) identified a number of key features. Young households are strong and better educated, but have not had enough time to accumulate assets like land, cattle, etc. The affluent are primarily middle-aged; they have accumulated assets, but could also have large families, including several homesteads, and may have substantial expenditures on health and education. The elderly are invariably in decline; their initially large holdings are probably already split among their children. In the case of widows, they have probably moved into the household of one of their children (most likely the eldest son). It is not rare, however, that grandparents take care of an expanding number of grandchildren whose parents have left for town, or who can no longer afford to feed them in town. Being physically weaker, such households are extremely vulnerable to disease and even hunger. Clearly, the needs of the various households along the life-cycle differ, as does the impact on them of an external disturbance.

2.5. Impacts of Economic Policies

With regard to the rural sector, the NRM government's ambition has been to bring about a rapid increase in the production of cash crops, such as coffee, and to encourage development of non-traditional exports like pineapples, and there has been much emphasis on the need to improve incentives to farmers. However, this ambition conflicted with the government's need to raise revenue (Kayizzi-Mugerwa, 1993): until the mid-1990s the government remained very dependent on coffee export-taxes, and the share of the world price that reached the farmer was small. The fact that farmers continued to produce coffee at all was due partly to domestic legislation which forbids the uprooting of coffee trees, and partly (and more convincingly) to the need for a reserve source of cash income, should food crops fail them. In the earliest stages of the adjustment process, relative coffee prices increased, but the coffee slump that followed, and government failure to compensate for it, led to a sharp deterioration in the producer prices. But improvement in urban economic activity, mainly due to expenditure of increased aid inflows, raised the demand for food, and farmers responded by abandoning cash-crop production for the more lucrative food market (see also Van der Willigen, 1986). The coffee boom that began in 1994 reversed some of the earlier effects, with visibly higher incomes in rural areas. But the price of market goods, including social services, has also risen (and could rise further when the cost-sharing proposals for health services are fully implemented) decreasing the real income of the rural sector, which could shift demand away from market goods towards increased subsistence production, resulting in failure to reincorporate the rural sector into the market economy.

3. The Masaka Survey

The survey was undertaken in April/May 1990, covering all sub-districts in Masaka except Ssese Islands.[5] From the Ministry of Local Government in Kampala and the District Administrator in Masaka we obtained lists of the parishes and villages in Masaka by county and subcounty. We then made a population-weighted selection of subcounties (RC3s), parishes (RC2s), and finally 20 villages (RC1s); within each of these we selected households at random, giving us a total of 220 households. Appendix Table B2 shows the percentage share of each county in the sample as compared with its share in the district population.

A household was defined as everyone living in the house at the time of the interview, including guests who had stayed for more than two weeks and shared meals. The main respondent was the head of household, but in most of the interviews other household members were also present and provided information on their activities.[6] The interviews focused on five major areas: household composition, income and time-use, assets and investments, expenditures on education and health, and an assessment of recent socioeconomic changes. The section on income and time-use was divided into several sub-sections: off-farm wage employment, business income, work on other people's farms, work on own farm including the cost of production, the amount and value of output, and the keeping of livestock.

4. The Structure of Rural Incomes

The average Masaka household had a labour force of 2.91 persons and labour input of 453 hours per month (Appendix Table B3) or about 32 hours per week per labour force member (not counting hours provided by children). Most labour time was in agriculture with women putting in more time than men, and children providing some hours, after school or during holidays (see Obura, 1982; Batarirana, 1981). The need for diversification into other activities had increased with the years of decline, but the scope for it was much more restricted in rural Masaka than in urban Kampala (see Appendix A). Though males dominated the rest of the activities (80 per cent of the work in business or in wage employment), females still provided 46 per cent of total labour hours. Since in-house activities were not included, the female total work load could have been substantial (see also Batarirana, 1981; Mwaka *et al.*, 1994).

Appendix Table B3: *Household Labour Input —Total Hours Per Month and Percentage Distribution Among Men, Women, and Children*

Activity	Total Hours	Men %	Women %	Children %
Agriculture	310	39	45	16
Business	73	79	21	0
Off-farm employment	55	80	20	0
Farm employment	15	80	17	3

4.1. Income Structures by Quintile

Appendix Table B4 shows household incomes by adult-equivalent quintile.[7] Quintile 1 consists of those households with the lowest income per adult equivalent, quintile 5 of the highest. Average income in the first quintile was very low mainly due to some households (23 per cent) with large reported losses in farming, which also makes income shares in this column difficult to interpret.

Appendix Table B4: *Rural Incomes by per Adult Equivalent Income Quintile (Ushs per month)*

	Quintile 1	Quintile 2	Quintile 3	Quintile 4	Quintile 5	Average
Wages	1,017	623	2,065	1,695	11,586	3,397
Allowances	280	125	568	945	975	579
Remittances	120	239	348	1,585	8,764	2,211
Labourer	132	728	582	1,370	10,176	2,597
Farm income[1]	−2,112	6,285	12,998	20,493	142,886	36,110
Profits[2]	1,430	3,652	2,632	9,367	39,488	11,314
Per capita income	345	1,389	2,577	4,457	26,149	6,983
Per adult eq. income	470	1,976	3,682	6,238	35,872	9,648
Household size	8.4	6.8	7.8	7.9	8.2	7.8
Adult equivalent	5.9	4.8	5.3	5.6	5.9	5.4
Age of head	46	46.5	46.7	44	46.2	45.9
Head's educ. (years)	5.6	7	6.8	7	6.7	6.7
% of total income:						
Wages		5	11	5	5	6
Allowances		1	3	3	1	1
Remittances		2	2	5	4	4
Labourer		6	3	4	5	5
Farm income		54	67	59	66	64
Profits		31	14	25	19	21

[1] Farm income includes own production for own use. The cash component is on average 15 per cent.

[2] Because of missing data it was not possible to derive business profits from reported sales and costs. The profits reported were estimated by respondents. Cross-checking indicates that they probably underestimated returns to business.

Note: at the time of the survey the official exchange rate was US$1 = Ushs 350.

By way of comparison we eliminated the 23 per cent of the households who had a negative farm income. Still, the remaining households had a farm income of less than 3000 UShs per month, that is less than half that of quintile 2.

Farming was by far the most important rural economic activity providing 64 per cent of rural income overall, including income from the sale of crops, the value of subsistence consumption,[8] and income (adjusted for valuation changes) from the sale of livestock and livestock products. The shares from this source were largest for the third and fifth quintiles.

Wages and allowances provided a small share of income in the countryside, an average of 7 per cent (rising to 12 per cent when income from working on other people's farms or estates is included). By comparison, the wage share in smallholder income in Kenya's Central Province in 1982 was 37 per cent and 26 per cent in poorer Nyanza Province; in 1983, after a long period of economic decline, the figure for Tanzanian smallholders was 6 per cent (Bevan *et al.*, 1988). The three countries had similar shares a couple of decades earlier, but Uganda seems to have declined as Tanzania did earlier (see also Tripp, 1989). On average, rural households also received 4 per cent of their incomes from members living elsewhere. The richer the quintile, the larger the monthly remittances received, the reverse being true for remittances-out. Possibly the richer households had been able to invest more in children who then provide a better flow of remittances. The share of incomes from working on other people's farms or estates was surprisingly even across quintiles.

A few rural households remitted out substantial amounts of money; it was not possible to ascertain its direction, but many children and other relatives lived in Masaka town and Kampala, so some of the money probably went to urban areas. Food remittances were not recorded but, on the basis of anecdotal evidence, seem to have been substantial.

Business accounted for 21 per cent of rural income, from small-scale operations ranging from milling, baking, and brewing, to cottage industry, construction, trade and services. In contrast with farming, the shares from this source were largest for the second and fourth quintiles. No clear pattern across quintiles emerged.

4.2. Income Structure by Age of Household Head

The age of the household head can be used to approximate the life cycle phase of the household. Households with the youngest households heads (up to age 30), constituting 17 per cent of the sample, had the smallest households (3.8 adult equivalents) and the second highest income per adult equivalent (Appendix Table B5).

Appendix Table B5: *Rural Income Structures by Age of Household Head (Ushs per month)*

	< 31	31–40	41–50	51–60	> 60	Average
% Households	17	26	20	20	17	100
Wages	2453	5640	1666	4179	1946	3397
Allowances	238	738	419	891	487	579
Remittances	54	542	258	4370	6568	2211
Labourer	6546	759	783	6996	4361	2597
Farm income	6333	13053	24165	61913	83934	36110
Profits	30113	10218	6716	5243	6914	11314
Per ad. eq.income	10929	6224	5127	9655	18733	5415
Adult equivalent.	3.8	5.1	5.8	6.8	5.8	5.4
Age of head	27.8	36	46	55.4	68	46
Schooling of heads	7.7	8.2	6	6.3	4.8	7.2
Wages (%)	6	18	5	5	2	6
Allowances (%)	1	2	1	1	1	1
Remittances (%)	0	2	1	5	6	4
Labourer (%)	1	3	2	8	4	5
Farm income (%)	16	42	71	76	81	64
Profits (%)	76	33	20	6	6	21

Business accounted for 76 per cent of the total income, farming 16 per cent, and other employment 5 per cent. Younger households probably had relatively little access to land, and were thus forced to seek other income generating opportunities. Barriers to entry in business were low and what was required most was stamina and mobility, both attributes of the young. The youngest cohorts also had the highest education levels. The share of business income fell substantially and consistently with age of household head, and conversely the share of farm income rose. There is no clear pattern regarding employment incomes, the years of chaos having wreaked havoc on the wage labour market. Remittances tended to increase with age.

The largest group of households, 26 per cent of the sample, had heads aged from 31 to 40. Business accounted for a third of total income, but now farm income contributed 42 per cent, and formal wage employment 18 per cent, by far the highest of any cohort; this group also had the highest education level (8.2 years). Still, this group had lower total income and a larger family size than the first quintile, resulting in much lower income per adult equivalent. For households with heads over 40, the shares of wages and business income declined, whereas the share of farm income increased dramatically. Households with heads 51–60 years old had the most adult equivalents, 6.8. Households with heads over 60 were slightly smaller and had even more farm income, and thus the highest income per adult equivalent. Since most of the farm income was calculated from subsistence, this reflects self-sufficiency in food more than a capacity to transact on the market. The potential vulnerability of this group is reflected in the low education level of the head, less than 5 years.

Robertson and Hughes (1978) had explained the life-cycle pattern of income in terms of agricultural accumulation, but the process of accumulation was disrupted by political and economic chaos during the 1970s and 1980s so younger cohorts have been unable to accumulate along the same pattern as before. In 1990 it was mainly older households which had more agricultural assets and higher farm incomes, but the youngest cohort had been able to compensate its lack of agricultural capital by engaging in own business ventures. These changes had altered the age pattern of income per adult equivalent, which now followed a U-pattern rather than the inverted-U predicted by Robertson and Hughes; with the return to normality, however, this pattern may shift back.

4.3. Income Structure by Size of Holding

Since farming was the most important single source of income, land was the single most important asset in the country-side, and land ownership was an important determinant of rural welfare. Appendix Table B6 shows household incomes and characteristics by size of holding; 70 per cent of the households had 2 hectares of land or less with an average of 1 hectare per family of 4.9 adult equivalents. This group was the most dependent on wages (10 per cent of total income), and had a large share of business profits (30 per cent). Lack of sufficient land has driven these households into business.

Three per cent of the households had an average holding of 60 hectares, mainly ranches. Affluence rose with the size of holding, but the share of business profits fell. Households holding 5–10 hectares (13 per cent of the sample) had the largest household sizes (8.3 adult equivalents), and supplied the most own labour (503 hours).

5. Analysis of Income Generation and Labour Allocation

In this section we analyse the different activities and the factors that determined income generation in them; we also estimate the relative returns.

5.1. Farm Production

Appendix Table B7 shows average revenues and costs of farming by quintiles including inputs of own labour and the amount of land owned by the household. For most quintiles, the largest component of incomes by far was the imputed value of subsistence consumption, but the richest quintile had more income from livestock. After the first quintile (which reported losses), the higher quintiles had larger holdings, an average of almost 11 hectares for the highest, and own labour also tended to increase.

Appendix Table B8 shows production structure by age of the household head. The youngest group had above average holdings, size of holding was smallest for the group aged 31–40, then peaked at 6.7 hectares for the group aged 41–50. The oldest household heads

Appendix Table B6: *Rural Income Structure by Size of Holding (hectares) (Ushs per month)*

	up to 2	2+ to 5	5+ to 10	10+ to 20	20+	Average
% Households	70	18	6	3	3	100
Average holding (has)	1	3.4	8.2	15.8	60	4
Wages	2291	6833	335	5083	12329	3397
Allowances	650	343	115	333	1429	578
Remittances	829	250	5038	25000	19043	2211
Labourer	1723	671	519	45405	0	2597
Farm Income	10308	33488	7477	106815	486307	36110
Profits	6845	29810	796	14500	7428	11314
Per adult eq. income	5026	12494	1029	33290	73592	9648
Household size	6.9	8.7	12.3	7.5	14	7.8
Adult equivalents	4.9	6.1	8.3	5	10.1	5.4
Average age of head	45	46	50	46.5	48	45.9
Wages (%)	10	10	0	3	2	6
Allowances (%)	3	1	0	0	0	1
Remittances (%)	4	0	6	13	4	4
Labourer (%)	8	1	1	23	0	5
Farm income (%)	46	47	84	54	92	64
Profits (%)	30	42	9	7	2	21

had an average holding of 2.7 hectares. Own labour per month increased with age of head. The first age group worked only 148 hours on its holding, but the oldest reported 415. This difference was not only due to household size, but also resulted from variations in dependence on farm income; older households had to work their smaller holdings more intensively to make ends meet. The sample seemed to miss households which were in complete decline, however.

Appendix Table B7: *Farm Revenue and Costs by Per Adult Equivalent Income Quintile (Ushs per year)*

	Quintile 1	Quintile 2	Quintile 3	Quintile 4	Quintile 5	Average
Crop sales[1]	17,786	19,075	55,770	77,394	295,395	93,084
Livestock income[2]	3,177	5,450	-1,739	26,627	1005,940	207,891
Value of subsistence food consumption	35,427	61,375	129,665	179,890	516,290	184,529
Production costs	81,731	10,476	27,714	37,998	103,000	52,184
% of costs:						
Labour	87	70	83	59	65	73
Seeds	5	12	9	11	3	6
Chemicals and fertiliser	8	18	8	30	32	21
Farm income/year	-25,341	75,424	155,982	245,913	1714,625	433,320
Farm income/month	-2,112	6,285	12,998	20,493	142,886	36,110
Size of holding (hectares)	2.9	1.2	2.8	2.8	10.9	4.1
Own labour (hours/month)	323	270	273	296	389	310

1 Includes value of cash crops not yet marketed.
2 Includes valuation change and value of own consumption.

Appendix Table B8: *Average Farm Revenue and Costs by Age of Household Head (Ushs per year)*

	< 31	31–40	41–50	51–60	over 60	Average
Crop sales	43,697	87,414	55,618	173,643	98,943	93,084
Livestock income	2,626	13,895	170,840	156,750	807,297	207,891
Value of subsist. food consump.	62,176	120,028	135,471	446,594	154,183	184,529
Production costs	30,142	64,492	71,949	34,025	53,213	52,184
% of costs:						
Hired labour	85	74	81	76	53	73
Seeds	8	6	6	9	3	6
Chemicals and fertilisers	7	20	13	15	44	21
Farm income/year	75,996	156,648	289,980	742,962	1007,210	433,320
Farm inc./month	6,333	13,053	24,165	61,913	83,934	36,110
Size of holding (ha)	4.2	2.0	6.7	5.7	2.7	4.0
Own labour (hours/month)	148	269	374	375	415	310

Appendix Table B10 shows the results of an estimation of an aggregate production function for agricultural output. The marginal productivity of labour will then be compared with returns to labour in other activities. The sum of elasticities was 0.82, implying slightly decreasing returns to scale. The coefficient for labour was rather low (0.16) and only significant at the 5 per cent level, but it is typical for estimates of smallholder production in Africa, where the coefficient for land is normally larger than that of labour. Evaluated at the mean, the value marginal product was 21 shillings per hour, very low. By comparison, the joint return to labour, land, and capital was 116 shillings per hour worked (see Appendix Table B7). We extended the production function with variables measuring the education level of

Appendix Table B9: *Average Farm Revenue and Costs by Size of Holding (Ushs per year)*

	< 2	2+ to 5	5+ to 10	10+ to 20	20+	Average
Average holdings (has)	1.0	3.4	8.2	15.8	60.0	4.1
Crop sales	33169	115653	227900	796933	428585	93084
Livestock income	17327	237610	111992	154630	4454214	207891
Value of subsist.						
food consump.	95250	157695	673035	415158	1197100	184529
Production costs	22041	109105	115596	84933	244214	52184
% of costs:						
Hired labour	74	76	60	52	82	73
Seeds	9	5	4	10	2	6
Chemicals and fertilisers	17	19	36	38	16	21
Farm income/year	123696	401856	897336	1281792	5835684	433320
Farm inc./month	10308	33488	74778	106816	486307	36110
Own labour (hours/month)	264	393	503	343	458	310

the head, but an F-test showed that they were not statistically significant (Appendix Table B11); education thus seems to have contributed relatively little to agricultural productivity, whereas output increased significantly and substantially with the age of the household head. Generally, education is assumed to increase productivity by raising the operational skills of the workers; it also improves information processing and makes the choices of input and output mixes more efficient, speeding up responses to changes in prices and technology. Earlier studies of the impact of education on agricultural productivity have shown that in fact it has a significant and substantial positive impact in modernising environments, that is, where new techniques and products are being introduced (Lockheed *et al.*, 1980). In stagnant or declining agricultural environments, on the other hand, we would not expect education to have much impact, since traditional knowledge would be sufficient; this seems to have been the case in Masaka in 1990. Using national survey data for 1992/93, Appleton and Balihuta (1996) found that household members with four or more years of education were significantly more productive than the less educated, but (as in our case) the education of the head (farm manager) was not significant (though positive) in the estimation of productivity, but it *was* significant in estimation of productive efficiency.

Appendix Table B10: *Production Function for Agricultural Output*

	Estimate	Standard Error	t-value
Intercept	7.762	0.460	16.886
Ln L	0.158	0.087	1.811
Ln A	0.495	0.077	6.415
Ln I	0.168	0.042	3.931

Note: A heteroscedasticity test showed that the null hypothesis of constant variances could not be rejected. Adj R^2=0.32, F=32.04

Diversification into business enabled many Kampala households to protect their income levels (see Appendix A), and a substantial number (14 per cent) relied on business alone. In rural areas, however, due to limited markets and many other constraints such as infrastructure and credit availability, the extent and variety of business engagements was rather limited. In the Kampala sample, 62 per cent of the households were engaged in some form of business activity, and even 49 per cent in rural Masaka, but the extent of eng-

Appendix Table B11: *Extended Production Function for Agricultural Output*

	Estimate	Standard Error	t value
Intercept	7.337	0.569	12.876
Ln L	0.088	0.088	0.993
Ln A	0.481	0.076	6.322
Ln I	0.096	0.028	3.439
ED1	0.111	0.334	0.334
ED2	0.229	0.372	0.616
ED3	0.663	0.444	1.494
AGEZ	0.623	0.253	2.458
AGEW	0.970	0.266	3.654
Adj R^2=0.35			

L: labour input in hours
A: land input in hectares
I: value of purchased inputs
ED1: primary education of the head (dummy variable equal to 1 if the head has some primary education but no further education, otherwise 0)
ED2: secondary education of the head (dummy variable equal to 1 if the head has some secondary education but no further education, otherwise 0)
ED3: post-secondary education of the head (dummy variable equal to one if the head had some tertiary education, otherwise 0)
AGEZ: head 31–50 years of age
AGEW: head 51 years of age or more

agement, in terms of both time and finances expended, was much smaller than in Kampala. In Masaka, business engagement was not so crucial for survival, which was largely taken care of by growing food. Nevertheless, business was a crucial source of cash income for the purchase of health care and education, and of life-sustaining goods not produced at home, such as paraffin.

5.2. Rural Business Activity

Business in rural Masaka was mainly a male activity (see Appendix Table B12); females owned only 12 per cent of the establishments, whereas in Kampala they owned 34 per cent. Informal trades and retailing was the most common form of activity (28 per cent of the businesses), and the most labour was devoted to it (an average of 230 hours per month). Service businesses, including transport and the professions, had the smallest number of participants, a mere 5 per cent, none women. Average age and education were fairly even across business types. Dividing estimated monthly profits by monthly hours devoted to the business yields total return to both labour and capital (profit per hour). This includes the owner's and others' hourly wages as well as the scarcity premium on the sector-specific capital input; for example, one could not enter the transport business without a vehicle. Cottage industry had a distinctly lower return than the others reflecting ease of entry: it is labour intensive with little capital requirements. The average total return for individuals was 178 Ushs/hour, compared with total return to land, capital, and labour in agriculture, which was 116 Ushs. We were not able to derive the implicit return to labour in business, but this simple comparison suggests that it may be somewhat higher than the return in agriculture.

Appendix Table B13 shows the results from a probit estimation of the determinants of business participation by individual labour-force members. The labour force was defined as all individuals from 15 to 65 years except students and the disabled. For explanatory variables we used human capital (primary, secondary, and post-secondary education), demographic characteristics (age, sex, head of household), income, and assets (land). The age and age squared variables, *AGE* and *AGE2*, were used as proxies for experience. The size of land holding (*SIZEE*) could influence business participation either way: it is a good proxy for the household's financial viability (land is often

Appendix Table B12: *Structure of Business Incomes by Main Business (Ushs/Month)*

	Grain Processing Related	Cottage Industry	Construction	Informal Trades and Retailing	Services	Other
			Type of Business ($n = 108$)			
% main business	18	12	16	28	5	22
% female owned	10	2	10	11	0	12
Profits (Ushs)	8953	7213	28457	36900	34000	25382
Days worked per month	7	20	19	23	21	15
Hours worked per day	5.8	6.3	6.7	10.2	8.8	8.7
Age of owner	43	38	34	36	38	41
Education of owner (years)	7.9	8.8	9.2	8.6	8.4	9.0
Profit per hour (Ushs)	220	57	223	157	184	195

Note: the structure of business incomes is presented by type of main business. Business types are defined as follows:

Grain processing related = milling, baking or brewing
Cottage industry = tailoring, shoe-repair, furniture making, carving
Construction = brick making, building and repairs
Informal trades and retailing = hawking, kiosk, shop, shoeshine
Services = transport services, professional services
'Other' includes landlords

Appendix Table B13: *Probit Estimate of Participation in Business Activity in the Rural Sector*

Variable	Parameter Estimate	Standard Error	t-value	Marginal Effect
Intercept	3.3010	0.9663	3.417	
ED1	−0.0334	0.2201	0.152	−0.013
ED2	−0.1839	0.2562	0.718	−0.073
ED3	−0.2458	0.3626	0.678	−0.098
AGE	−0.1505	0.0381	3.947	−0.060
AGE2	0.0021	0.0005	4.343	0.00083
SEX2	−0.2326	0.1782	1.305	−0.093
HEAD	0.9882	0.1987	4.973	0.393
SIZEE	−0.0042	0.0040	1.029	−0.002

$n = 108$

SIZEE: size of land holding
ED1:   dummy for primary education
ED2:   dummy for secondary education
ED3:   dummy for post-secondary education
SEX2:   dummy for females
HEAD: dummy for heads of household.
Log likelihood = −215.03

used as collateral for credit). One could also have sold land in order to get into business, or for land-scarce households, business could be a substitute for farming.

Education had no significant impact on participation (though the three variables were consistently negative); the business undertaken in Masaka thus seems to have made minimal demands on education. Grain processing businesses, for example, are in many respects mere extensions of farming. Being female had no significant effect, although again the sign was negative. Age and age-squared were highly significant, the former with a negative coefficient. It was primarily the young who were drawn to business, which seems to require more stamina than experience. Heads were much more likely to venture into business leaving the farming to their spouses and others; the coefficient was both highly significant and substantial. This might have implications for the intra-household distribution of income. The land variable had a negative but not statistically significant coefficient.

5.3. Formal and Other Wage Employment

Formal wage employment was a minor contributor to total incomes (7 per cent, compared with Kampala's 44 per cent), but 32 per cent of households had someone engaged in wage employment. Wage incomes where much lower than in Kampala: 65 per cent of the respondents earned below 5,000 Ushs per month, including almost all public sector employees (Appendix Table B14), compared with 44 per cent in the capital, 49 per cent earned less than 3,000 Ushs per month (less than US$5), while only 5 per cent earned more than 20,000 Ushs. The overall average was just above 10,000 Ushs per month. In Kampala, allowances were also more than the wages themselves, but in the countryside they seemed confined to medical and housing allowances, and played an insignificant role (only 1 per cent of total income). Food, transport and night allowances that were common in the capital, were unknown in Masaka.

Nevertheless, allowances helped somewhat; with allowances included, the average monthly income was 12,494 Ushs. Assuming a 40 hour week, hourly income was 72 Ushs, roughly equal to the median farm income of the average household. An advantage of wage employment was that it generated cash income, which helped ameliorate the cash constraints to business activities and agricultural innovations (see Bigsten, 1984, on Kenya).

Appendix Table B15 shows the results from a probit estimation of the determinants of participation in formal employment, while Appendix Table B16 shows estimates for farm and estate employment. Given the small sample size, earnings functions were not estimated.

Appendix Table B14: *Wage Incomes in Rural Masaka by Class*
(Ushs per month)

	Over 3000	3001– 5000	5001– 10000	10001– 20000	Over 20000	Average
% of persons employed	49	16	20	10	5	na
% in public sector	29	54	7	0	0	24
% female	32	27	0	14	0	21
Age (years)	32	34	31	28	43	32
Experience (years)	10	12	6	4	13	9
Wages	2,456	3,851	7,104	16,000	102,500	10,676
Allowances	2,002	1,757	2,786	110	0	1,818
Total	4,458	5,608	9,890	16,110	102,500	12,494
Gap	–19,750	–42,450	–16,833	–19,814	–89,666	–26,566
Wage/total %	45	69	72	99	100	85
Gap/total %	–443	–756	–170	–123	–87	–213

n = 70

It was secondary and post-secondary education that had the most significant impact on formal employment (Appendix Table B16), which was of limited importance for agriculture and business in Masaka; in formal employment it could be put to some use. The land variable was also somewhat significant (and positive), but the marginal effect was very small. Our hypothesis was that land pressure drives people into the labour market, but this did not seem to be the case.

Higher education reduced participation in farm or estate employment; secondary education was especially significant, and the negative marginal effect quite large. This employment was chosen by those without access to other employment. The probability of participation was 36 per cent lower for females than males, but although it was mainly males who participated, household heads were less involved. The jobs were inferior alternatives, either because the work was hard and tightly supervised, as opposed to, say, government employment, or possibly because these jobs were considered to have low status. Again the land variable was somewhat significant.[9]

Appendix Table B15: *Probit Estimate of Participation in Formal Employment*

Variable	Parameter Estimate	Standard Error	t-value	Marginal Effect
Intercept	−1.8279	0.9065	2.016	
ED1	−0.0267	0.2592	0.103	−0.011
ED2	0.6001	0.2768	2.168	0.238
ED3	1.4710	0.3546	4.149	0.585
AGE	0.0436	0.0341	1.278	0.017
AGE2	−0.0003	0.0004	0.691	−0.00012
SEX2	−0.1318	0.1891	0.697	−0.052
HEAD	0.3102	0.0060	1.325	0.123
SIZEE	0.0107	0.0060	1.767	0.004

$n = 70$
Log likelihood = −173.67

Wage employment was thus of limited importance in Masaka in the early 1990s, as indeed in other parts of Uganda (see Whyte, 1987), constrained by the collapse of the formal economy; business was a more important supplement to farming. Of those who entered employment, two contrasting patterns emerge: formal employment was mainly open to males with post-primary education, while farm and estate employment was the option open to those without education or other income sources.

Appendix Table B16: *Probit Estimate of Participation in Farm or Estate Employment*

Variable	Parameter Estimate	Standard Error	t-value	Marginal Effect
Intercept	3.8999	1.0565	3.691	
ED1	−0.2996	0.2263	1.178	−0.119
ED2	−0.8766	0.3371	2.600	−0.349
ED3	−0.2668	0.4381	0.609	−0.106
AGE	−0.0392	0.0396	0.940	−0.012
AGE2	0.0005	0.0005	1.053	0.00021
SEX2	−0.9097	0.2177	4.179	−0.362
HEAD	−0.4769	0.2531	1.884	−0.190
SIZEE	0.0529	0.0311	1.699	0.021

$n = 40$
Log likelihood=−127.79

6. The Efficiency of Labour Allocation

We found the return to labour in agriculture to be only 21 Ushs per hour, whereas the combined return to assets (mainly land) and labour was 116 Ushs per hour worked. In business, the combined return averaged 178 Ushs. (It was not possible to impute the return to labour in business separately.) The average return to labour in formal employment was 73 Ushs per hour, that is considerably higher than the return to labour in agriculture; this gap was not unexpected, since formal employees possessed substantially more human capital than the rest of the labour force, and there were restrictions on access to formal jobs. The average return to work on other people's farms or estates was as high as 173 Ushs per hour, which seems surprisingly high, perhaps partly explained by the seasonality of farm employment and partly by the existence of non-wage benefits in formal employment.[10] There may also have been a certain status connected to formal-sector jobs, or an expectation that they would pay better in the long run (see for instance Oberschall, 1969).

The persistence of the gap between wages in other agricultural employment and returns to labour on one's own farm is more difficult to explain; there were no administratively set minimum wages that could account for this gap. Part of the disparity could be attributed to the undervaluation of subsistence production, but there were also indications that other farm and estate jobs were unattractive. The work was often hard, offered few possibilities for extra income, and working for your fellow peasant as a labourer might have been considered degrading. Farm labourers were often from other parts of the country, and high wages were required to attract them in sufficient numbers.

7. Changes Under Early Adjustment 1985–90

In 1986 the NRM took power in Kampala with the goal of bringing about 'a fundamental change' in the country. The rural sector seemed to be the new rulers' natural constituency (Museveni, 1986), agriculture was emphasised. The reforms after the departure of Idi Amin had included a strong shift in relative prices in favour of cash crops, particularly coffee: from 1980 to 1986 the price of coffee relative to domestic manufacturing had increased over 500 per cent, and twice that in relation to non-tradables. However, despite the NRM's emphasis on agriculture this trend reversed. Coffee prices slumped in the second half of the 1980s, while the government was hard pressed for revenue and fell back on the time-honoured method of squeezing cash crop producers; relative to domestic manufacturing the price of coffee fell by more than 50 per cent. Since food prices essentially kept pace with general inflation during this time, there was a dramatic shift of relative prices in favour of food crops, which hampered growth in coffee production: there was practically no investment in new coffee trees. The most notable improvement in terms of income generation since 1986 were in the urban areas; rural dwellers only benefited indirectly as suppliers of food and, to some extent, labour.

To capture the impacts in Masaka of the regime shift, we asked respondents how their holdings of land, livestock and houses changed between 1985 and 1990. Land is a key asset in the rural sector, and 51 land transactions, involving about a quarter of the sample households, were recorded between 1985 and 1990. Crop sales were the main source of finance for 30 per cent of the households, whereas 40 per cent named 'business'. Wages, loans, and land sales were about 10 per cent each. About a quarter of transactions, and most of those who sold land, said they wanted cash for their children's school fees. New home constructions and improvements to dwellings were spread fairly evenly across quintiles, though the richest quintiles spent 5 times more (an average of 2.3 million Ushs) than the poorest.

Respondents were also asked to provide information on children and spouses who had left the household, and their current area of residence. From the dates of departure and the ages of the relatives, we may infer some of the push and pull factors before and after 1985. The sample households had a total of 422 spouses and children living 'elsewhere', while slightly more than half had 'migrated' before 1986. Of those, almost 70 per cent had remained in the countryside, with the rest moving to Masaka town or Kampala. Of the group that migrated during the first 5 years of the NRM, over 40 per cent opted for Masaka or Kampala; the attractiveness of urban life had evidently increased. However, data collected from respondents on migrated members suggested that their earnings were not high; perhaps the increase in the share of migrants going to urban areas after 1985 was due to increases in informal sector activities, rather than to sharp increases in wages (or in wage-employment opportunities).

We also asked respondents to name an aspect of social infrastructure in which they had noted the most improvement since 1985, and one in which they would most wish for improvements. Over 30 per cent of the respondents saw the return of peace as the most notable improvement in their well-being since 1986. The government had emphasised rehabilitation of major trunk roads, and roads were singled out by about half the respondents as having shown the most improvement, despite the fact that rural feeder roads have not been improved and were easily flooded during the rainy season. Less than 20 per cent mentioned improvement in the supply of medical and educational services, while two thirds desired improvement. Less than 10 per cent thought further road improvement to be a priority, whereas 30 per cent wanted improvement in local administration, especially streamlining of the functions of the resistance councils (RCs).

8. Summary and Conclusions

Livelihood in rural Masaka is very much attached to food production. Indeed, most quintiles reported most income as subsistence consumption, although the pattern was more variable by age of household head and size of holding. Households seem to have been well endowed with food supplies, producing a variety of crops and keeping substantial numbers of animals on holdings that were generally not desperately small. Food storage and processing techniques were still rudimentary, and the weak rural transport network made access to markets difficult, so in spite of the adverse circumstances in the coffee sector, coffee was still thought to be the best source of cash income. Its prominent place as the source of prosperity at the time of independence seemed long lost, however (Kajubi, 1965).

The next biggest source of income was business. In the cash-starved rural environment, business was weak; yet even the modest demand for modern-sector goods provided opportunities for intermediation. Youthful households were more apt than older ones to be engaged in business, perhaps because they were less risk averse or simply less attached to the soil; they also had less access to land than older households. Formal employment played a minor role in the dynamics of rural income generation, in contrast with Kampala, where a formal-sector job was a source of useful contacts that could be transformed into informal business deals.

The endowments of the household, such as land and human capital, had an impact on the pattern of income generation; it was necessary to possess a large tract of land to belong to the richest groups in the countryside. It was not necessary, to have an education in order to generate high income in the rural sector, however. Thus, one of the adverse effects of economic decline was the decoupling of education from technical innovation and income generation in the countryside, probably the result of decreased contacts with the urban areas.[11] Agricultural production was the biggest source of income for the richest households in Masaka. The position of the household along the life-cycle (proxied by the age of the head) was also crucial for its response to shocks. Business incomes fell as households became older, the opposite of farm income. Other things equal, a free-wheeling business atmosphere thus benefited young households, while improved marketing of food crops boosted older ones.

We analysed how rural smallholders in Masaka responded to the years of economic decline and early adjustment in Uganda. The long period of decline resulted in a weakening of the rural-urban link. Not only did the flow of remittances from urban relatives slow down, but the supply of urban goods and services diminished markedly as well. It has been argued by some that this delinking forced peasants to find survival strategies independent of the government, making them less vulnerable to external shocks and the *de facto* urban taxation of cash-crop production, and thus that the economic decline at the national level was something of a blessing at the rural level.

We argue instead that the lack of functioning markets and reliable information and increased risk raised the constraints on rural households and reduced their capacity to respond to the decline. Whereas a market for goods and services enabled Kampala dwellers to engage in the informal sector, rural households mainly resorted to subsistence production. Due to the fertility of the land, people in Masaka produced enough food to survive, but the households also needed cash incomes for a variety of purposes. For example, both education and health services were heavy financial burdens. On average households reported spending 30 per cent of their income on these services and many households had children not going to school for lack of fees. Because of negative relative price shifts and corrupt marketing organisations the traditional role of coffee as income-generator was partly taken over by food crops. Apart from the desire to achieve an income maximising allocation of labour. The need for cash was also a stimulus for undertaking wage employment and business activities.

Labour returns were lowest on the family farm, higher in business and formal wage-employment, but highest in farm and estate employment. The gap between business and formal wage incomes, on the one hand, and own-farm returns on the other, could be rationalised on the basis of the better physical stamina and higher education of those engaged in the former. There are also barriers keeping people out of formal employment, at least. Correcting for these factors might eliminate the disparity between the returns to raw labour. However, work on other people's farms and estates is hard, tightly supervised, and possibly also socially degrading. Farmers mentioned in interviews that they found it difficult to recruit labour, despite the high wages which they also complained about.

Formal schooling did not contribute significantly to agricultural productivity; to raise subsistence crops, traditional knowledge was sufficient. Lack of education was not a barrier to entry in business either; only in formal wage-employment, which generates but a small share of total rural income, was education important. One of the far-reaching impacts of the crisis thus seems to have been the reduction of the role of education in income generation. Since education is important for productivity in a modernising agricultural environment, educational investment is still essential for long-run agricultural growth once such an environment is recreated.

Notes

1. There is little intercropping between coffee (or bananas) and other crops in Uganda.
2. See for instance Whyte (1987) for an interesting account of rural response in eastern Uganda.
3. Delays of more than a year were common before the recent liberalisation measures.
4. See Singh *et al.* (1986) for an extended discussion of smallholder modelling.
5. The islands have only one per cent of the population and were excluded for logistical reasons.
6. The interviews were carried out by students from Makerere University, with university lecturers as supervisors. They checked the questionnaires every evening, and also made random checks on the interviewers in the field.
7. A child under 15 was assumed equivalent to 0.5 of an adult. The use of income per adult-equivalent rather than per capita did not substantially influence the relative incomes of the quintiles; it reduced the relative welfare level of quintiles 1 and 5 slightly. It would have been desirable to have a welfare index which corresponded more closely to long-run utility. Anand and Harris (1990) suggested per capita food expenditure, but unfortunately we did not collect expenditure data. We experimented with subsistence production per capita and per adult-equivalent as proxies for expenditure, but the results were poor.
8. For all unsold and domestically consumed products we imputed a value of two thirds the average price in the nearest market. The reason for valuing own consumption at less than the full price is that the latter includes a marketing margin; it was not possible to measure this empirically, but a third of the market price seemed reasonable. The results are not very sensitive to this choice, however. Average total income would have been 12 per cent higher if the subsistence component had been valued at the full market price. Since subsistence food consumption increases very strongly with income, the distribution of income would also have been more skewed in favour of the rich if consumption had been

multiplied by a factor larger than two thirds, and the reverse for a smaller factor. The valuation of subsistence output was also problematic due to the varying access to market of various regions, some extremely remote. For example, a bunch of bananas in Bukoto, close to Masaka town and the main routes to Kampala, had a high market value and consequently received a high imputed subsistence value; the same bunch would have had a much lower value in some remote part of Bukomansimbi. To estimate the local price we used the price and marketing channels information given by the respondents in the villages.

9. In the past, however, rural wage employment, however menial, was a source of social prestige; it provided a permanent cash income enabling individuals to expand into business, or acquire another wife (Hayley, 1940).

10. A position in the formal-sector network might have provided a basis for both legal and semi-legal side activities; see Appendix A.

11. In a study of rural-urban linkages in Kutus, Kirinyaga District, Kenya, Evans (1992) found a mutually reinforcing pattern of linkages between town and hinterland that spurs the growth of both agriculture and non-farm activities; he also noted that as households diversified into other activities outside the farm, their income started to rise, whereas households that relied most on agriculture for income generation were also the poorest.

Appendix B1: Sample Counties, Parishes and Villages, Masaka District (Rural)

County	Sub-county	Parish (RC II)	Village (RC I)
Bukoto	Kaswa	Bisanje	Kingo
		Kabonera	Kindulwe
		Kabonera	Kyakayinda

cont ...

Appendix B1 cont ...

County	Sub-county	Parish (RC II)	Village (RC I)
Bukoto	Lwengo	Nakyenyi	Kafuzi
		Nakyenyi	Lwensinga
		Kito	—
		Mbirizzi	Trading centre
		Kyawaggonya	—
	Kisekka	Kinoni	Western zone
		Nakateete	—
	Buwunga	Kanywa	Kanamusabala
		Kanywa	Bukeli
	Kyanamukaka	Kyantale	Kagologolo
		Kyantale	Kamungu
		Buyinja	—
Kalungu	Kalungu	Kalungu	—
		Bwasandeku	Kawule
		Bwasandeku	Seeta
		Nabutongwa	—
	Mukungwe	Bugabira	Ndegeya
Bukomasimbi	Kibinge	Kiryasaaka	Kyankoole
	Butenga	Kawoko	Kiwenjula
		Kisagazi	Ntuma
		Kisagazi	Mbulire
Mawogoola	Mateete	Manyama	—
		Kayunga	Katimba
		Kayunga	Muguluka

Note: in comparison with Kampala, it was not always possible to get a complete list of all the villages (RC1s) in a parish (RC2) in rural Masaka. In all such cases, we avoided the related boundary problems by sampling at the parish level.

References

Adam, C., A. Bigsten, P. Collier, E. Julin and S. O´Connell (1994a) *Evaluation of Swedish Development Cooperation with Tanzania,* SASDA, DS 1994:113, Ministry of Foreign Affairs, Stockholm.

Adam, C. P.Ă. Andersson, A. Bigsten, P. Collier and S. O'Connell (1994b) *Evaluation of Swedish Development Cooperation with Zambia,* SASDA, DS 1994:114, Ministry of Foreign Affairs, Stockholm.

Adyanget, N. (1994) 'Brewing Booms in City Suburbs', in *The New Vision,* 5 January, Kampala.

Agrawal, N., Z. Ahmed, M. Mered and R. Nord (1993) 'Structural Adjustment, Economic Performance, and Aid Dependency in Tanzania', Policy Research Working Paper Series, No.1204, World Bank.

Agricultural Policy Committee (1989) *Proceedings and Recommendations of the Workshop on Land Tenure, Resource Management and Conservation Studies, Jinja 1989,* Ministry of Planning and Economic Development, Kampala.

Anand, S. and C. Harris (1990) 'Food and Standard of Living: an Analysis based on Sri Lankan Data', in J. Drèze and A. Sen (eds) *The Political Economy of Hunger,* Oxford: Clarendon Press. Oxford.

Anas, A. and K.S. Lee (1992) 'Costs of Deficient Infrastructure: the Case of Nigerian Manufacturing', *Urban Studies,* 29 (7).

Appleton, S. *et al.* (1995) 'Gender Differences in the Returns to Schooling in Three African Countries', *Working Paper* No. 83 Centro Studi Luca D'Agliano, Oxford: Queen Elizabeth House.

Appleton, S. and A. Balihuta (1996) 'Education and Agricultural Productivity: Evidence from Uganda', *Journal of International Development,* 8 (3).

Appleton, S. and J. Mackinnon (1995) 'Status of Poverty in Uganda', mimeo, EPRC, Kampala.

Azam, J-P., D. Bevan, P. Collier, S. Dercon and J.W. Gunning (1994) 'Some Economic Consequences of the Transition from Civil War to Peace', mimeo, Centre for the Study of African Economies, Oxford University.

Bank of Uganda (1970) *Banking in Uganda,* Kampala.

– (1986) *Annual Report 1985,* Kampala.

218

- (1988) 'Review of the Operation and Strategy of Uganda's OGL System of Importation', mimeo, Research Department, Kampala.
- (1991) *Economic Report 1986–1991*, Kampala.
- (various issues) *Quarterly Economic Report*, Kampala.

Banugire, F. (1989) 'Employment, Incomes, Basic Needs and Structural Adjustment Policy in Uganda 1980–87', in Onimode (ed.) *The IMF, the World Bank and the African Debt*, London and New Jersey: Zed Books.

Batarirana, J.J. (1981) 'The Measurement of Time Spent by Women on Farm and Non-farm Activities in Nyakagyeme Sub-County, Rukungiri District', Project Paper, Faculty of Agriculture and Forestry, Makerere University.

Berkeley, S. (1988) 'Uganda Primary Health Care Review, 1987', *Health Information Quarterly* (Entebbe), 4 (4).

Bevan, D., A. Bigsten, P. Collier and J. W. Gunning (1988) 'Incomes in the United Republic of Tanzania During the 'Nyerere Experiment'', in W. van Ginneken (ed.) *Trends in Employment and Labour Incomes. Case Studies of Developing Countries*, Geneva: ILO.

Bevan, D., P. Collier and J.W. Gunning, with A. Bigsten and P. Horsnell, (1989) *Peasants and Governments: an Economic Analysis*, Oxford: Clarendon Press.

- (1990) *Controlled Open Economies: a Neoclassical Approach to Structuralism*, Oxford: Clarendon Press.

Bigsten, A. (1984) *Education and Income Determination in Kenya*, Aldershot: Gower Press.

- (1993) 'Regulation versus Price Reforms in Crisis Management: the Case of Kenya', in M. Blomström and M. Lundahl (eds) *Economic Crisis in Africa. Perspectives on Policy Responses*, London: Routledge.

Bigsten, A., R. Aguilar, L. Hjalmarsson, G. Ikiara, A. Isaksson, P. Kimuyu, M. Manundu, W. Masai, N. Ndungu, S. Kayizzi-Mugerwa, H. Semboja and C. Wihlborg (1994) *Limitations and Rewards in Kenya's Manufacturing Sector: a Study of Enterprise Development*, Report to the World Bank, Washington DC.

Bigsten, A. and P. Collier (1995) 'Linkages from Agricultural Growth in Kenya', in J.W. Mellor (ed.) *Agriculture on the Road to Industrialisation*, Baltimore: Johns Hopkins University Press.

Bigsten, A. and S. Kayizzi-Mugerwa (1992) 'Adaption and Distress in the Urban Economy: a Study of Kampala Households', *World Development*, 20 (10).

- (1993) 'Macroeconomic Adjustment and Trade Liberalisation in Kenya, Uganda, and Zambia', in G. Hansson (ed.) *International Trade and Economic Development*, London: Routledge.
- (1995) 'Rural Sector Responses to Economic Crisis in Uganda', *Journal of International Development*, April.

Blundell, R., J. Hay and C. Meghir (1987) 'Unemployment and Female Labour Supply', *Economic Journal*, 97 (Supplement).

Brett, E.A. (1989) 'Political Reconstruction and the Agrarian Problem in Uganda: Policy Management and Organisational Restructuring', mimeo, Institute of Development Studies, Brighton.
- (1993) *Providing for the Rural Poor, Institutional Decay and Transformation in Uganda*, Kampala: Fountain Publishers.
- (1994) 'Rebuilding Organisation Capacity in Uganda Under the National Resistance Movement', *Journal of Modern African Studies*, 32 (1).
- (1995) 'Neutralising the Use of Force in Uganda: the Role of the Military in Politics', *Journal of Modern African Studies*, 33 (1).

Bunker, G.S. (1991) *Peasants Against the State: the Politics of Market Control in Bugisu, Uganda, 1900–83*, Chicago and London: University of Chicago Press.

Campbell, H. (1979) 'The Commandist State in Uganda', PhD Dissertation, Sussex University, Brighton.

Calvo, G.A. and C.A. Veigh (1992) 'Inflation, Stabilisation and Nominal Anchors', *IMF Paper on Policy Analysis and Assessment*, No. 4.

Chew, D.C.E. (1990) 'Internal Adjustments to Falling Civil Service Salaries: Insights from Uganda', *World Development*, 18 (7).

Ciantia, P. (1989) 'Report on Nutrition Survey in Kitgum District September, 1988', *Health Information Quarterly* (Entebbe) 5 (1, 2).

Collier, P. (1994) 'Economic Aspects of the Ugandan Transition to Peace', in J.P. Azam, D. Bevan, P. Collier, S. Dercon and J.W. Gunning (eds) 'Some Economic Consequences of the Transition from Civil War to Peace', mimeo, Centre for the Study of African Economies, Oxford University.
- (1995) 'The Marginalisation of Africa', *International Labour Review*, 134 (4–5).

Collier, P. and D. Lal (1986) *Labour and Poverty in Kenya 1900–1980*, Oxford: Clarendon Press.

Collier, P. and J.W. Gunning (1991) 'Trade Liberalisation and the Composition of Investment: Theory and African Applications', May.

– (1995) 'War, Peace and Private Portfolios', *World Development*, 23 (2).

Collins, C. and A. Green (1994) 'Decentralisation and Primary Health Care: Some Negative Implications in Developing Countries', *International Journal of Health Services*, 24 (3).

Commonwealth Secretariat (1979) *The Rehabilitation of the Economy of Uganda: a Report by a Commonwealth Team*, 2 Vols, London.

Cornia, G.A. (1987) 'Adjustment at the Household Level: Potentials and Limitations of Survival Strategies', in G.A. Cornia, R. Jolly, and F. Stewart (eds) *Adjustment with a Human Face: Protecting the Vulnerable and Promoting Growth*, Oxford: Oxford University Press.

Cragg, J.G. (1971) 'Some Statistical Models for Limited Dependent Variables with Applications to the demand for Durable Goods', *Econometrica*, 39 (5).

Dercon, S. (1993) 'Supply Response and Macroeconomic Policies: Cotton in Tanzania', *Journal of African Economies*, 2 (2).

Dornbusch, R. (1991) 'Credibility and Stabilisation', *Quarterly Journal of Economics*, 106.

The East African, various issues

Edwards, S. (1984) 'Coffee, Money and Inflation in Colombia', *World Development*, 12 (11–12).

Elbadawi, I.A. (1990) 'Inflationary Process, Stabilisation and the Role of Public Expenditure in Uganda', mimeo, Macroeconomic Adjustment and Growth Division, World Bank.

Elliott, C. (1973) 'Employment and Income Distribution in Uganda', Development Studies Discussion Paper, No. 1, University of East Anglia, Norwich.

Evans, A. (1994) 'Growth and Poverty Reduction in Uganda', in Poverty Reduction and Development Cooperation, *Report from a Conference in Copenhagen 23–25 February, 1994*, Center for Development Research, June.

Evans, E.H. (1992) 'A Virtous Circle Model of Rural-Urban Development: Evidence from Kenya', *Journal of Development Studies*, 28 (4).

Fuller, B. (1989) 'Eroding Economy and Declining School Quality: the Case of Malawi', *IDS Bulletin*, 20 (1).

Flood, L. (1988) 'Measurement and Estimation of Male Labour Supply', Working Paper, Department of Economics, University of Göteborg.

Gertzel, C. (1990) 'Uganda's Continuing Search for Peace', *Current History*, May.

Gibson, B. (1991) 'The Inflation-Devaluation-Inflation Hypothesis in Nicaragua', *Journal of Development Studies*, 27 (2).

Gilson, L. (1995) 'Management and Health Care Reform in Sub-Saharan Africa', *Social Science and Medicine*, 40 (5).

Gilson, L. *et al.* (1993) 'Prescribing Practices: a Tanzanian Study', *International Journal of Health Planning Management*, 8 (37).

Goetz, S.J. (1992) 'Economics of Scope and the Cash Crop-Food Crop Debate in Senegal', *World Development*, 20 (5).

Green, R. (1981) 'Magendo in the Political Economy of Uganda: Pathology, Parallel System or Dominant Sub-Mode of Production?', *Discussion Paper* No. 115, Institute of Development Studies, University of Sussex, Brighton.

Greenstone, J.D. (1966) 'Corruption and Self-Interest in Kampala and Nairobi: A comment on Local Politics in East Africa', *Comparative Studies in Society and History*, 8 (2).

Haggblade, S., P. Hazzel and J. Brown (1989) 'Farm Non-farm Linkages in Rural Sub-Saharan Africa', *World Development*, 17 (8).

Hansen, H.B. and M. Twaddle (eds) (1988) *Uganda Now*, Eastern African Studies, Kenya: Heinemann, Athens: Ohio University Press, and London: James Currey.

- (1991) *Changing Uganda: the Dilemmas of Structural Adjustment and Revolutionary Change*, Kenya: Heinemann, Athens: Ohio University Press, and London: James Currey.

- (1994) *From Chaos to Order*, Kampala: Fountain Publishers, and London: James Currey.

Harvey, C. (1992) 'The Role of Commercial Banks in the Recovery from Economic Disaster in Ghana, Tanzania, Uganda and Zambia', presented at a conference *From Stabilisation to Growth*, Marstrand, Sweden.

Hayley, T.T.S. (1940) 'Wage Employment and the Desire for Wives Among the Lango', *Uganda Journal*, 8.

Hazari, R.B. and P.M. Sgro (1991) 'Urban-rural Structural Adjustment, Urban Unemployment with Traded and Non-traded Goods', *Journal of Development Economics*, 35 (1).

Helleiner, G.K. (1981) 'Economic Collapse and Rehabilitation in Uganda', *Rural Africana*, 11 (Fall).

Henstridge, N.M. (1994a) 'Stabilisation and Structural Adjustment in Uganda: 1987–90', in W. Van der Geest (ed.) *Negotiating Structural Adjustment in Africa*, London: James Currey and Portsmouth: Heinemann.

– (1994b) 'Does Money Cause Prices?', Memorandum, Ministry of Finance and Economic Planning, Kampala.

– (1995) *Coffee and Money in Uganda: an Econometric Analysis*, PhD Thesis, Exeter College, Oxford University.

Herbert, J.R. (1987) 'Nutrition in Uganda', *Health Information Quarterly* (Entebbe) 3 (2).

Heyneman, S.P. (1979) 'Why Impoverished Children do Well in Ugandan Schools', World Bank Reprint Series, No. 111, World Bank.

Hoppers, W. (1989) 'The Responses from the Grassroots: Self-reliance in Zambian Education', *IDS Bulletin*, 20 (1).

House, W.J. (1991) 'The Nature and Determinants of Socioeconomic Inequality among Peasant Households in Southern Sudan', *World Development*, 19 (7).

Huber, J.H. (1993) 'Ensuring Access to Health Care With the Introduction of User Fees: a Kenyan Example', *Social Science and Medicine*, 36 (4).

ILO (1995) *Employment Generation and Poverty Reduction in Uganda, Report of an ILO/UNDP Employment Advisory Mission*, Eastern Africa Multidisciplinary Team, Addis Ababa.

IMF (various years) *International Financial Statistics*, Washington DC.

Ingham, K. (1994) *Obote: a Political Biography*, London: Routledge.

Jamal, V. (1976) 'Asians in Uganda, 1880–1972: Inequality and Expulsion', *Economic History Review*, 19 (4).

– (1987) 'Ugandan Economic Crisis: Dimensions and Cure', in Wiebe and Dodge (eds).

– (1988) 'Coping Under Crisis in Uganda', *International Labour Review*, 127 (65).

Jamal, V. and J. Weeks (1993) *Africa Misunderstood*, Macmillan Series of ILO Studies, London: Macmillan.

Jitta, J., M. Migadde and J. Mudusu (1992) *Determinants of Malnutrition in Under-Fives in Uganda: an Indepth Secondary Analysis of the Uganda DHS (1988/89) Data,* Child Health and Development Centre, Makerere University, Kampala.

Kabwegyere, T.B. (1974) *The Politics of State Formation,* Nairobi: East Africa Literature Bureau.

Kaheru, Z. (1990) 'Health Cost Sharing Policy', Policy Paper, Ministry of Health, Entebbe.

Kajubi, W.S. (1965) 'Coffee and Prosperity in Buganda: Some Aspects of Economic and Social Change', *Uganda Journal,* 29 (2).

Kanbur, R. (1995) 'Welfare Economics, Political Economy and Policy Reform in Ghana', *African Development Review,* 7 (1).

Kapoor, K. (1995) 'Restructuring Uganda's Debt. The Commercial Debt Buy-Back Operation', Policy Research Working Paper No. 1409, Washington DC: World Bank.

Kasekende, L. and G. Ssemogerere (1994) 'Exchange Rate Unification and Economic Development: the Case of Uganda, 1987–92', *World Development,* 22 (8).

Kasekende, L. and M.T. Malik (1993) 'An Interbank Foreign Exchange System for Uganda?', draft for discussion, Bank of Uganda, February.

Kasfir, N. (1983) 'State, Magendo and Class Formation in Uganda', *Journal of Comparative and Commonwealth Politics,* November.

Katabira, E.T. (1988) 'Looking After Aids Patients', *Health Information Quarterly* (Entebbe) 4 (4).

Katumba, A.B. (1988) 'The State of the Industrial Sector — 1984', Occasional Paper, No. 6, Makerere Institute of Social Research.

Kayizzi-Mugerwa, S. (1989) 'Economic Recovery Credit II: Report to SIDA on the Work of the World Bank's Pre-Appraisal Mission to Uganda, 13 February – 4 March, 1989', mimeo, Department of Economics, University of Göteborg.

– (1990) 'Corruption, Rent-seeking and Economic Adjustment', mimeo, Department of Economics, University of Göteborg.

– (1993) 'Urban Bustle/Rural Slumber: Dilemmas of Uneven Economic Recovery in Uganda', in M. Blomström and M. Lundahl (eds) *Economic Crisis in Africa, Perspectives on Policy Responses,* London: Routledge.

– (1994) 'Uganda: Stabilisation at Last? Analysis of an Aid-led Recovery', *Macroeconomic Studies,* 49, Stockholm:Sida.

– (1995a) 'Income Diversification Under Pressure: the Case of the Gambia', mimeo, Research and Development Policy Department, African Development Bank, Abidjan.

– (1995b) Chapter 7 in *African Development Report 1995,* African Development Bank, Abidjan.

Kayizzi-Mugerwa, S. and A. Bigsten (1992) 'On Structural Adjustment in Uganda', *Canadian Journal of Development Studies,* June.

Kigozi, J. (1995) in *The East African,* October 9–15.

Kikafunda, J., L. Serunjogi and M. Migadde (1992) 'Final Report on the Establishment of an Absolute Poverty Line for Uganda', mimeo, PAPSCA, Ministry of Finance and Economic Planning, Kampala.

Killick, T. and S. Commander (1988) 'State Divesture as a Policy Instrument in Developing Countries', *World Development,* 16 (12).

King, K., C. Aboudha (1991) 'The Building of an Industrial Society. Change and Development in Kenya's Industrial Sector 1970–1990, Occassional Paper, No. 30, Centre of African Studies, Edinburgh University, Edinburgh.

Knight, J.B. (1967) 'The Determinants of Wages and Salaries in Uganda', *Bulletin of Oxford University Institute of Economics and Statistics,* 29 (3).

Knight, J. and R. Sabot (1990) *Education, Productivity and Inequality: the East African Natural Experiment,* Oxford: Oxford University Press.

Lockheed, M., D. Jamison and L. Lau (1980) 'Farmer Education and Farm Efficiency: a Survey', *Economic Development and Cultural Change,* 29 (1).

Loxley, J. (1989) 'The IMF, the World Bank and Reconstruction in Uganda', in B. Campbell and J. Loxley (eds) *Structural Adjustment in Africa,* London: Macmillan.

Lufumpa, C.L. (1995) 'Nature and Magnitude of Poverty in Uganda', Environment and Social Policy Working Paper Series No. 11, African Development Bank, Abidjan

Lwanga-Ntale, C. (1995) 'Poverty in Selected Districts of Uganda', presented at a World Bank Workshop, Kampala, December.

Macrae, J., A. Zwi and H. Birungi (1995) 'A Healthy Peace? Rehabilitation and Development of the Health-Sector in the 'Post-conflict Situation. The Case of Uganda', London School of Hygiene and Tropical Medicine, *Conflict and Health Services,* 1.

Mackinnon, J. (1995) 'Health as an Informational Good: the Determinants of Child Health Nutrition and Mortality During Political and Economic Recovery in Uganda', WPS/95.9, Oxford: Centre for the Study of African Economies.

Malik, P. (1995) 'The Central Bank, the Treasury and Monetary Autonomy — The Experience of Uganda', Annex 3.1, *African Development Report 1995*, African Development Bank, Abidjan.

Maliyamkono, T.L., M.S.D. Bagachwa (1990) *The Second Economy in Tanzania*, Kenya: Heinemann, Athens: Ohio University Press, and London: James Currey.

Mamdani, M. (1976) *Politics and Class Formation in Uganda*, London: Heinemann.

– (1988) *NRA/NRM: Two Years in Power*, text of public lecture, Makerere University, Kampala: Progressive Publishing House.

– (1992) 'Uganda, Contradictions of the IMF Programme and Perspective', *Development and Change*, 33 (2).

– (1993) 'The Uganda Asian Expulsion, Twenty Years After', *Economic and Political Weekly*, January.

Martin, M. (1994) 'A Sustainable Proposal for Reducing the Burden of Uganda's Multilateral Debt', mimeo, London.

Maxwell, D.G. (1995) 'Alternative Food Security Strategy: a Household Analysis of Urban Agriculture in Kampala', *World Development*, 23 (10).

Maxwell, D.G. and S. Zziwa (1990) *Urban Agriculture: a Case Study of Kampala*, Makerere Institute of Social Research, Kampala.

Mayanja-Nkangi, J. (1994) 'Country Economic Review — Uganda', presented at a DANIDA Conference on Structural Adjustment, Harare, November.

Mazrui, A. (1975) *Soldiers and Kinsmen in Uganda: the Making of a Military Ethnocracy*, Beverly Hills and London: Sage Publications.

– (1991) 'Privatisation versus Market: Cultural Contradictions in Structural Adjustment', in H.B. Hansen and M. Twaddle (eds) *Changing Uganda: the Dilemmas of Structural Adjustment and Revolutionary Change*, Kenya: Heinemann, Athens: Ohio University Press, and London: James Currey.

Mbire, B. and J. Mackinnon (1993) 'Modelling Money Demand in Uganda', mimeo, Centre for the Study of the African Economies, University of Oxford.

Meagher, K. (1990) 'The Hidden Economy: Informal and Parallel Trade in Northwestern Uganda', *Review of African Political Economy*, 47.

Mohammed, N. (1996) 'Military Expenditures in Africa: a Statistical Compendium', mimeo, Development Research and Policy Department, African Development Bank, Abidjan.

Morris, S. (1989) 'Macroeconomic Features of the Ugandan Economy and Some Policy Implications', mimeo, Ministry of Planning and Economic Development, Kampala.

Mudoola, D. (1988a) 'Political Transitions since Idi Amin: a Study in Political Pathology', in H.B. Hansen and M. Twaddle (eds) *Uganda Now*, Eastern African Studies, Kenya: Heinemann, Athens: Ohio University Press, and London: James Currey.

– (1988b) 'Civil-Military Relations, the Case of Uganda', Occassional Paper, No. 5, Makerere Institute of Social Research.

– (1993) *Religion, Ethnicity and Politics in Uganda*, Kampala: Fountain Publishers.

Mulema, P. (1986) *Budget Speech*, Entebbe: Government Printer.

Murinde, V. (1993) 'Budgetary and Financial Policy Portency Amid Structural Bottlenecks: Evidence from Uganda', *World Development*, 21 (5).

Museveni, Y.K. (1986) *Selected Articles on the Uganda Resistance War*, Nairobi.

Mwaka, V.M., M. Mugyenyi and G. Banya (1994) 'Women in Uganda: a Profile, Draft Report', Department of Women's Studies, Makerere University.

Mwega, F. (1995) 'Towards Currency Convertibility: the Case of Kenya', Annex 3.2 to *The African Development Report 1995*, African Development Bank, Abidjan.

Nabuguzi, E. (1993) 'Peasant Responses to Economic Crisis in Uganda: Rice Farms in Busoga', *Review of African Political Economy*, No. 56.

Nelson, J.M. (1984) 'The Political Economy of Stabilisation: Commitment, Capacity, and Public Response', *World Development*, 12 (2).

New Vision Newspaper (various issues).

Nsibambi, A. (1976) 'The Politics of Education in Uganda', *Uganda Journal*, 38

Oberschall, A.R. (1969) 'Rising Expectations and Political Turmoil', *Journal of Development Studies*, 6 (1).

Obura, A. (1981) 'An Analysis of the Participation of Children in Productive Economic Activities in Apach District with Particular Emphasis on Oyam County', Project Paper, Faculty of Agriculture and Forestry, Makerere University.

Odaet, C.F. (1990) 'Implementing Education Policies in Uganda', World Bank Discussion Papers, 89, Washington DC.

Odeke, A. (1994) '$5m Nytil Sell-off Raises Controversy', *The New Vision*, 5 January.

Ofcansky, T.P. (1996) *Uganda: Tarnished Pearl of Africa*, Boulder Westview Press.

Okune, J.W. (not dated) 'Framework for PAPSCA Review and Possible Re-Design', mimeo, PAPSCA Secretariat, Kampala.

Opio-Odong, J.M.A. (1993) *Higher Education and Research in Uganda*, Nairobi: Acts Press, and Stockholm: SAREC.

Oundo, G.B. and T. Burton (1992) 'A Hungry Child Does not Learn: Factors Affecting the Feeding of Children in Primary School, Kiyeyi project Area, Tororo District', Report, Child Health Development Centre, Makerere University.

Pain, D.R. (1987) 'Acholi and Nubians: Economic Forces and Military Employment', in P.D. Wiebe and C.P. Dodge, *Beyond Crisis Development Issues in Uganda*, Kampala: Makerere Institute of Social Research, Kampala.

Pinckney, T.C. and P.K. Kimuyu (1994) 'Land Tenure Reform in East Africa: Good, Bad or Unimportant?', *Journal of African Economies*, 3 (1).

Planning Department, Ministry of Animal Industry and Fisheries (1988) *Agricultural Sector Survey 1984–87*, Kampala.

Robertson, A.F. and G.A. Hughes (1978) 'The Family Farm in Buganda', *Development and Change*, 9.

S.G. Warburg and Co. (1991) 'Inventory of Outstanding Medium-term Public Sector External Debt', June.

Saha, S.K. (1991) 'The Role of Industrialisation in the Development of Sub-Saharan Africa. A Critique of the World Bank's Approach', *Economic and Political Weekly*, November 30.

Sathyamurthy, T.V. (1986) *The Political Development of Uganda: 1900–1986*, Aldershot: Gower Publishing House.

Sentongo, J.A.P.M. (1979) *Budget Speech*, Entebbe: Government Printer.

Sharer, R.L., H.R. De Zoysa and C.A. McDonald (1995) 'Uganda: Adjustment with Growth 1987–94', Occasional Paper 121, International Monetary Fund.

Singh, I.J., L. Squire and J. Strauss (eds) (1986) *Agricultural Household Models: Extensions, Application and Policy*, Baltimore: Johns Hopkins University Press.

Ssemogerere, G, (1990) 'Structural Adjustment Programmes and the Coffee Sector in Uganda', Research Paper, No. 1, African Economic Research Consortium, Nairobi.

Stren, R.E. (1992) 'African Urban Research Since the Late 1980s: Responses to Poverty and Urban Growth', *Urban Studies*, 29 (3–4).

Swedish Technical Mission (1992) 'Recovery and Reform. Assistance to Uganda the Next Five Years', Final Report, Stockholm: Swedish International Development Authority.

Tindigarukayo, J.K. (1988) 'Uganda, 1979–85: Leadership in Transition', *Journal of Modern African Studies*, 21 (4).

Tripp, A.M. (1989) 'Women and Changing Urban Household Economy in Tanzania', *Journal of Modern African Studies*, 27 (4).

Tumusiime-Mutebile, E. (1990) 'A Critique of Professor Mamdani's 'Uganda, Contradictions of the IMF Programme and Perspective'', Discussion Paper 4, Ministry of Planning and Economic Development, Kampala.

Uganda (1964) *The Patterns of Income and Expenditure of Coffee Growers in Buganda 1962/63*, Statistics Division, Ministry of Planning and Economic Development, Kampala.

– (1965a) *Uganda 1964*, Kampala: Ministry of Information, Broadcasting and Tourism.

– (1965b) *Background to the Budget 1965–66*, Kampala: Ministry of Finance.

– (1965c) *Annual Report of the Agricultural Department*, Kampala: Ministry of Agriculture, Forestry and Cooperatives.

– (1966a) *Budget Speech*, Kampala: Ministry of Finance.

– (1966b) *Uganda's Second Five-Year Development Plan 1966–71*, Entebbe: Government Printer.

– (1966c) *Statistical Abstract 1965*, Kampala: Statistics Division, Ministry of Planning and Economic Development.

- (1967a) *Statistical Abstract, 1966*, Kampala: Statistics Division, Ministry of Planning and Economic Development.
- (1967b) *High Level Manpower Survey, 1967*, Kampala: Statistics Division, Ministry of Planning and Economic Development.
- (1969) *Budget Speech*, Kampala: Ministry of Finance.
- (1970) *His Excellency the President's Communication from the Chair of the National Assembly on 20th April, 1970*, Entebbe: Government Printer.
- (1971) *Budget Speech*, Kampala: Ministry of Finance.
- (1972a) *Budget Speech*, Kampala: Ministry of Finance.
- (1972b) *Uganda's Third Five-Year Development Plan 1971/72–1975/76*, Entebbe: Government Printer.
- (1972c) *Enumeration of Employees, June 1971*, Kampala: Statistics Division, Ministry of Planning and Economic Development.
- (1977) *The Action Programme*, Entebbe: President's Office.
- (1979a) *Economic and Social Policy of the Uganda National Liberation Front*, October.
- (1979b) *White Paper on the Report of the Commonwealth Team of Experts*, October.
- (1981a) *The Challenge of Recovery*, Communication from the Chair by A.M.Obote, Kampala.
- (1982a) *Budget Speech*, Kampala: Ministry of Finance.
- (1982b) *Background to the Budget 1982/83*, Kampala: Ministry of Finance.
- (1983) *Budget Speech*, Kampala: Ministry of Finance.
- (1986) Press Release, Kampala: Ministry of Finance, 27 May.
- (1987a) *Report of the Commission of Inquiry into the Local Government System in Uganda*, Entebbe: Government Printer.
- (1987b) *Budget Speech*, Kampala; Ministry of Finance.
- (1987c) *An Address by H.E. Hon Yoweri Kaguta Museveni*, 7 April, Entebbe: Government Printer.
- (1989a) *Manpower and Employment in Uganda*, Kampala: Ministry of Planning and Economic Development.
- (1989b) *Programme for the Alleviation of Poverty and the Social Costs of Adjustment (PAPSCA)* Kampala: Ministry of Planning and Economic Development.
- (1989c) *Uganda Health and Demographic Survey*, Entebbe: Ministry of Health.

- (1989d) *National Manpower Survey: Census of Civil Servants*, Kampala: Ministry of Planning and Economic Development.
- (1990a) *The Way Forward*, Kampala: Ministry of Planning and Economic Development.
- (1990b) *Household Budget Survey 1988–1989*, Entebbe: Statistics Department, Ministry of Planning and Economic Development.
- (1990c) *Statistical Bulletin No GDP/2, Gross Domestic Product of Uganda 1981–1989*, Ministry of Planning and Economic Development, July.
- (1990e) *Background to the Budget 1990/91*, Kampala: Ministry of Finance and Economic Planning.
- (1991) *Final results of the 1991 Population and Housing Census*, Kampala: Ministry of Finance and Economic Planning.
- (1992) *Background to the Budget 1992/93*, Kampala: Ministry of Finance and Economic Planning.
- (1993a) *Integrated Household Survey 1992–93*, Kampala: Ministry of Finance and Economic Planning.
- (1993b) *Report on the Integrated Household Survey 1992–93*, Vol. II Kampala: Ministry of Finance and Economic Planning.
- (1993c) *Background to the Budget 1993/94*, Kampala: Ministry of Finance and Economic Planning.
- (1994) *Decentralisation in Uganda: the Policy and its Implications*, Kampala: Decentralisation Secretariat.
- (1995a) *Budget Speech*, Kampala: Ministry of Finance and Economic Planning.
- (1995b) *Background to the Budget 1995/96*, Kampala: Ministry of Finance and Economic Planning.
- (1996a) *Background to the Budget 1996/97*, Kampala: Ministry of Finance and Economic Planning.
- (1996b) *Statistical Abstract 1996*, Entebbe: Statistics Department, Ministry of Finance and Economic Planning.
- (various years) *Quarterly Economic and Statistical Bulletin*, Kampala: Statistics Division, Ministry of Planning and Economic Development.
- (various years) *Background to the Budget*, Kampala: Ministry of Planning and Economic Development.
- (various years) *Key Economic Indicators*, Kampala: Ministry of Planning and Economic Development.

Uganda Cooperative Alliance Limited (1989) *Agricultural Cost of Production and Price Survey*, Kampala.

Uganda Commercial Bank (various years) *Quarterly Economic Review*, Kampala.

Uganda Constitutional Commission (1991) *Guidelines on Constitutional Issues*, Kisubi, Kampala: Marianum Press.

Uganda National Council for Children (1994) *The State of Ugandan Children in 1994*, Kampala.

Uganda Protectorate (1952) *The Distribution and Price of Goods Ordinance*, Entebbe: Government Printer.

– (1961) *Lipoota y'Akakiiko Akabuuliriza eby'Entabagana Wakati w'Ebitundu bya Uganda* (Report of the Uganda Relations Committee) Entebbe: Government Printer.

– (1962) *Report of the Committee on Wages and Conditions of Service of Government Unestablished Employees*, Entebbe: Government Printer.

Uganda Manufacturers Association (1996) *Uganda International Trade Fair Catalogue 96*, Kampala, UMA.

UNICEF (1989) *Children and Women in Uganda — A Situation Analysis*, Kampala: UNICEF.

– (1994) *Children and Women in Uganda — A Situation Analysis*, Kampala: UNICEF.

United Nations (1993) *Report on Social Conditions*, New York.

United Nations Secretariat (1995) *Population Newsletter*, 59 (June).

Van der Geest, W. (1994) *Negotiating Structural Adjustment in Africa*, London: James Currey, and Portsmouth: Heinemann.

Van der Heijden, T. and J. Jitta (1993) *Economic Survival Strategies of Health Workers in Uganda*, Study Report, Child Health and Development Centre, Makerere University, Kampala.

Van der Willigen, T.A. (1986) 'Cash Crop Production and the Balance of Trade in a Less Developed Economy: a Model of Temporary Equilibrium with Rationing', *Oxford Economic Papers*, 38 (3).

Vandermoortele, J. (1993) 'Labour Market Informalisation in Sub-Saharan Africa', in G. Standing and V. Torkman (eds) *Towards Social Adjustment: Labour Market Issues in Structural Adjustment*, Geneva: International Labour Organisation.

Wade, R. (1985) 'The Market for Public Office: Why the Indian State is not Better at Development', *World Development*, 13 (4).

Weekly Topic (various issues).

Whyte, M.A. (1987) 'Crisis and Recentralisation: 'Indigenous Development' in Eastern Uganda', Working Paper 87/1, Center for African Studies, University of Copenhagen.

Wiebe, P.D. and C.P. Dodge (1987) *Beyond Crisis Development Issues in Uganda*, Kampala: Makerere Institute of Social Research, Kampala.

World Bank (various years) *World Development Report*, Washington DC.

- (1982) *Uganda — Country Economic Memorandum*, Washington DC.
- (1988) *Uganda — Towards Stabilisation and Economic Recovery*, Washington DC.
- (1989a) *Uganda — A Review of the Economic Recovery Program*, Eastern Africa Department, Washington DC.
- (1989b) *World Tables, 1988–1989 edition*, Washington DC.
- (1992) *Uganda — Growing Out of Poverty*, Washington DC.
- (1994a) *Adjustment in Africa — Reforms, Results and the Road Ahead*, Washington DC.
- (1994b) *Adjustment in Africa — Country Studies*, Washington DC.
- (1995) *Uganda: The Challenge of Growth and Poverty Reduction*, Washington DC.

World Data 1995, Socio-economic indicators from the World Bank, CD-ROM.

World Trade Organisation (1995) *Trade Policy Review of Uganda*, June, Geneva.

Index

Note: page numbers in *italic* refer to tables or figures.